A Voice in
the Wilderness

"Joe Bayly's creative works powerfully influenced more than one generation of evangelicals. The stories and incisive prose both opened windows and drove down stakes. Now new generations can be thus stimulated and older generations dip again into this stream of lively discourse."

Harold Myra, President
Christianity Today, Inc.

A Voice in the Wilderness

Joseph Bayly

Victor is an imprint of
Cook Communications Ministries, Colorado Springs, Colorado 80918
Cook Communications, Paris, Ontario
Kingsway Communications, Eastbourne, England

Printed in the United States of America.

1 2 3 4 5 6 7 8 9 10 Printing/Year 04 03 02 01 00

Consulting Editor: Timothy B. Bayly
Design: David Carlson Design

Library of Congress Cataloging-in-Publication Data

Bayly, Joseph.
  A voice in the wilderness by Joseph Bayly.
    p. cm.
  ISBN 1-56476-787-6
  1. Meditations. I. Title.

  BV4832.2B365 2000
  242--dc21   99-039738

After graduating from Wheaton College and Faith Theological Seminary, Joe Bayly served as New England regional director with the fledgling InterVarsity Christian Fellowship—followed by terms as editor of *HIS* magazine and director of InterVarsity Press. In 1963 Joe joined David C. Cook Publishing Company where he served in various editorial and management positions.

For twenty-five years Joe wrote a column, "Out of My Mind," for *Eternity* magazine. "Joe wrote with grace and good humor, but he was fearless in confronting evangelicals about questionable practices, false piety, and pompous pretense," said former *Eternity* editor Russell Hitt. Shortly after writing his final column in July 1986, Joe joined three sons who had preceded him in death, leaving behind his wife of forty-three years, Mary Lou, and four children involved in Christian service.

Joe will be remembered as a man of insight and wit, a man keenly sensitive both to the law of God and the weakness of man.

Contents

Joe Bayly 9
AFFLICTING THE COMFORTABLE

I Saw Gooley Fly 13

Ceiling Zero 17

I Saw Gooley Crash 22

Rehoboam's Gold Shields 27

Protest Until Pizza 29

Black Gold 33

Still Small Roar 43

How Shall We Remember John? 47

The Gospel Blimp 50

I Love to Tell the Story 90

How Silently, How Silently 131

Christmas Voices 143

Is Holiness Possible Today: With a Warning from Esau 148

Out of My Mind 152

What Would Happen If .152

Is Every New Bible Version a Blessing? 154

Lord, Raise Up a Negro Prophet 156

Beauty Out of Cinders .158

Hush, Hush about Morality 161

The Truth—But Not the Whole Truth 163

The Teaching We Have Neglected 166

Oh, for the Good Old Days 168

Is There a Parallel Between Infant Baptism
    and Early Decisions for Jesus? 170

The Missing Ingredient in the New Bibles 171

Are We Undermining Authority? 174

Does Christian Coffee Save Men? 176

High Price of TV 179

Raison d'Être 181

Wrong Fences 184

Women's Lib and the Bible 186

If We Could Rewrite the Bible 188

Revise Our "Sexist" Scriptures? 190

Why Don't Sinners Cry Anymore? 193

Power of Providential Praying 195

Bloodthirsty or Biblical? 198

Empty Calories 202

New Fig-Leaf Dictionary 204

One Sage's Testament 208

Unlikely American Hero 213

The Birth of an Ethic 214

Who Are We to Judge? 217

Our Reich of Indifference 220

The End of an Era 222

Rome Fell While Moralists Slept 228

COMFORTING THE AFFLICTED

When a Child Dies 235

The Last Thing We Talk About 241

   The Predictable Event 241

   Death's True Colors 243

   "Why Would a Kind God...?" 245

   Two Kinds of Death 248

   "Death Be Not Proud" 251

A Psalm on the Death of an Eighteen-Year-Old Son 254

Heaven 256

The Severity and Goodness of God 265

Ordination Charge 269

Index 271

Acknowledgments 285

Joe Bayly

In the economy of God and in His sovereignty, He puts certain people among us who will be up to the task He will place before them. Joe Bayly was such a man. He was my friend. He was the father of several of my patients. Three separate times I shared with him the bone-crushing grief when one of his children died. Indeed, as a surgeon I was involved in one way or another with each of these tragic deaths—deaths that to some people seemed as humanly unavoidable as they were tragic.

What was the real Joe Bayly like in the midst of drinking deeply from the cup of sorrow? He was like he always was—concerned for the spiritual welfare of others, available to go the extra mile for a friend (when it should have been the other way around), and apparently unflappable. Yet, entirely human.

No one could have lived through the sorrow of Joe Bayly's life with such equanimity without an abundant portion of the grace of God—which of course Joe acknowledged. But I said he was human.

Joe reminded me of Jesus praying in the twenty-sixth chapter of Matthew. God the Son talking with God the Father, and while mindful of His divine mission, nonetheless talking about the suffering to come in most human terms.

Joe wasn't a dishrag who said, "Thank You, Father," as each new blow was rained down upon him. He was human. He knew it was part of a sovereign plan of God but he hated it—naturally. After all, didn't Joe write *Psalms of My Life* and like the biblical psalmist run the gamut of emotion from wonder to sorrow to questioning to rebellion . . . finally to acceptance and praise? That was Joe.

Joe's eldest son always stood out from the crowd. When the boy wrote his essay for the National Merit Scholarship competition, it was about his faith in Christ. When he went to secular college, his testimony was strong and clear, while his winsome personality and personal achievement attracted not only those who shared his faith, but also those who didn't.

When he sustained a minor bump while sledding, his hemophilia allowed uncontrollable internal hemorrhage to threaten his life. When the young man lay dying in a suburban hospital near Philadelphia, Joe called me to ask that I see his son in consultation. It was too late.

For the third time in my career I told the same friend that his child was just a step away from heaven.

As I drove home from the hospital, I was terribly burdened, saddened by the apparent unfairness of it all. I was only the surgeon; Joe was the father. What unspeakable thoughts must have been going through his mind. And yet as I left him at the hospital elevator, he was apparently stoic, certainly resigned, at once a figure most pitiable, but among his son's attendants a tower of strength. That was Joe Bayly. No wonder he was the source of so much sage advice to the countless young people who sought his counsel over the years.

The memorial service for that boy in the Blue Church in Delaware County, Pennsylvania was the most heart-wrenching, yet triumphant, hour I can remember. The church was packed not only with Joe's friends, but also with all the new friends his son had made at college. These young people felt inexplicably deprived of a truly unique person to whom they had become unusually attached, but whose special view of life—and death—they could not understand.

After few preliminaries, Joe Bayly went to the front of the church. The lump in my throat was so large I could barely swallow. The lump in Joe's throat was so large he could barely talk. But he did, and his opening words are burned forever in my mind: "I want to speak to you tonight about my earthly son and his Heavenly Father . . ."

Joe poured out his heart. Tears streamed down the faces of almost everyone present. That night, the message Joe brought to his son's college friends started a large number of them down a path in search of what Joe and his son had—and many of them found it in faith in Jesus Christ. That was Joe Bayly.

—C. EVERETT KOOP, M.D.

Afflicting the Comfortable

Joe Bayly wrote parables, and those with ears to hear heard. Aside from his classic, "The Gospel Blimp," Bayly's best-known parables are the following three centered around an "ordinary sort of guy" named Herb Gooley.

I Saw Gooley Fly

HERB GOOLEY WAS just an ordinary sort of guy until the night he stepped out of his third-floor dorm window and fell away into the wild blue yonder.

But I'm getting ahead of my story.

I first met Gooley in that little hamburger and malt joint just off campus—Pete's Place. I'd never have noticed the guy except that he dropped a mustard bottle, and the stuff squirted down the front of his storm jacket. Now I'm a sophomore at the time, and this guy's a frosh. (No mistaking them during those early weeks of the quarter.) But he's making such a mess out of wiping the stuff off that I help him. Brother, what a mess. But Herb was the sort of fellow who could hardly wipe his nose himself, let alone the mustard.

When we had the stuff pretty well wiped off his coat and shirt (you could still see these bright yellow streaks), I ask him where he sacks out.

"Pollard," he says.

"That hole. Must be a frosh, huh? You'll learn. 'Course you can transfer after a quarter. Me, I'm at Sigma Phi House. Know the place that looks like a country club over on Lincoln?"

He doesn't know it. So we pay Pete and walk out. That is, I walk out. Herb trips over a cigarette machine that stands near the door.

Next time I notice the guy is at homecoming.

It's during the frosh-soph tug-of-war. (They really had pressure on those fire hoses that year.) We're ready for the final pull and the gun goes off. Suddenly the whole frosh team's yelling to stop pulling. So, after they turn the hoses on us, we stop; and here's Gooley, looking sort of dazed, with the rope twisted clear around his arm. I'll never know how he did it. They get it

13

off and take him to the infirmary. Nothing broken, but he sure must have had a painful arm for a few days.

I remember—sometime the following fall—seeing a crowd gathered around the front of Hinton's department store. So I pull over to the curb, and here is the college station wagon half-in, half-out of Hinton's show window. What a scene. Bodies all over the place, one of them broken in two across the hood. Gooley's standing there holding a plastic head.

Maybe losing his driving privileges for a while got him interested in flying. At any rate, he comes back from Christmas vacation, his junior year, able to fly. Able to fly, mind you, not just able to fly a plane.

His roommate (Jerry Watson, it was) told us about it the next day. Seems Gooley had been studying late, and finally he turns the book over, switches off his desk light and says, "Think I'll go down to Pete's for a malted."

"Too late," Jerry says. "It's three minutes to twelve and he closes at midnight."

"I'll fly down." Gooley says it matter-of-factly, just like he's saying he'll run or something.

So over to the window he goes (Jerry all the while thinking Gooley is suddenly developing a sense of humor), lifts it up, and steps off the ledge.

Their room is on the third floor.

Jerry waits a second for the thud, then dashes into the hall and down the stairs yelling, "Gooley fell out the window! Somebody call a doctor!"

No Gooley on the ground, or anywhere around. So they think Jerry's pulling their leg.

"Honest, fellows, Gooley stepped out of our window. Said he'd fly down to Pete's. Honest, he did."

So they wait around for Gooley to come back, and when he does, they start firing questions.

"Sure I can fly. Jerry was telling you the straight stuff. Here, I'll show you." And with that he takes off into the wild blue yonder.

None of us believed the story when we heard it. Would you? In the first place, people can ride bicycles, people can row boats, people can fly planes even, but nobody can fly.

In the second place, if anybody could fly, Herb Gooley wasn't the man. That guy couldn't even walk.

It began to snow about suppertime the next day, and it snowed all through the night. Next morning the ground is covered, but some of the walks are shoveled off. I'm walking down the cleared path at the quad when I notice something. Fresh footprints go out on the snow a few yards, then there's nothing. Nothing. No trampled snow, no feet turning around. Just footprints going out and stopping.

Within a few days nobody needs any more circumstantial evidence. We've all seen it—Gooley flying.

He'd be walking along with you, and suddenly he's airborne. Nothing spectacular. I mean it was all very quiet. His rise was almost vertical, and he flew along at about fifteen or twenty miles per hour. Just above the treetops. He'd sort of bank to turn.

That winter and spring you should have seen Gooley come into class on the third or fourth floor of Old Main. Brother, that was a sight to behold. It got to be a regular custom to open the window just before the bell. I'll never forget the day we had a visiting lecturer. Nobody had told him.

Let me tell you, there was a run on the library for books on aerodynamics, aircraft design, and any other subject that even faintly bears on flying. Guys were spending all their free time soaking up all they could learn. So were most of the girls.

I don't want you to get the idea that we talked about it. Nobody would admit that he wanted to fly, but most everybody did. Nothing in the world I wanted more. (Seems sort of funny now.)

The college flying course tripled in size. (Flying planes, that is—but it was as close as we could come to personal flight.) In bull sessions we talked into the small hours about how Gooley probably did it.

You see, Gooley wasn't saying.

Of course, later there was some reaction—a lot of people began to call Gooley a freak. It sort of made us laugh, though, when one of the most outspoken anti-Gooleyites was found with a brain concussion at the foot of the Old Zach monument. (He got over it all right.)

I think the college administration was sort of ashamed to have Gooley as a student. So they bring in this guy Sevorsky for a special lecture series called "Flight Emphasis Week." Brother, were those lectures packed out. Standing room only.

Halfway through the week we realize that Sevorsky can't fly. We're standing outside Old Main, waiting for him to leave the president's office, which is on the second floor. So how does he come down? Why, he walks down the stairs and out the front door. This guy can design airplanes, we say; he has the latest scoop on jets and helicopters; but he can't fly.

About a dozen students show up for his final lecture.

Most of us had heard a myth about some ancient Greek who could fly until he got too near the sun. So we think maybe there's a clue. Interest switches to books on ancient Greek mythology, and the library puts them on the reserve shelf.

You know, I've always been surprised that Gooley didn't tell us how to do it, or at least how he did it. He couldn't help knowing how interested we all were. But he kept his mouth shut. So none of us learned to fly.

It's a funny thing, but I still have a sense of loss of not learning Gooley's secret. And the other grads have confessed the same thing to me.

What happened to Gooley? I've often wondered about that. He transferred that fall to another college where, they say, all the students know how to fly.

Ceiling Zero

M Y ROOMMATE IS a guy named Gooley. Herb Gooley.
He transferred to this crummy little school in the boondocks about six months ago. When he first arrived, we were all asking why he left a big, well-known college at the beginning of his senior year. Everybody's heard of it; nobody's heard of us.

Only thing we have that they don't have is a flight school. What they have, and we don't have, would fill a book.

One night I ask Herb straight out, "Why did you come here?"

"One reason," he says. "Last Christmas vacation I learned to fly. So I decided to switch to a flight school, a place where everyone could fly. That's why I'm here."

I should explain that I don't mean flying planes or gliders or balloons or anything. I mean we can fly, period.

We can step out of a window and be airborne. I remember my first flight—it was while I was still in high school—off a barn in the Blue Ridge Mountains. Some of the guys and girls here have been flying ever since they were little kids.

So the reason Herb Gooley gave for coming here made sense. Except for one thing, which he couldn't have known before he came. It's the sort of thing you don't learn from a catalog.

Gooley is a sensitive guy—withdrawn. Doesn't talk to many people. But there's some reason for being as he is: for one thing, he got off to a bad start.

I've never seen a happier freshman than Gooley, when he first showed up. I don't mean that he was actually a freshman—like I said, he was a transfer senior. But he had that same stupid innocence.

One of those hot afternoons in September—like so many days when school has just begun—I was stripped to the waist, arranging my clothes on

17

hangers, when this new student comes through the window. He flew in—our room is on the third floor of Derwin Hall.

"I'm Herb Gooley," he says. "Boy, have I ever been looking forward to coming here."

"To this crummy school? Why?" I ask.

He looks sort of surprised. "Why, because it's a flight school. You can fly, can't you? The other guys in this dorm can fly, can't they? And the girls—just think of having a flying date. Wow!"

Should I tell him straight off, or should I let him find out for himself?

I guess I'm sort of chicken, because I decide not to say anything. Let someone else tell him.

"Yeah, this is a flight school, all right. We can all fly, including the profs—and the administration. You can have that bed over there by the door, Gooley. And that dresser, and either closet, except that I've got my things in this one. The public relations department can fly, too. They prepare the catalog."

He doesn't say anything, but begins to unpack. First thing out of his suitcase is a copy of *Aerodynamic Theory*. It goes on his desk.

Around five-thirty I head for the dining hall. "Coming along?" I ask.

"Not yet," Gooley says. "Don't wait for me. I want to finish here first. I'll be along before it closes."

So I walk on over and go through the cafeteria line. I find my crowd and sit down to eat with them.

We're on the dessert, when there's a little stir over by the door.

"What do we have here?" someone asks.

"An exhibitionist."

"A new student, you can tell that. Nobody else would fly on campus."

Sure enough—it's Herb Gooley, my new roommate. He comes through the door and touches down gently, by the stack of trays and the silver holder. He's got a smooth technique.

Everybody gets sort of quiet. I don't know about the others, but suddenly I'm thinking about some of my flights in high school days.

"You're too late," this battle-ax who runs the cafeteria says. "We close at six-thirty." The clock on the wall says six-thirty. She's absolutely right, which is what she always is.

"Serves him right," a girl going back for seconds on iced tea says, loud enough for Herb to hear. "He's just a show-off."

Gooley looks sort of hurt, but he doesn't say anything, either to battle-ax or to battle-ax, junior grade. He just heads out the door. Walking.

"He'll learn," someone at my table says. "We all learned."

And he did, during the next few weeks.

First thing he finds out is that here nobody flies. In spite of this being a flight school, and everyone can fly—theoretically—we're all grounded.

There's a lot of talk about flight, of course, a daily flight hour. But nobody flies.

Some of us came here planning to be flight instructors. I myself wanted to teach Africans how to fly, but that didn't last long.

Actually, the deadest things are the flight courses. They use *Aerodynamic Theory* as the text, but you'd never recognize it. One flight out of a hayloft has more excitement to it than a year of that course.

One night we get into a discussion on our floor of the dorm.

"Look, Gooley," one of the guys says, "tell us about the college you were in before you came here. Is it true that they have more exciting courses than we do here?"

"A lot of them, yes," Gooley says. "But they don't know anything about how to fly."

"Are the girls there real swingers?"

"I guess so. But they can't fly."

The way Herb answers sort of frustrates the guys who are asking the questions, because they would jump at a chance to transfer to the school he came from.

"I think this flying isn't all it's cracked up to be," one of them says.

"I feel the same way," another chimes in. "And besides, it seems sort of selfish to me to fly when the rest of the world is walking."

"Not only selfish. To them you look like some kind of a nut, up there above the ground. From here on in, any flights I take are going to be when there's nobody around to see me."

"Besides, the world needs to be taught how to walk. And pavements and roads need to be improved."

"Did any of you read John Robin's book? It's a pretty strong critique of *Aerodynamic Theory*, and he does an effective job of questioning the usual foundations of flight. The significant thing is that Robin is a flyer, not a walker."

That was the only time I ever heard Herb Gooley swear. "Oh, hell," he says, and dives out the window. (It was a cold night, but fortunately we had opened the window because the room was getting stuffy. If we hadn't, I think Herb would have gone right through the glass.)

He didn't return until early next morning. I heard him at the window and got up to open it. It had begun to snow, and he was covered. He looked nearly exhausted, but happier than I'd seen him since the day he first arrived.

That night marked a change in Herb Gooley, a change that came to affect the whole school. Only, I didn't know it at the time.

He began to fly again. On campus.

Now when you're with flyers, flying isn't remarkable—actually it's the basic minimum, it's taken for granted. What worries us is perfection, and it's sort of embarrassing—around other flyers—to try an extra little maneuver, or to stay aloft longer than usual. There can be such a letdown. And the competition is so keen. There's always someone who can fly better than you.

That's the reason nobody flies here. At least they didn't, not until Gooley took it up again.

Like the flight prof says, "This is a school for flying, not an airport. You've come here to learn more about flying, not to fly. We want to teach you how to fly with real conviction." Then he draws diagrams on the blackboard. And he walks across the campus.

Meanwhile, Herb is getting better and better. I mean his flying is improving. You can see him on a moonlit night, trying all sorts of flight gymnastics.

Moonlit nights. That brings me to another side of the change in Gooley.

He began to have flying dates. Not many—none of the girls, except one or two, would be caught dead on a flight date, especially with Herb.

What can you talk about on a flying date? What can you do? I ask you.

We discuss it while Gooley's out of the dorm. He's out a lot those last months of school. Not just flying or on flight dates, but teaching a bunch of kids to fly at the community center in town, studying *Aerodynamic Theory* with a little group of students. The guys can't understand why Herb keeps at it.

"Sure we can fly—at least as well as that guy Gooley. But after all, real life is down here on the earth. It's not as if we were birds."

"Besides, we've got to learn to relate to the walkers. And that's a lot harder to do than flying."

"I've found—I don't know about the rest of you guys—but I've found that they're not much interested in my flying ability. I mean, the walkers aren't. So it's important to show them that I can walk."

"Don't get me wrong. It's not that I'm against flying. I'm not. But you don't have to fly to be for flying."

So the year ends.

We graduate.

I ask Gooley, while we're packing, what he plans to do next year.

"Grad school," he says. "In a walking university. You see, I was reading *Aerodynamic Theory* the other day, where it says that you can take off best against the wind."

I Saw Gooley Crash

I'M HERB GOOLEY'S WIFE. At least I was until recently. You've read about it in the papers.

We met at flying school; our first date was a moonlight flight in the springtime. I still remember the fragrance of apple blossoms floating up to us from an orchard. Later, we worked together at a community center teaching children how to fly.

A few months after graduation we were married. Both of us were dedicated to flying and we thought our happiness would never end. But I guess happiness is like anything else: you don't own it, it can be repossessed at any time.

Herb had this obsession with flying. As far as he was concerned, there was nothing else in life. Maybe it would be more accurate to say that everything else came in a distant second, including me.

Not that I objected. I was committed to flying, too. For the first few years after we were married, flying took first place for both of us. We went everywhere, living out of our suitcases, establishing flight training centers. What did we do during those years of itinerant life? We taught young flyers advanced techniques, and we also taught a lot of nonflyers the joy of flight. Then, after several years, Herb had a Big Idea.

"Look," he said, "we're limited to one place at a time. I know we travel all over, but it's still here or there. Nobody can be here and there. —Except it is possible. You can be all over the country, all over Canada, all over the world if you want to." (He had this triumphal look on his face like he got when he executed a particularly tricky flying maneuver.)

"How's that?" I asked. "I don't follow you."

"Television," he said. "The means of teaching millions of people how to fly at the same time. Besides, I'm getting tired of living out of suitcases all the time."

That conversation, forever vivid in my mind, marked the beginning of Herb's new career.

It was a struggle at first. We weren't living out of suitcases any longer, but Herb had to scrounge for money. Big money. He took it in stride, though, and there were plenty of flyers who owed their knowledge of flight to Herb's instruction—he'd been the first one to get them airborne. So they chipped in money, and one beautiful day in October Herb flew in the kitchen window (I was making supper) and shouted, "Here I come, Johnny Carson! I've got enough money to start my own flying program on TV!"

Herb's first show was the Saturday after Thanksgiving Day. It was spectacular; maybe semispectacular would be a better way to describe it since there wasn't much time to put it together. But it was impressive and it brought a surprisingly big response—especially considering that the program was local.

It didn't stay local. Inside of a year "Fly with Herb Gooley" was on a major network, and Herb, my husband, was teaching millions to fly. Maybe it would be more accurate to say that he was teaching them the principles of flight. I'm not sure how many actually had the thrill of stepping off a building and being airborne. They saw others do it, they knew how it was done (I think), but did they really do it? I'll never know.

I hope those millions of people learned, especially the young people. There's no thrill like stepping off the railing of a bridge, like the George Washington in New York, and following the river as it goes up past West Point—or in the other direction, out to the ocean. Or flying through the snow (incidentally, Herb later developed these funny glasses for snow flying with tiny windshield wipers that he gave away to people who sent in a hundred dollars for his show). Or flying over the Grand Canyon—I did that last summer, after Herb left me.

You can tell I'm crazy about flying, can't you? I always was—since I first took off, that is—and I always will be. There's a sort of closeness to the heavens when you're up there, earth becomes remote. The silence is unreal, but your thoughts scream.

I gradually came to realize that Herb was losing that vision of flight. It was becoming what I think they called in college *utilitarian* to him. If you learned to fly, you could make more money, for instance. How? Delivering boxes and packages across town in a hurry, especially during rush hours. Taking aerial photographs. Performing at malls and fairs. Locating lost dogs, rescuing cats out of trees.

You get the drift. Nothing wrong with any of those things, I guess, but should the glories of flight be lowered to financial success, to finding dogs?

Herb lost sight of the Grand Canyon. He was too busy walking on Wall Street. The money really began to come in. He was on a roll. We bought a big tract of land and built a headquarters building on it. There was a forty-foot statue of Daedalus out in front—you know, the man in ancient Greek mythology who made wings for himself and his son so that they were able to fly.

I say "we" bought the land and built the headquarters because I was on Herb's board at the time, the so-called governing body of Herb Gooley Flight Ministries International, Inc. There were three others in addition to Herb and me, all of them his employees.

We next built a seminar center where people came to learn more about flying, especially how it could enrich their lives. This became Herb Gooley University. (When I asked Herb why we couldn't just give the money to the college where we'd met and perfected our flying instead of building our own university, he said, "That little school in the boonies? Don't make me laugh.")

Nobody was making him laugh those days, unless it was his director of development or his accountant. And nobody was laughing at him—Herb was a Success.

Our lifestyle changed radically. No more suitcases. No more cheap hotels, or poor flyers' homes. (Should it be flyers' poor homes?) Everything became first class for us, all the way. We flew (longer flights that is, the ones on planes) first class, we stayed in first-class hotels, we wore first-class clothes, we had a first-class bank account.

I'll be honest with you: I didn't fight it. I enjoyed the condominium on the beach with its live-in maid and the expensive automobiles as much as anyone else would. I got my kicks out of looking like a million when Herb took me to one of those Big Affairs where he often spoke. I felt honored to meet the President and his wife, even have lunch with them at the White House.

I didn't fight it, that's for sure. Except one night, maybe I did. We were lying in our canopied king-size bed (I'm laying it all on the line—there's no reason to hide anything anymore). We'd been at some sort of banquet; the night-light was on and I could see my diamond glittering on the dressing table.

"Herb," I said, "what about the kids?"

"What kids?" he asked. "I'm trying to get to sleep."

"Not that," I quickly answered. "I mean the kids at the community centers where we taught flying, it seems ages ago."

"What about them? They're probably grown now, in college or the service or somewhere."

"I don't mean those kids. I mean other kids like them. Who's teaching them to fly? Here we are in our palace, the king and queen of flight, bloated with speeches and food. Who's teaching the kids?"

"Somebody is. Good night."

"I was thinking about something else too, Herb. We took the Jag to the banquet. Only ten miles away and we don't fly, we take the Jag. I can't remember the last time I saw you fly—you can probably say the same thing about me."

So he says, "Listen, if you want to talk, go in a guest bedroom. I'm going to sleep." So that ended that.

Our conversation must have made Herb think, though. Several weeks later he had several poor kids around eight or nine years old on his program. And I mean poor.

He stood them up one at a time on his desk, the one he sat behind to pontificate about flight. "Now fly!" he said, and they jumped off. But since they couldn't, they fell. He caught two of them; the third one wasn't hurt because there were mattresses on the floor.

Then he says, with tears running down his face, "Those poor children, and millions more like them, can't fly. They need to be taught how to fly. I'm setting up a program called Junior Wings. It'll cost a lot of money, but I know I can count on you partners to stand behind me. After all, we're in this together. Now make the telephone ring and the cash registers sing!"

Of course the money came in, the program was set up, and he soon had a Learjet to take him to his more distant appointments. I've sometimes wondered why flyers, and some nonflyers, supported him as they did. I'm not letting him—or myself—off the hook, but there's been a big audience out there acting as if he were Daedalus reincarnated, as if he could do no wrong. Didn't they see how he'd changed? —Maybe not, since they didn't know him before. Did they get a sort of vicarious satisfaction out of the way he lived? (Me too, until recently.)

Where were the real flyers during those years, the veterans who should have seen the direction Herb was taking and tried to turn him around? —It seems as if they were either critical of him or they got on the bandwagon with him.

Some of them really did have a place on the bandwagon. I remember when his book *Fly to Success* hit its millionth copy. They were almost ready to give him the flight publishing house. I've been asked if I had any premonition of disaster. I have to answer no, it seemed as if Herb and his organization would go on and on and grow forever. Like I said, he was on a roll.

How do I explain what happened? I can't. I've seen Herb step off the ledge of a window seven stories off the ground and take off, flying toward the stars. I've seen him fly through rain, snow, in heat and bitter cold. I've seen him land in wind shear that had 727s circling the field.

Of course, all that was years ago. With a Learjet, Jaguar, and Mercedes, he didn't need to fly. But to fall over a sawhorse on the third floor of the Hospitality Center they're building, and go over the edge . . .

I think of Daedalus and his son, Icarus, who flew too close to the sun and melted. Maybe Herb wasn't Daedalus reincarnated after all, but Icarus.

Rehoboam's Gold Shields

REHOBOAM CHECKED IN TODAY, about four o'clock this afternoon. He walked into the dorm, looked around the way every freshman does, and headed for the room he'd been assigned to. Then he went back out to the car and brought in his gear.

Nothing unusual about Rehoboam's arrival—except that among his things were some gold shields. And those shields are the cause of no little comment around the dorm. He can tell.

A shield is an awkward thing, difficult to wrap, impossible to stow away so it doesn't show. Maybe Rehoboam wouldn't have been so conspicuous if anybody else had brought shields. But nobody had.

"Why does a guy bring shields to a university?" he hears as he enters the john. But that's the end of the conversation, at least until he leaves.

Those first few days everyone finds some excuse to come to Rehoboam's room. "What's the text for Chem 101?"

"When's the deadline for dropping a course?"

"Do you know how much an extra season ticket costs?"

Sometimes they don't even wait for the answer before they wander over to the dresser, where the gold shields are stacked. (The things are too wide to fit in a closet.)

"Hey, look at the shields," they say. "First ones I've seen here at the university."

Always there's the same feeble, half-apologetic explanation by Rehoboam. They were his dad's shields, but his dad gave them to him. Then he warms to his subject a bit and explains that they're gold—believe it or not. Sure, they're worth a lot.

So they begin to call him the "Gold Shield Boy." Word gets out about the shields. Pretty soon it's all over the campus—even the profs know. Worst of all, the girls think it's a big joke.

Hardly a day passes that one or two guys don't come over to Rehoboam's dorm to see the shields. Several upperclassmen advise him to hang on to them—"They're worth more than most of the garbage you'll pick up around here"—but the general opinion seems to be that shields are out of place in a university, and a man must be some kind of nut to own them. Especially gold ones.

After four or five weeks of this, day after day, night after night, a certain change begins to take place in Rehoboam. Defending his shields is wearing him down. He spends as little time as possible at the dorm, hangs around the union a lot, and studies at the library. A conviction grows in his mind that he's a fool to have brought those gold shields along to the university.

One morning, as he dresses hurriedly so he can grab breakfast before an eight o'clock class, he notices something. One shield is missing. Sure enough— it's gone. No time to look for it now, though. Later on, after class, he'll come back and find it. But later in the day, when he gets time to hunt for the missing shield, he can't locate it. And it doesn't turn up later in the week.

Before long, a second shield disappears, then another. Rehoboam is determined to keep the last one from being stolen, for he values that one especially. But when he returns to his room one morning at 4 A.M., after spending a night in town, he finds that the last shield is gone too.

Surprisingly, his feeling, in the face of this great loss, is one of relief. Those gold shields won't make him stand out anymore. Now he's the same as everyone else. At last he can feel thoroughly at home in the university.

And he does. The gold shields gone, his defense of them ended, Rehoboam becomes a popular figure on campus.

As Christmas vacation approaches, however, some misgivings trouble him. What to do about the shields when he goes home?

The solution, when he finally thinks it through, is simple. He decides to replace the gold shields with others made of highly burnished brass.

He takes the counterfeit shields home with him when vacation begins, and his deception appears to be complete. None of his family seems to notice the substitution. The reaction pleases Rehoboam, for it would upset his family to learn of his loss, which he knows is a great one.

Protest Until Pizza

S O WHAT ARE you going to do?"

"Do? What can I do — what can anyone do? It's done now, over, finished, kaput."

"No marches?"

"Are you kidding?"

"No placards? No demonstrations?"

"Look, about the seventeenth-century lit assignment . . ."

"You're a great one. March for better food in the dining hall, march for Professor Fliedner, march for graffiti on the library walls. Now suddenly, halt, one two."

"Come off it. Let up, will you? Those things were free speech. This would be free suicide. Anything now would be putting our heads in a noose. Besides, I didn't see you at any demonstrations, even the big sit-in for Fliedner. You never carried a placard for free speech. So don't start trying to make me feel guilty. By the way, what do you intend to do now?"

"Nothing. I'm not going to change my pattern, which means I'm consistent."

"So am I. It's just a new element, a radically different element, has entered the picture."

"Meaning Irving was dragged out of the dormitory?"

"Right. That and the Supreme Court decision last Friday. Now there's no longer any doubt about it."

"But what happens to free speech, if that's so?"

"It's still there. Nothing's happened to it."

"Provided you use it harmlessly—like trying to get visiting privileges in the girls' dorms extended to all night or something else that's strictly university."

"Sure, like that."

"But not Irving, picked up by the federal police last night. Not the prison camp outside of Peoria. Not the genetic test or fallout."

"Cool it. After all, I can't do anything about those things."

"You mean they're not like getting more steak in the dining hall, or pressuring the university to renew Fliedner's contract after they discover he's a Communist?"

"Right. There's some hope for results on protests like that. But Irving, prison camps—no hope. Absolutely none."

"What if Irving's headed for the extermination chamber?"

"All the more. Who knows—say I did protest—that the federal police wouldn't be knocking on my door tomorrow night. Then my days of usefulness would be over."

"Just like Irving's."

"Sure, like Irving's. Only he had no choice. I do."

"Thank God you're not Jewish."

"Right. And you can, too."

"I do. Never more than today. But I got sidetracked. We were talking about demonstrations and free speech."

"You were talking. I'm finished."

"Don't you feel any responsibility to demonstrate against the government's policy toward Jews?"

"What good would it do?"

"I don't know. I guess it wouldn't change things."

"Right. The Supreme Court's decision makes it final."

"So Irving is thrown to the dogs."

"He has lots of company, if you've been reading the papers."

"But I know Irving personally. He's someone I've gotten my physics assignments from. I've talked about the World Series with him. I've eaten pizza late at night with Irving."

"But he's Jewish, and there's nothing you can do about it."

"I'd like to make a sign, *Free Irving Greenhow*, or *The United States Is Murdering Jews*, or maybe even, *Get Haman Out of the White House*."

"What would you do with the sign?"

"Why, I'd carry it downtown—maybe to the newspaper office. Then I'd march with it."

"For two minutes maybe. After that you'd be on your way to Peoria. With only your teeth smashed in, if you were lucky."

"But what a glorious two minutes! It would almost be worth it."

"Nothing's worth dying for."

"But Irving's not a thing. He's a person endowed with certain inalienable rights."

"Not any longer, he isn't. He's a nonperson without any rights at all. Maybe he's dead already."

"So steak is more important to you than Irving."

"I guess so. Or—give me the benefit of the doubt—Fliedner's right to teach although he was a Communist? Some of the protests were more significant than others."

"You'd demonstrate for Fliedner's right to speak, but not for Irving's right to live?"

"I wouldn't put it quite that way, but I guess that's about it. The point is, we had a chance of gaining what we were after in Fliedner's case; none at all in Irving's. So why demonstrate?"

"Maybe to let them know we don't agree with what they're doing to the Jews. Or to say—here's Irving Greenhow—he's got as much right to live as anyone else. As me. Even as the President."

"But he doesn't. The Supreme Court answered that question last week. The Bill of Rights is relative; it's conditional."

"Isn't there any higher appeal than the Supreme Court?"

"Not in this country, there isn't. The Supreme Court is the end of the line."

"I know that. But beyond the court, even beyond the country. Isn't there any higher authority?"

"The UN stopped meeting two years ago. What's left?"

"What about you and me?"

"What about us?"

"Don't we have any responsibility to a higher authority?"

"Who? If you mean Irving—if you mean human dignity or something like that—it's too late. He's probably dead. Or soon will be."

"I mean God."

"God? What's He got to do with this? God's in church on Sunday mornings, not in demonstrations. God isn't carrying any placards. Not even for Irving."

"Maybe I owe it to God."

"Owe it to God? If you did, the preachers would be telling you, don't forget that. They're not."

"Maybe they value their lives as much as we do ours."

"Of course they do. If they got killed, or even put in prison, who'd keep church?"

"So everybody is silent because they—I mean we—might get killed if they spoke."

"Not might. Would. There's no doubt about it."

"That means life is more important than anything else in the world."

"Right. You'd better believe it."

"It also seems to say that life is more important than God."

"And it is, except for some misguided people in history who had a martyr complex."

"Including Jesus?"

"I don't really know. He's a hard one to figure out."

"And He didn't keep silent."

"And died for it."

"You know what? We've been talking so much we missed supper."

"Let's go downtown and get a pizza."

Black Gold

JUDSON DORMER CAME out of China in 1949. He was swept out
by the Communist regime, along with thousands of other missionaries
and their dependents. They left the church behind, its hospitals and schools
and other institutions possessed by the enemies of God.

After a short rest in the small town in upper New York from which he
had first gone to China, and to which he had returned several times on furlough, Dormer began to accept meetings in various places. In the early fifties,
people were immensely concerned about Communism, both in China and
also in our own country. Senator Joseph McCarthy was then alerting
Americans to the danger of our own Trojan horse.

So this returned missionary, Judson Dormer, was much in demand as a
speaker. Primarily he took church engagements, but he also spoke at Kiwanis
and Rotary and other service clubs, as well as at high school assemblies.

Let me tell you, he was an imposing person. He had what we've come to
call charisma, at least as far as I understand it. He stood up there on the platform and looked you straight in the eye, and you just had to believe that
what he said about the Red Menace was true. When you went home afterward, like I told my wife, even the headlights of passing cars looked red.

I guess the big reason for this was that Dormer had himself suffered at the
hands of the Communists. He was able to tell us what they were like up close.

First time I heard him was at Second Church in Iowa City. I had supported his missionary society for some years—actually, it was one of the first
obligations we had taken on after we were married—and so I decided to
drive in to the meeting when I heard he was to be there.

Marian was in the midst of canning, and she said, "You go alone. I can
hear him some other time." So I got into the pickup truck and drove into
the city by myself.

A lot of speakers start out by telling how glad they are to be in Iowa City, or feeling at home in a Baptist or Presbyterian church. Or they tell a funny story.

Not Judson Dormer. He stood up there in the pulpit, right after the pastor had introduced him, and looked us straight in the eye. He was silent for maybe a minute, then he held up five slender, pointed sticks.

"These bamboo rods," he said, passing them from one hand to the other, "were pounded down under my nails with a hammer by my Communist jailers. They interrogated me for as long as fifteen hours at a stretch, trying to get me to deny my faith and admit that I was an American imperialist agent. But God brought me through, and I'm here tonight to warn you that what happened in China can happen tomorrow—tonight even—in the United States of America."

He told us how he had been arrested at the missionary compound, separated from his wife, and hauled off to prison in an army truck. He was in that prison for ten months, he said, and those months were the closest thing to hell that anyone could imagine. Interrogations for long periods of time, under a single lightbulb, with teams of fanatical, sadistic Communists taking turns questioning him. Almost daily beatings, living in an isolation cell with only a bucket: these were the things he endured.

Those bamboo sticks pounded under the nails were almost the least of his sufferings. He could not describe others in a mixed group. (He probably could today, things have changed that much.)

I don't remember everything he said that night, but I do remember thinking, during my fifty-mile drive back home, that America was in tremendous danger. I also thought how proud I was, although that may not be the right word, to have had a part all these years in his mission's work. I might be an Iowa farmer, but I had done something to stem the Red Tide in China.

When I pulled into the yard, I went right into the house, not even stopping to check the barn. I headed straight for the kitchen.

"Marian," I said, "did you ever miss something tonight. Judson Dormer was just great. You'll have to go tomorrow night."

"I will, if I get this canning done," she said.

She was tying spices up in a piece of old sheet to put in the vinegar that was boiling on the stove. It smelled good, like fall.

"Look," I said, "you've got to go, whether it's done or not. I almost feel ashamed of myself, coming back to the land and cattle and house—even cucumber relish—after what I heard tonight."

"Tomato relish, green tomato relish," she corrected me. "What did this man have to say?"

So I told her, as best I could. By the time I finished, she was ready to call it a night and go to bed.

The next night we both drove in to Iowa City. If anything, he was better than the night before, including more details of his ten-month imprisonment.

We went up to the front to speak to him after the service was over. I introduced myself and Marian to him, and told him how much his messages had meant to me. He looked me straight in the eye and said, "Don't thank me, thank God."

Then he asked me what I did, and I told him about the farm. I didn't say much, because there were other people waiting to shake his hand. I also told him that we had supported the work of his mission in China for a number of years.

Before he turned away from us, Dormer took out a little black book and asked me to write down our name and address. The book was filled with other people's names.

Driving home, I asked Marian what she thought about Judson Dormer.

"He is certainly a good speaker," she said. "He holds your attention, and you're surprised, when he stops, at how long he's spoken. At the same time ..."

"What?" I asked. "Was there something about him you didn't like?"

"Not really." And I couldn't get anything more out of her.

To Marian's credit, in all the years since, she hasn't mentioned the misgiving, or early warning signal, she had that first night. But that's the sort of woman she is.

A couple of months later, we had a letter from Dormer. It wasn't on his mission's letterhead—in this letter he told how the Lord had led him to establish a new work, an independent testimony to the faith. He called it "Truth Against Communism," and there was also the verse on the letterhead, "Ye shall know the truth, and the truth shall make you free."

He appealed for money to support his work, and of course we added him to our list of missionaries and Christian works. This wasn't too hard, since the corn harvest that year was especially good, and prices were high.

I'll pass over the next few years, only explaining that every fall Dormer returned to Iowa City. The meetings outgrew Second Church, and were held in the municipal auditorium. Thousands of people heard him, and hundreds became members of Truth Against Communism. (For a ten-dollar contribution, you got a membership card for your wallet, and a subscription to *Alarm!*—his monthly paper.)

One fall when he was there, he accepted our invitation to come out to the house for dinner. It was a long trip out and back, but he seemed to appreciate getting to see the farm, and—of course—Marian's cooking. We had a steer butchered and put in the locker that week. So we had some good steaks. And, recalling that first night I ever heard Dormer, I got Marian to break out some of her green tomato relish.

After dinner, while Marian was getting ready to go in with us, I took Dormer for a little walk through the pasture.

"You know," he said, "I grew up on a farm. It wasn't at all as big as this; farms in New York State usually aren't. It's a very simple life, but once you leave it, you never can go back. Shanghai, or even Iowa City, I guess, gets in your blood, and you're sunk."

I must admit, when he said that, I felt a little dissatisfaction with my life. What had I done, where had I been, except live in Cambridge, Iowa, all my life? Still, when I thought about it later, I got some satisfaction out of thinking that Marian and I had at least sent our money to China and the Congo and other places, to serve the Lord there.

One day, about four or five years after we had first met Dormer, we had a different kind of letter from him. The letterhead said, "Reclamation Mining, Ltd." Judson Dormer's name was there as president, and the address was a Canadian one. I had a moment of surprise that he was in business rather than his anti-Communism mission work, but that was soon dispelled. I kept the letter—here it is.

Dear Brother and Sister in Christ:

As you know, I have given my life to stamping out the brushfires of Communism in China and theUnited States.

One serious obstacle to mounting an all-out attack on the enemy is the lack of money. This is true not merely of Truth Against Communism; it is true of every other work of the Lord.

How much more could you do if you had ten times as much money—even a hundred times as much money—to give to the Lord's work as you are now giving?

God has now made that possible. I am writing to let you know about a miracle by which your money can be multiplied like the loaves and fishes.

As you doubtless know, there are many worked-over gold mines in the West. They are worked over, but not exhausted. Hundreds of millions of dollars worth of gold still lies there, some on the surface, some underground in abandoned mines, just waiting to be reclaimed.

Why was this gold missed? Because it was too expensive to separate the ore. And it would still be too expensive if it were not for the miracle I mentioned.

That miracle is a new mining machine, representing a totally new concept in ore separation, that has just been invented. I am teamed up with the inventor (his name is at the top of this letter, as vice president and treasurer), and we are announcing the availability of shares in Reclamation Mining, Ltd., on the following basis.

1. Anyone may invest at $1,000 a share (Canadian or American). You may buy as many shares as you wish, with the following proviso: Since I want this whole project to benefit the Lord's work, every investor must agree to give a minimum of 10 percent (a tithe) of the profits to Christian work. You need not give this to Truth Against

Communism, although I hope many of you will do so.

2. *For every $1,000 you invest, I guarantee you will receive $500 per month, starting one year after you have bought into the operation.*

3. *Anytime after six months, you may get your money back, with 10 percent interest per annum, simply by requesting it.*

Some of you may want more information about the Miracle Machine. I regret that I cannot describe it for you, except in the broadest terms. The inventor has no intention of even registering it for patent purposes, since that would enable any unscrupulous person to duplicate it.

But I can tell you that a prototype is now operational. I have seen black ore transformed—by God's wonder of modern technology—into the purest gold. Gold, I might add, that is like the product of suffering in the Refiner's fire. We will soon be closing this offer, so I appeal to you not to be overly long in deciding to invest . . . for His kingdom and your financial independence. . . .

I read that, and I read it again. Then I took it in the house and got Marian to read it.

"What do you think?" I asked. "Do you think we should invest?"

She folded the letter and put it back in the envelope. "You've decided about buying the farm and farm machinery and cattle up to now. You're the one who decides when to sell the corn. And I've been pretty well satisfied. So I don't see why I should have to be a part of this decision. You make up your mind and I'll go along with it."

"But we'd have to mortgage the property."

"If you decide to mortgage, I'll sign for it with you. But you decide."

Two days later I went to Cambridge State Bank and arranged for a $7,000 mortgage loan. I explained that it was for an investment. Since we had finished paying off the old mortgage on the property several years before, I had no trouble getting the money.

I had the check made out to Reclamation Mining, Ltd., and sent it off airmail. I enclosed a short letter to Judson Dormer, explaining that Marian and I were with him in this, and that we wanted seven shares.

A few weeks later, we got a receipt for the money.

The next year passed pretty fast. That was the year we had torrential spring rains, and you couldn't get a tractor into the fields until late in May. Whenever I got worried about the crops, I'd think about our shares and be at peace. That's how much confidence I had in Judson Dormer.

As the end of the year approached, Marian got enthused too. We'd talk about what we'd do with the money after we paid off the mortgage. One thing was to buy a camping trailer. Another was to increase our giving substantially—way beyond the tithe—to the Christian works we were interested in.

I never expected a check right on the anniversary of our investment. But when two weeks passed, and then a month, and then two months, I began to get a little concerned. So I wrote a letter to Judson Dormer, asking if maybe the check had gotten lost in the mail.

Several weeks later I had this mimeographed letter from Dormer in reply.

Dear Friend,

Unexpected complications in securing machine parts have delayed our reclamation mining project. I regret that this has delayed the payments on your investment that I guaranteed. This is doubtless a disappointment to you, as it is to me.

Be assured that we are working night and day to become operational, and will keep you informed by regular progress reports.

It will be worth it, I think you'll agree, when your monthly checks begin to arrive. . . .

I hated to show the letter to Marian, but I did. She just said, "I guess all of life has its complications. So we shouldn't be surprised if this does too."

Six months later, we had another mimeographed letter. This one was signed by Ernest Madling, Certified Mining Engineer.

Dear Investor in Reclamation Mining, Ltd.,

At the request of our mutual friend, Judson Dormer, I am writing to give you my professional opinion about the ore separation process and related machinery in which you have purchased shares.

The process is absolutely sound in chemical engineering theory.

Of more importance, I have seen the machine working at an abandoned mine in the West. (Discretion forbids my identifying its location more precisely.) Quality and quantity of gold reclaimed for the ore are excellent . . .

Well, that encouraged us. So we just waited eight months more, and had the mortgage on the farm converted to run a longer term. It still wasn't easy making the payments.

By this time, I was writing to Reclamation Mining, Ltd., every six weeks or so, sending a letter to Truth Against Communism at the same time. The last letter I sent, I asked them to return our total investment of $7,000, as Judson Dormer had promised he would at the very beginning. I sent the same letter to both addresses, by registered mail.

When this letter produced no results, I wrote to the missionary society Dormer had served under in China. They replied that he had resigned from the mission about six years earlier, and they regretted that they could supply no information about him.

A month or so later, reading the Saturday church newspaper of the Iowa City paper, I noticed that a missionary of this society was going to be speaking at a church there the following day. So Marian and I drove in to that service on Sunday morning, instead of our own church in Cambridge.

The missionary was good, but I could hardly wait for the service to end. I wanted to ask him a lot of questions.

Marian and I waited around until everyone else had left the church, except a few people talking at the front. Then we introduced ourselves to the missionary.

"I'd like to ask you about one of your former missionaries," I said. "That is, a former member of your mission."

"Judson Dormer?" he asked.

"Yes. Do you know about his mining project?"

"That's why I thought you wanted to ask about him. Did you invest any money?"

"Seven thousand dollars. Is there any hope, do you think, of getting any of it back?"

"I'm afraid not. I was just up in Canada, and it's a pretty big mess. If an investor who's Canadian would lodge an official complaint, the government would investigate. But nobody will."

"How about here in the States?"

"It was a Canadian operation. The Securities and Exchange Commission won't get involved. Incidentally, I lost two thousand dollars myself. Money I had saved for retirement."

"I'm sorry. With the farm and all, it isn't so serious for us."

Marian had been silent up to this point. But now she said, "You know, it's sort of strange how he hoodwinked us—and a lot of other people, too."

"No doubt about it," the missionary said. "And most of the people couldn't afford it any more than we could."

"Makes you wonder," Marian continued, "about all those other things he told us—about the things that happened to him when the Communists took over in China."

The missionary was quiet for a few moments. Then he spoke. "You know, he never was in any Communist prison."

"He wasn't?" we both exploded.

"No, he made that whole story up. Very few people in the mission even knew that, and when he resigned, our leaders decided not to say anything about it. I guess they thought he was no longer answerable to them, and it would be an act of Christian love to cover it up."

"Love for whom?" Marian asked. "The people who believed him and supported Truth Against Communism, and later invested in his mining scheme?"

"Nobody could have known at the time—before it all happened—how it would turn out," the missionary said.

"What about that report from the certified mining engineer?" I asked. "He said the machine really worked."

"Ernest Madling isn't a mining engineer," the missionary said. "He's a pastor out in the prairies. Dormer evidently persuaded him to write that letter and sign it as he did."

"Do you have anywhere to go for dinner?" I asked. "We're going to eat here in Iowa City before we head for home, and we'd like to have you join us."

"Sorry, I'd really like to," the missionary said. "But I'm going home with the pastor."

So we said good-bye and went out and got into the pickup truck.

"Do you know what?" Marian said. "You're going to take me to the best restaurant in town for Sunday dinner."

"Sure," I said. "Anything else?"

"Yes, one more thing. I like that missionary. He wasn't flashy, but he had a lot to say that was worth saying. I'd like us to think about giving to his support."

The dinner was great, except the relish wasn't as good as Marian's.

Still Small Roar

IN THE KINGDOM of ideas lived a word.

The word was unspoken in real-world language, not through mere ignorance, but through inability to contain it.

Thus the word continued in the unapproachable realm of ideas.

Now other words were easily contained, readily expressed. These were the dread words, the dead ones, fearsome, morbid, evil, beautiful.

There were a few in the real world who affirmed the unspoken word's existence. "It is there," they said, "even though we cannot perceive it. We are in a box that excludes the word. We cannot break through to it, but it is there. Just outside the box."

Some vaguely felt their need for such a word, although they had little hope that the word really existed.

But the other real-world inhabitants, in overwhelming numbers, denied that there was such a thing as an unspoken word. "Whether the word is or not makes little difference," they said. "What counts is here and now. Go back to sleep, or to sex, or to stocks or clubs, even to rosebushes. Why waste your mound of minutes with a word that isn't spoken? There are enough other words to satisfy—three- and four-letter words, seven-letter, even twelve-letter ones. And for all and always, the single-letter one."

Those who knew the four-letter words, and the twelve-letter ones, were least interested in the unspoken word.

And so it continued from generation to generation. Words became longer, new words were formed, the one-letter word continued at the center and perimeter of life in the real world.

Still the word continued unspoken, and hope dimmed among some who had affirmed that there was such a word.

Others, the feeling and sensitive ones, shaped substitute words to which they gave allegiance. "It has come out of the idea world to reality," they said. "The unspoken word has finally been spoken"—but it hadn't. And no new word survived prolonged encounter.

One day the word was spoken.

In a whisper.

This surprised everyone, but most of all those who had insisted that there was such a word: they expected a shout, a roar, a waterfall thundering of sound.

In a real barn, in a whisper. When the word left the barn, it went throughout the countryside. Country people heard it, not kings—the small, not great.

"Yes, it's the word," they said, "the word we never knew we wanted because we never knew it was."

They took the word from a barn into their peasant homes. It was spoken at their tables, their picnics, their weddings and funerals.

Strangely, the four-letter-word people heard the word most eagerly. The fifteen-letter people scorned it, explaining it away.

More strangely, most of those who had lived expectant for the unspoken word now refused the spoken one. "This is scarcely the word we awaited," they said. "It isn't even shouted."

"If it were really the once unspoken word, it would conform to our expectations. Since it doesn't, it can't be. We prefer no word to this word we hear."

Those who had most wanted the word to be uttered came to despise the uttered word. They scorned it and turned from it.

But to those who listened, the word was powerful, more powerful than howling storm or waterfall, marching army or creeping lust.

And the power was implosive; the word shattered all other words. All of them, but especially the one-letter word, concealing the word that it revealed.

What was true of the one-letter word was true of the rest. Even the four-letter ones were changed, made beautiful, by the spoken word.

Those who turned from the word were irritated, aghast that such a thing should happen. "Four-letter words are to be buried, not changed. The one-letter word is to be affirmed, not torn to shreds."

"And besides," said others, "if it were the true word, it would be spoken in temple and palace, not hovel and sailboat."

Children loved the word. They laughed it, sang it, danced it. And they could understand it, even when the fifteen-letter-word older people were puzzled at the word's meaning.

"It means 'I love you,'" they'd say. "It means 'Come here. Don't be scared.'"

For the people were afraid.

"What will the end be?" they asked. "The word casts doubt on all our other words. It is not at home in the real world, yet soon it will fill our every nook and cranny."

At increasing pace, resistance to the word—bitter, vengeful, calculated resistance—grew among the people.

"The word could destroy us," they said. "We have no choice—come, destroy the word. Or be destroyed by the word. Our world is at stake."

And so, impelled by hateful fear, or fearful hate, temple and throne joined to destroy the word.

And they did.

They erased it from pavement, wall, and book, that word first whispered in a barn. They silenced it, whisper and shout, from hill, field, lake, desert, tree.

They erased the word, expunging hope. For while the word existed outside the box, within was hope, dim hope. And when the word was spoken, hope flowed.

But the word removed killed hope.

Children and four-letter-word people cried for the word that no longer was, the hope that was dead. So did some five- and seven-letter ones.

The twelve-letter and fifteen-letter people decided that they should bury it. For it was a worthy word, they agreed.

They put the word in a dictionary, contained it with all the other words. That seemed to be the proper place for it, a place that was safe. "After all, a word is only a word," they said. "And all words are on an equal footing in a dictionary. So that's where the word belongs."

But the dictionary couldn't contain the word, nor could all the dictionaries. It broke out, grew, and filled the box.

The word broke out of the box and left a gash through which the beyond idea world could be glimpsed for the first time from the real world.

Children waited wide-eyed, looking up at the gash. In all their games and hurts they watched the gash.

"We'll hear the word again," they said. "Next time it'll roar. And it will tear up the box."

How Shall We Remember John?

M Y BIG BROTHER John and I were great pals. In fact, our whole family was close, including Mom and Dad, my sister, the brother I'm telling you about, and me. We were close in a way that you find few families today.

Breakfast was always a special time. We sat around this round oak table with a red, checked cloth on it. Mom almost always served the same thing: steaming hot oatmeal with brown sugar cooked in it (we piled a lot more on top of it too), and milk. A big, white pitcher full of milk.

We'd talk about what we were going to do that day, and maybe we'd joke some. Not that we had a lot of time—we didn't, but we had enough to talk some before Dad went off to work, and us kids went to school.

John and I were two grades apart in school. That was sort of hard on me, because the teachers who had had him were always comparing us when I got into their classes. And the comparison wasn't too flattering to me.

Don't get me wrong. John wasn't a teacher's pet or a bookworm. He was a regular guy, and the kids all liked him, including the girls. Maybe one guy who was sort of a bully didn't, but everyone else did.

Life went on like that; breakfast of oatmeal and milk, walk to school, classes, walk home, chores, supper, study around the kitchen table—and you never thought about anything else. Except vacation. Vacation was always stuck in your mind.

You know the kind of life, day after day, when it's so great you hope it never ends. Maybe you cry at night sometimes, if you think of your mom or dad dying. You know they will someday. But then you go to sleep, next to John, who's already sawing wood.

It was Christmas vacation, when I was in sixth grade and John was in eighth, that it all suddenly came to an end. Actually, it was two days after Christmas.

John and I had gone to ice-skate on Big Pond. It was a real cold day, cold enough so that your scarf got ice on it from your breath. I put on my skates in a hurry and sailed out to the middle of the pond. I noticed a slight cracking sound from the ice, but it wasn't much and I wasn't worried. It had been pretty cold for about a week. So I showed off some for John, who was still lacing up his skates, sitting on a log, and then I headed for the opposite shore.

John stood up and went real fast, right out to the middle too. Just as he got there, I heard this sickening cracking noise, the ice broke up, and John fell through.

I got a long branch and went out as far as I could on the ice. But I couldn't see John anywhere. He had just disappeared. I yelled for him, and I went even farther out, but he wasn't there.

I must have panicked, because first thing I knew, I was running into the house shouting for Mom, crying my eyes out, yelling that John was in the pond. It was awful.

They found his body later that afternoon.

A few days after the funeral, we were sitting at the table, eating breakfast one morning. Nobody was saying anything, all of us were thinking about that empty chair over against the wall.

You could tell Mom was trying to talk. Finally she just sort of blurted out, "Look, we all miss John terribly. We loved—love him, and we'll always miss him. Now I have a suggestion to make. Do you remember how he liked oatmeal and milk?"

"Do I!" I said. "He used to pile on the brown sugar until—"

"That's enough. He liked his oatmeal sweet and so do you. What I want to suggest is this. Let's think about John every time we eat oatmeal and drink milk. Let's talk about him—"

"Yeah, like the time he and I went swimming in Big Pond and . . ." I knew before Sis spoke that I had said something I shouldn't have. Everyone was sort of choked up.

"Time for school," she said.

And Dad said, as we all left the table, "We can continue this later."

Well, we did. And we agreed with Mom's suggestion. So each morning, when that big pitcher of cold milk went on the table, and our bowls of steaming oatmeal were set in front of us, we'd talk about John.

It wasn't sad talk, but happy. Remembering. I don't mean we never said anything that made us choke up—other people besides me did. But mainly it was happy talk. And we still talked about what we were going to do that day, and even—after a while—joked some.

One day, some months later, Mom said, "I don't think what we're doing is respectful enough for John's memory."

"Respectful?" I said. "Why, it's fun. Sometimes it's almost like John is here with us. I like it."

"So do I," Mom said. "But I think we're too casual about it. So I think we ought to set aside a time when we're not rushed like we are at breakfast. Let's say Saturday morning. And we'll remember John in a more fitting place than the kitchen. We'll sit in the parlor, and we'll have a special time worthy of John's memory."

"Aw, Mom," I said, "John always liked breakfast in the kitchen. Lots of oatmeal with plenty of brown sugar on it. And milk. Why make a big deal out of it?"

"Son," Dad said, "we'll do as your mother says."

So every Saturday morning, after we had eaten our regular breakfast in the kitchen, we went into the parlor and remembered John. Mom had gotten some little silver cups for the milk, and some tiny plates for the oatmeal.

Later we only went into the parlor once a month, instead of every week, and now we only did it every three months. It doesn't seem right to me, but I'll soon be leaving home, so it doesn't much matter.

I still wish we had never begun that "fitting" remembrance, and had just kept on remembering John every time we ate breakfast.

The Gospel Blimp

One: Conception of an Idea

THE IDEA REALLY began that night several years ago when we were all sitting around in George and Ethel Griscom's backyard.

We'd just finished eating an outdoor picnic supper (a real spread), and there wasn't much to do except swat mosquitoes and watch fireflies. Every so often an airplane flew over, high in the sky. You could see the twinkling red and white lights.

I guess that's what got us started on the Gospel Blimp. Or maybe it was George and Ethel's next-door neighbors, who were playing cards and drinking beer on the porch.

Anyway, we began talking about how to reach people with the Gospel. Herm's active in the local businessmen's group (he and Marge were there that night, their first time out after the baby was born). So when we started talking about reaching people, Herm says, "Let's take those folks next door to you, George, for example. You can tell they're not Christians. Now if we wanted to give them the Gospel, how'd we—"

"Herm, for goodness' sake, keep your voice down," Marge interrupted. "D'you want them to hear you?"

"Herm's right, they're not Christians," George agreed. "Go to church— a liberal one—Christmas and Easter. But drink and play cards most other Sundays. Except the summer. In a few weeks they'll start going to the shore each weekend until Labor Day."

"OK now. Any suggestions?" Herm is a good discussion leader.

"Hey, look at the plane. It's really low. You can almost see the lights in the windows."

"Portholes. More potato chips, anyone?"

"Like I was saying, here's a test. How do we go about giving the Gospel to those people over there?"

And Herm motioned toward the house next door.

"Too bad that plane didn't carry a sign. They looked up from their card playing long enough to have read it if it had carried one."

"Hey, you know, you may have something there. Any of you seen those blimps with signs trailing on behind? You know, 'Drink Pepsi Cola', or 'Chevrolet Is First'?"

"Volkswagen sales are really increasing. I read the other day—"

"What I mean is this. Why not have a blimp with a Bible verse trailing—something like 'Believe on the Lord Jesus Christ, and thou shalt be saved'?"

"I can see it now. The world's first vertical blimp, straight up and down like that tree. Anchored by a sign."

"Stop making fun. We could get a shorter verse."

"Sounds like a terrific idea. Really terrific. Why, everybody would get the Gospel at the same time."

"Everybody except blind people and children who aren't able to read."

"Nothing's perfect. Anyway, it does sound terrific, like Marge said."

"How'd we go about it? And wouldn't it be awfully expensive? I mean, buying the blimp, and blowing it up, and everything."

"Hey, it's time for the 'Maxie Belden Show.'"

"Aw, who wants to watch TV on a night like this, stars and breeze and all? Well, if everybody else is going inside . . ."

I guess we'd have left it at that—just one of those crazy things you talk about when a group gets together for supper and the evening—if it hadn't been for Herm.

Like I said, Herm's a good organizer. (I mean, I said he's a good discussion leader. But he's a good organizer.)

So the next Thursday Herm brought the idea up at our weekly businessmen's luncheon. He asked to make an announcement, and then he began. You could tell he was excited.

"Look, we want to reach people. And I've got a proposal to make. As you can see, we're not reaching them with our luncheons—" Here he paused and looked around the room. I did too, and I guess everybody else did. Not that we needed to. The regulars were there: three preachers and sixteen businessmen, two of them retired. And, of course, there was old Mr. Jensen. He doesn't do much anymore, but he still owns about half the real estate around town. I mean, a lot of houses and buildings—not necessarily half. And all of them Christians—the men at the luncheon, that is.

Well, Herm summarized the Gospel Blimp idea. He really did a good job. You could just tell that different ones were getting excited as he talked. Nobody even started on their ice cream until he was through.

"And so I suggest," Herm ended, in a real loud voice, "that we appoint a committee. Maybe it's for the birds. Maybe not. But anyway," and here he paused and looked around the room again, "we ought to be reaching people somehow."

He'd hardly sat down when old Mr. Jensen was on his feet, real excited. "Herm," he said. "I'm all for it. One hundred and ten percent. 'Course, there'll be problems, but nothing ventured, nothing lost. I think you ought to be chairman of the committee, Herm. Young fellow like him has lots of spizzerinkum, Fred," he finished, with a wink at our president, Dr. Gottlieb.

That afternoon we were a little late ending the luncheon, but by the time we did, a committee had been formed, with Herm as chairman.

"All you fellows on the committee, stay behind a few minutes," Herm called out above the scraping of the chairs as we rose to go. "We'll have to settle on a meeting time. This'll take work—lots of it."

Two: Labor Pains

Lots of work. That was the understatement of the year—maybe of the century.

First off we found we'd have to incorporate, otherwise the businessmen's group would have been liable, or maybe us personally. Liable financially, that is.

That constitution was a bear. It took two trips to the state capital before we got it approved. But finally, there we were, International Gospel Blimps, Inc. (We made it blimps instead of blimp because someone suggested the idea might spread. And if it did, we'd be in on the ground floor. Then Herm said, well, if it did spread, or if it might, why not be sure we take care of all eventualities. Why not make it international right from the start? So we did.)

Next we got stationery and receipts printed up. Since we'd gotten incorporated as a nonprofit organization, we could include the line on the receipt about contributions being tax-deductible.

This took all our time, and I mean all our time, for the next couple of months. That summer my lawn looked like a jungle. Especially after that week of rain late in the summer.

I remember that third week in August, because it was Friday evening, and I had gone over to George Griscom's to decide on accounting procedures. Money had begun to come in, and we'd just opened a bank account. It was about nine-thirty, and we were coming along OK when someone knocked on the screen door.

George got up and went. I heard him thank whoever it was for mowing his lawn. Then they talked for a few more minutes, and the man went away. I heard him call out, "Sorry you can't come," as he went off the porch.

"I'm sure glad you got that screen door closed," I said, half serious. "This place is crawling with mosquitoes."

"Listen," George says, and I can tell something's on his mind, "that was my next-door neighbor. Remember the guy who was drinking beer and playing cards with his wife on the porch when you were over in June? The night we dreamed up this Gospel Blimp idea? He just invited me, that is, Ethel and me, to go down to the shore with them this weekend. Of course I told him we couldn't go. Tomorrow's the full committee meeting, and Sunday afternoon's the IGBI prayer meeting.

"But that's not what I'm getting at," George continued. "What I mean is this. Wouldn't it be tremendous if he'd be the first fruit of the blimp? Both of them, I mean. It would sort of put a seal on it all if they'd become Christians. After all, they were why we thought of it in the first place."

So before I left, Ethel came in, and the three of us had prayer together that their neighbors would be saved through the Gospel Blimp.

Somehow as I drove home through the darkness, there was a peaceful sense of rightness about the IGBI plan. Maybe I'd had it before, maybe not. But tonight I knew. This was for people. And people would be saved. People like the Griscoms' next-door neighbors.

I've sometimes wondered whether we'd have started on the whole thing if we'd known at the very beginning all that was involved.

Not the money. I don't mean that. Like somebody once said (maybe it was that fellow who started missions in China), "Have faith, think big, and tell the people. You'll get the money." And we did. It really came rolling in.

We were able to get an article about the Gospel Blimp in a Christian magazine, and did that ever stir up interest. We followed it up with a big advertisement. Money came in from all over. Also requests for information, suggestions of verses to be used at the blimp's tail, offers of hangar space, offers of uniforms for the crew. All kinds of offers.

At first I handled the correspondence, until I got swamped so bad I couldn't see my way out (complicated by it being Christmas and the kids having the measles). Honest, I never knew so many Christians were sign painters or had had experience on Navy blimps and ground crews. I answered twenty-six letters from sign painters and nineteen from Navy blimp Christians (not counting about a hundred Air Force guys) before I gave up and handed the job over to Herm.

One old gentleman even wrote from Germany to say he'd be honored to give us technical advice. (Doc Gottlieb read it for me—it was in German.) Seems he'd served on the Hindenburg—missed its last trip because he'd fallen off a ladder the day before it left Frankfurt. He was willing to serve without compensation—only wanted his passage money across the Atlantic.

Like I said, the whole thing mushroomed like an inverted pyramid until we just had to do something. It was wrecking my home. I was out every night, and the only time I saw the kids was at breakfast. Love in our home meant "A bowl of cereal, a glass of milk, and you." (That's the year we celebrated Christmas five days late. At least the tree didn't cost us anything.)

So Herm finally decided to give up his job at the meat packing plant and go into the Gospel Blimp full time. It was a big decision for him to make, giving up a good job with security and a pension and relatively safe work. On the other hand, as he pointed out to us, there was no real security in the Gospel Blimp, even though it looked promising. But he was willing to take a step of faith if we were behind him.

And we were. Especially me, for reasons that should be obvious. I was about at the end of my rope.

Three: The Blimp Is Delivered

The blimp was delivered in April. It drifted in, sort of lazylike, from the East, where it had been manufactured.

We were all on hand, plus about five hundred other people, to see it come down into the hangar. (Did I tell you old Mr. Jensen gave some ground just beyond the city limits, down near the sewage disposal plant, for the hangar?)

It was a beauty. I've never seen Herm so touched—said it made him think of a perfect sausage, a perfect one.

That night we had a sort of send-off dinner up at Second Church. Speeches by the mayor (that was before the time when persecution began), by the head of the ministerial association (he, too, was extremely friendly still), and by a Christian Navy commander.

Afterward we all got in our cars and drove out to the hangar, where the Gospel Blimp was christened. Herm's little girl broke a bottle of 7-UP over it. (We originally thought of Coke, but someone suggested that seven is the number of perfection, so we used 7-UP.)

George Griscom invited us over to his house afterward—everybody who'd been there that night we had the original idea for the blimp, almost a year ago. We were sort of sober, thinking of all that lay ahead.

"You know," George said, "if only my next-door neighbors are saved. If they are, it'll be worthwhile. All the work and money and time."

"Listen," Herm said, "it can't fail. They can read, can't they? Well, tomorrow morning at eight sharp they'll see the Gospel in the sky. Right over their house. I promise you, George, in my capacity as general director of International Gospel Blimps, Incorporated. And not just your next-door neighbors. The whole block. My block. Every block in the city. Every last one. But we'll start with your block, George. Seems only right, doesn't it?" And he looked around the room for approval.

We all nodded or said yes, it sure did.

"What verse are you starting out with, Herm?"

"That would be telling. You'll see tomorrow morning, bright and early. Well, everybody, guess we'd better call it a night."

Next morning I drove past George's house on my way to work, starting a little early so I'd get there just at eight. Sure enough, there was the blimp. And trailing on behind was the sign. It was really beautiful, with the early morning sun highlighting those bold red letters.

Why, the Gospel could be seen for blocks!

Maybe it was too early in the day, but I didn't see anyone out looking up at it. So after stopping the car for a minute across from George's house, I went on to work.

I went out for lunch that day (often I'd bring it in a bag, and just get a cup of coffee at the soda fountain on the first floor). But I went out, and first thing I did was look up between the buildings at the sky. No blimp.

So I walked several blocks to this little sandwich shop some of us go to, hoping I'd run into one or two of the fellows. Sure enough, George and a couple of others were there.

"Seen the blimp?" George asked me.

"First thing this morning, on my way to work."

"Boy, is it beautiful. You can see that sign almost a mile off."

"Wonder where it is now. Herm should have brought it downtown for the lunch hour."

"Well, there's going to be a lot of lunch hours before we're finished with that bag."

We didn't know it then, but we were almost finished with the blimp right at that moment. In fact, we found out later that's the reason Herm didn't have it downtown for the noon hour.

Seems Herm and the other guy (this graduate of a Christian flying school we had hired) were cruising along just over the rooftops when there was this tremendous jolt, followed by a hissing sound. Next thing they knew they were losing altitude, but fast.

Must have been a frightening experience. (Herm said later he expected the whole thing to go thrrp-l-p-sss, the way a balloon does when you blow it up and release it in the air without tying it, that is, the end you blow into. But it didn't.) In a few minutes they came to rest, sort of wedged between two houses.

I wish I'd been there to see those two women come running out of their front doors. One of them had been making beds upstairs when suddenly all the light from the outside was extinguished. So she ran over to the window, threw it open, and there was this thing. It sort of gave when she pushed against it, and there was this hissing sound. Well, she ran screaming into the street.

The other lady called the fire department, and they soon had a hook and ladder truck there.

"I've gotten cats out of trees, and kids out of bathrooms, but this is the first time I've gotten two guys off a blimp," this fireman in charge of the truck said, according to Herm. Herm says he used some other language, too, which was the opportunity for a witness.

It took a few weeks to get the blimp back in shape again. Seems they were flying too low, and the pilot wasn't watching carefully the way he should have been. Besides, he wasn't yet familiar with our little city. The big thing he didn't know was that a radio station's tower was located plumb in the middle of this residential section. So first thing, he'd ripped the blimp's bottom on the tower. But finally it was ready to return to the air. (I mean the blimp. The radio station's programs weren't interrupted. That was no factor in the later persecution.)

Four: Togetherness

Meanwhile we'd gotten prepared for the long haul. By that I mean we learned a lesson from that first day. This job wouldn't be done overnight. There would be opposition; the Enemy had already tried to ruin the blimp.

So we started prayer meetings for the safety of the blimp and those whose lives would be constantly endangered by flying in it. These prayer meetings were held downtown each noon hour for those of us who could come, in the International Gospel Blimp, Inc., office. (I forgot to tell you we'd rented three rooms in the Bender Building.) Thursdays we didn't meet there, since that was the day of the businessmen's lunch, too.

The wives had their prayer meeting every Tuesday night. They combined their praying with work on these fire bombs, which they filled.

But I'm getting ahead of my story.

After the rip in the blimp was repaired, Herm got the thing running on a regular schedule. This was possible because we let this other fellow, the first one we had, go. He was undependable, and besides, he didn't know enough about flying, as witness the radio tower episode. But we really got a wonderful replacement who had spent four years flying Navy blimps out of Lakehurst, New Jersey. He was a young married fellow who'd been considering the mission field. In fact, he'd applied for South America or Africa or someplace. But, with his wife's help, we finally convinced him that this was much more strategic, because look at all the kids and young people he could influence for missions with this job.

Just so I won't forget this part of the blimp's ministry, let me tell you that this new fellow wasn't with us very long before he convinced the board that we should have a missionary emphasis on the blimp. So we decided that every Saturday afternoon would be Missionary Blimp Afternoon. (We chose Saturday because we knew the Christian kids don't go to the movies then, like so many other kids.) We used missionary signs on the blimp and released junior missionary bombs.

I was interested to see how my own kids would be affected by this new missionary emphasis, especially because they'd sort of come to resent the time I (also their mother) was spending on blimp work. Maybe resent is too strong a word. It was more a matter of their saying, "Aw, another night out working on the blimp? You haven't been home since a week ago Saturday." They also were rather bitter about what happened at the football game.

Anyway, I was really happy when this one Sunday on the way home from church my boy brought up the subject. He said he'd been thinking about the blimp, and the missionary sign the blimp had pulled the afternoon before (it was, I believe, the "One Billion Unreached" one).

As a result of all this thinking, he said, "I've decided to learn to pilot a blimp when I grow up. I'm going to enlist in the Navy."

"It's not fair," says his little sister. "It's really not fair at all. Boys get to do everything. I could never be a missionary. Girls don't get to learn to fly blimps. All they get to do is play with dolls and wash the bathroom floor and—" She stopped for breath.

"Huh," says our oldest girl, the one who's in high school. "Who'd want to have anything to do with a blimp, anyway? Only a creep. A real, square creep. Brother, I mean, that Gospel Blimp is—"

"Judy, be careful of your mouth," her mother warns her. "It can get you in trouble."

"Trouble? What do you call what I and the other Christian kids got in over what happened at the game with Central? I guess the blimp had nothing to do with that. My mouth didn't get us into that trouble. There we were, ahead at the half, and then that darn blimp has to come along and—"

"Judy, that will be enough. You may set the table when we get home."

"Besides," I felt constrained to add in the blimp's defense, "everyone agrees that it was one of those freak accidents. One chance in a million of its happening. You can't really blame the blimp."

I think I told you about the fire bombs we were using. We named them that because they represented revival fire falling on the unsaved.

The IGBI Women's Auxiliary fixed them, like I said, at their weekly meetings. There wasn't really much to making them—they just took a tract and wrapped it up in different-colored cellophane. There were loose ends sticking out, so that when they were dumped overboard from the blimp, they sort of floated to earth.

At first the kids chased them all over—I hear someone spread a rumor that there was bubblegum in them. But after a couple of days, no one got particularly excited when they fell.

The Commander (Herm wanted us to call him that now) made quite an affair out of dumping the load, according to the blimp pilot.

"Bombs away!" he'd shout, and then he'd shoot them down, alternating colors (each color was a different tract).

And always, when he'd have a new tract, he'd try to dump some on George Griscoms' next-door neighbor's lawn. He wasn't forgetting, the Commander wasn't, our covenant with George about his neighbor.

Not that there was any encouragement along that line. Once, I recall, I stopped at Griscoms' to return George's power drill. I'd been getting the PA system ready to install on the blimp. So I asked Ethel about their neighbors.

"Nothing new," she says. "I mean, nothing to get excited about as far as their salvation is concerned. But she hasn't been well. I think they took her to the hospital two or three days ago. We can see him eating over there alone at night. And always a bottle of beer. Sometimes two."

"What hospital's she in?" I asked.

"I don't know. I'll tell George you stopped with the drill. By the way, how's the sound system coming?"

"Oh, some bugs yet. But give us a few more nights like tonight and we'll be ready to roll."

"Will people really be able to hear it?"

"With a hundred-watt output? And three cone speakers? Listen, they'll be able to hear it anywhere—even in a basement. No worry about that."

"The Women's Auxiliary is really thrilled about the sound system. You know, we've been concerned about blind people, and children who can't read yet, and people who are nearsighted. And people who can't get outside to see the blimp, like invalids, and old men and women in convalescent homes, and people in hospitals. It'll be comforting to know we're doing something for them."

"Well, tell George I stopped. And thanks for the drill."

Five: A Small Cloud

When we started using the PA system about a week later, a new epoch in the Gospel Blimp's ministry began. In a sense, it seemed to give final assurance that the total evangelism of our little city was a distinct possibility.

But it also marked the beginning of the period of active opposition. Forces were unleashed that we hardly knew existed beneath the calm surface of life all around us.

I'll never forget that first night. I had gone down to the drugstore to get a box of candy and a card (having been reminded during dessert that it was our wedding anniversary), when suddenly I heard it.

In loud tones, on the wings of the night, as it were, came the sound of "Rolled away, rolled away." Honest, it was tremendous.

People came out of houses, cars stopped, everybody tried to figure where it was coming from.

Of course I knew. For I had put the last Phillips screw through the third speaker only that afternoon. But the rest of the people were puzzled because the blimp was nowhere in sight.

Next came the vibraharp rendition of the "Glory Song," followed by about fifty kids singing the "Hash Chorus." But it wasn't until the music had stopped, and the Commander's voice came on, "Now hear this, all you people," that the blimp hovered into sight. It wasn't a full moon, but it was still bright enough to see the blimp clearly outlined against the sky.

I suppose the Commander preached about ten minutes that first time. Or maybe it took ten minutes for the blimp to get out of earshot. But even though it was short, he was able to get in two invitations. The vibraharp came on for a few bars of "Almost Persuaded" each time. (I should explain that the music was recorded on tape, although Herm's messages were live. It was only later that he taped the full program, including his own preaching. But that was while he was out of town.)

I tell you, I was really thrilled. When I got home with the candy, I phoned up the Griscoms to tell them the good news.

"I know why you're calling," says George before I have a chance to tell him.

"Listen." And he holds the phone away from his head. In the background, coming through clear as a bell, I can hear, "Hallelu, Hallelu, Hallelu."

Were we ever enthused! I think, looking back, that night was the high point of the whole blimp project. But we were totally unprepared for the next morning.

I picked up the *Trib* on my way to the office. And there on the front page, down toward the bottom, was a story about the "airborne sound truck." It was the first time the blimp had hit the papers. (Earlier there had been a few lines about the christening, and a notice of the public meeting, but nothing like this.)

I guess I must have been sort of walking on air when I came into the office. Of course the guys I work with had known for a long time about my interest in the blimp. But they had sort of treated it something like—well, like the guy who bowls every night, or the fellow who's a scoutmaster. So now they could see the significance of my project., and they had probably even heard the Gospel the night before.

Anyway, I sort of remarked casual-like after I'd hung up my coat, "You fellows see the newspaper story on the blimp?"

"Which one?"

"Why, there is only one," I say. "You know, the one I'm interested in, the Gospel one."

"No, I mean which story? There are two, or didn't you know?"

"Where's the other one? I only saw the one on the front page." And suddenly I'm sort of sorry I brought up the subject, because everybody's quiet, and nobody's smiling.

"Well, then, maybe you'd better read the one on the editorial page, Buster."

So I sat down at my desk and read it. It was an editorial entitled, "The Right to Peace." And it began—here, I have a copy—

For some weeks now our metropolis has been treated to the spectacle of a blimp with an advertising sign attached at the rear. This sign does not plug cigarettes, or a bottled beverage, but the religious beliefs of a particular group in our midst. The people of our city are notably broadminded, and they have good-naturedly submitted to this attempt to proselytize. But last night a new refinement (some would say debasement) was introduced. We refer, of course, to the airborne sound truck, that invader of our privacy, that raucous destroyer of communal peace. That the voices of some of our city's beloved schoolchildren were used does not take away from …

Well, that's enough for you to get the general drift.

It seemed as if lunch would never come. When it did, I hurried over to the place I mentioned before, even though I'd brought my lunch. I mean the lunchroom where the Christian fellows often eat.

As soon as I saw them I knew we'd all had the same experience.

We talked it over, including all the angles. And when it came time for us to get back to work, someone—maybe it was George—seemed to sum it up when he said, "Well, we were told we'd be persecuted for righteousness' sake, and I guess this is it. So we'll just have to stand together, foursquare."

That night our IGBI board of directors held an emergency meeting downtown to discuss the situation. We'd hardly gotten started when the phone rang. It was the pilot—he'd just returned from supper to take the blimp out for its final run of the day. When he got inside the hangar, he found someone had broken in and sabotaged the blimp's PA system. Nothing else was touched.

The Commander told him to lock up and go on home for the night, and not to talk to anybody about what had happened. Then we settled down to discuss what to do. Somehow it seemed a much more pressing matter than it had before the phone call.

When we broke up around midnight, we'd come to certain decisions. In the first place, we decided that we'd continue to use the PA system on the blimp, no matter what happened. But we'd turn down the volume a bit. Next, we'd see if we couldn't get the sign electrified so that people could see where the sound was coming from when we broadcast at night. And finally, on the Commander's recommendation, we decided to hire a public relations man who'd be responsible for keeping the blimp in good with the general public. The Commander also said such a man could get money from Christians to pay for the blimp and the salaries and the sound system and the office and everything else.

The whole operation was costing about five thousand dollars per month, and even with contributions coming in from all over the country, it was still a strain. So we gladly voted to accept Herm's recommendation. I might even say that we breathed a sigh of relief. At least I did, because we were in a whole lot deeper than we ever imagined we'd be that Thursday afternoon about ten months ago, when Herm first brought the blimp up at our businessmen's lunch.

Six: Architect of Goodwill

That new public relations fellow really knew his business. First thing he did was arrange a big dinner—to recoup our forces and make new friends, he said. The IGBI Women's Auxiliary worked on it, and it was really well planned. Ham and sweets and everything else, with ice cream blimp molds for dessert. For favors they had little blimp banks—to save up money so you could pay your pledge, that is, if you made one. The whole dinner was gratis—there were no tickets and no offering. Just the opportunity to pledge at the end.

It was a bit disappointing that some of the people we invited didn't come. The mayor declined because of a previous engagement, and he was also too busy to write us a letter to be read at the dinner.

But the dinner was just the beginning of this public relations fellow's activity. As he expressed it, "Any item of interest about the blimp or its ministry is legitimate news. And news builds goodwill."

So he got little items in the papers about how much helium the blimp contained and where the helium came from, about the Commander moving to his new house, about the church affiliations of members of the board, about the Women's Auxiliary luncheons and parties, about the electric generating plant on the blimp, about all sorts of other things. One or two of these items even made the radio news summary.

He also had a regular news service for Christian magazines with plenty of photographs. Pictures of the Commander releasing the one millionth fire bomb were published by about ten different periodicals. Another time a picture of the Commander at the wheel made the front cover of a big Christian magazine.

This public relations fellow was working on the theory that International Gospel Blimps was too impersonal. People couldn't feel "empathy," as he put it, with a nonprofit corporation, or even with a blimp. Too big and fat and cold. So more and more he built up the Commander as the blimp's personification. He got the Commander to grow a beard (like those guys in the magazine advertisements), and also to wear a new uniform. The old one was something like a policeman's, but the new one was beautiful, powder blue, with shiny gold buttons and gold stripes on the sleeves. That visor had enough braid on it for an admiral.

The Commander was spending less and less time on the blimp. At our new public relations man's suggestion, he joined the best golf club so he could meet the people whose influence really counts, and who could contribute substantially to IGBI. He also began taking speaking engagements all over—not just churches, but service clubs and women's clubs and other meetings of that sort.

That summer he wasn't around much because he had a full schedule of engagements at Bible conferences. Sometimes he took Marge with him, but mostly he'd just go off in his Mercedes-Benz alone.

I'm told he had quite a ministry at these conferences, especially in terms of getting young people to dedicate their lives to Christian service. He talked a lot about sacrifice, and told about how he'd given up a successful career in business when he felt the call. No holding back, no looking around from the plow. Straight ahead, whatever the cost.

And the money really came in. There was no doubt about that public relations fellow knowing what he was doing.

Funny thing happened about this time. The Commander was leaving on one of his trips this particular Thursday afternoon, and he came to the businessmen's luncheon first. He wasn't able to come very often anymore, so we were all glad to see him.

Herm gave a report, and then we reminisced some, recalling how enthusiastic old Mr. Jensen (the one who gave us the land on which the hangar was placed) had been that first time we ever discussed the blimp. Most of us had been at Mr. Jensen's funeral a few weeks before. (Incidentally, he left $5,000 in his will to IGBI, some to the Commander, too, in view of his sacrifice.)

Anyway, after the meeting, while Herm got in the driver's seat, we told him we'd loaded the bombs for him to drop on his trip. As far as we were concerned it was just a practical joke. We were all standing around ready to empty the bombs back into the basket and take them away.

But Herm didn't take it as a joke. He sort of froze, didn't even say goodbye, and drove off. Later we found them dumped on the ground out near the hangar.

Seven: Cloudburst

That fall everything was going fine, and all of us had sort of settled down to the kind of life we'd known before the blimp came along.

The blimp was on a regular schedule, flying all over the city during the daytime, concentrating on shopping centers and special events at night. People had come to accept the blimp—fact is, there was a sort of community pride of ownership. No other place had a Gospel Blimp, you know, although a lot of them had expressed interest.

Opposition to the blimp had all but died out, largely as a result of turning down the volume on the PA system and the public relations work.

There was one new development: foreign language programs. Although they weren't large, our city had several foreign sections. These included Chinatown, Italian and Polish communities, and one suburb that was largely German. So we rigged up signs in these languages and also recorded foreign language programs on tape. Then we had regular days and nights during the month when the blimp concentrated on each of these foreign groups.

It was one of these nights, the Polish one, when all the goodwill Herm and the public relations fellow had been building up came crashing down around us. And not just the non-Christians; Christians were screaming for our hides just as loudly.

That Tuesday evening began in our home about the same as it did in thousands of other homes, I guess. We'd finished supper and the kids were hurrying to get the dishes done so they wouldn't miss any of the television programs. Tuesday night was, of course, the best night on TV. That was our downfall.

Let me explain at this point that the Gospel Blimp took to the air about seven o'clock that night. Everything was shipshape: the Polish sign was already lighted up, the baskets were full of fire bombs, the tape recorder was loaded and ready to roll with a completely Polish program. Everything was shipshape with one exception. But we couldn't have known ahead of time. Even the Federal Communications Commission later admitted that at the public hearing.

At any rate, we had just settled down in front of the TV set to watch "Pistol Bark" when the sound sort of fades, and instead of hearing what's happening on the program, we're listening to some sort of foreign gibberish.

"Hey, what's happening?" I ask. "Turn it to some other channel and let's see if it's just on the one station."

One station, every station: the same foreign-language program.

"Boy, is some radio station going to get it in the neck for this blooper," I say.

And then it happens. The speaking ends and a vibraharp rendition of "Sunshine, Sunshine, in My Soul Today" begins. Four verses.

A guy gets pumped full of lead, lips move, a horse gallops away. But no sound. Just "Sunshine, Sunshine, in My Soul Today."

The program ends, and little cigarettes march around on the screen, out of step, to the tune of "Sunshine, Sunshine, in My Soul Today."

By this time I'm on the phone, and so are fifty thousand other people. I wait and wait for the dial tone and finally give up.

Besides, what can I do? What can anyone do?

Next comes the "Maxie Belden Show," the most popular program on TV—or at least it was then. Maxie comes on with a great big smile and begins talking Polish. This girl with the low-cut dress sings, only her voice is bass, and the words are, "Dwelling in Beulah Land." In Polish. It was horrible. I can't describe how I felt.

My oldest girl, the one in high school, begins to cry.

"What's the matter?" I ask. "Don't take it so hard. You can see what's going on even if you can't hear it."

"It's not that," she sobs. And then she lets out a real wail. "What am I going to say tomorrow at school? This is awful—much awfuller than what happened at the game with Central. Oh, that darn, horrible blimp." And she runs upstairs to her room.

"Maybe," I suggest, but without much conviction, "maybe it's not on all the TV sets. Maybe ours is an exception."

But just a few seconds later any lingering, hopeful doubts were dissipated by the sign. It was printed rather crudely, I guess by the local station engineer: "Due to circumstances beyond our control, interference prevents listeners in this area from receiving sound on this or any other channel. Steps are being taken to correct this situation. Meanwhile, keep tuned to this station."

Just then the phone rings. George Griscom is really upset. He's been trying to get hold of the Commander but he's out of town. Marge doesn't know where he is, except that he left early this afternoon.

"What are we going to do?" George practically shouts over the phone. "Every minute that goes by, our stock gets lower with people. Maybe they'll even tar and feather us—I wouldn't put it past them. Not when you interfere with the 'Maxie Belden Show.'"

"Nothing we can do," I admit. "After all, there's no telephone connection to the blimp. Let's see, it's about eight-thirty now. He's due to stay up there another two hours, maybe longer on a clear night like this."

"What in the world's causing it? The TV interference, I mean."

"I'm not sure, but somehow or other the blimp's amplifier is broadcasting on television frequency. It shouldn't really be transmitting at all, but it is. And it's a freak that the picture is okay. I'd expect it to go with the sound."

"Maybe we could build a big fire or something," George suggests in a hopeless sort of any-port-in-a-storm tone of voice.

"How'd he know we meant him? And how'd we get him to bring the blimp down?"

Every television station in town had the same idea, though. Before long we heard guns and rockets going off. But who up in a blimp is going to think they're trying to attract his attention? It's just a big celebration in town that he didn't know about. Maybe, since it seems to be mainly localized beneath him, it's a Polish holiday.

And even when some private planes begin to buzz the blimp, it doesn't mean anything to him. Just crazy pilots, having some sort of drag race, using the blimp as their turning mark.

The one man who could have changed the situation in a moment was the one man who was totally unaware that anything was happening. Just the flip of a switch and peace would have flooded the community. But he didn't know. And so for two more hours the switch was left unflipped. Vibraharp, ten-minute sermon, invitation, "Almost Persuaded," hymn or chorus, vibraharp, on and on, around and around. Everything in Polish except the vibraharp.

And it came out here, on TV. Every channel, every set.

Some people called it a night and went to bed about nine-thirty, we found out later. They were in the happiest frame of mind, relatively speaking, next day.

Like I said earlier, it was a clear night. So the pilot kept going until about ten to eleven. Then he turned off the lights and the PA system and headed back to the hangar, blissfully unaware of what awaited him there.

He said later that he wondered why the big crowd. But he sure found out soon enough after he'd maneuvered the blimp into the hangar.

First were the police, with a summons for disturbing the peace. Then the reporters and photographers. And everywhere the crowd of people, raving mad, some of them shouting, "Let us have the bum! Burn the blimp!"

And in the background, waiting around until the police dispersed the crowd, were the board members of International Gospel Blimps, Inc.

Somehow or other, I think all of us realized that night was the beginning of the end. The end of the blimp as we had known it, the Gospel Blimp, which had come into our lives and filled them and crowded out almost everything else.

The wonderful, shiny blimp. The "darn" blimp, to use my oldest girl's usual description. The blimp that had its origin almost two years ago, that summer evening in George Griscom's backyard.

I look over at George, sitting on a box by the fence, waiting. Good old George, so faithful all these months to the blimp and its ministry. George and Ethel, so anxious for their next-door neighbors to be saved through the Gospel Blimp. Here the end is in sight, and they're not yet saved. All that praying for them, and they're not saved. All those special trips the blimp has made, flying low over their house, PA blaring away, fire bombs dropping. And they're not yet Christians. No wonder George looks so discouraged, sitting over there.

It seems forever, but finally the police get the crowd cleared away from the hangar and the people begin to get in their cars. A little group has found a basket of fire bombs, and they're standing around the fire it makes in the middle of the field. But even that group is beginning to joke, and seems to be getting in a better mood. For one thing, the pilot's reaction was so honest when he found out what happened that the crowd had to laugh.

"Think we'll post a couple of men here for the night, just in case," the police lieutenant says to the pilot. "Never can tell. Not that I'd mind, particularly. Not after what happened to the 'Maxie Belden Show' and getting that emergency call out here when I was all comfortable at home. But duty's duty. Want an officer to drive home with you, just in case?"

"No," says the pilot. "I've got to see some friends first, anyway—the Gospel Blimp board members. That's them over there. I guess we'll have a lot of talking to do."

"Well, call your precinct if you need us during the night. Think I'll get on home to the late-late show. And by the way, I think I'd keep that thing in the hangar the next few days."

"Thanks for the advice. Also for the help earlier. I thought for a while they might be thinking about lynching me, or at least they'd throw me in the sedimentation pool at the sewage disposal plant over there."

"You were lucky, my friend. But don't push it. 'Night." And the lieutenant swung into the police car.

"Hi, fellows," the pilot says to us as we close in on him. "Where's Herm? Where'll we go to talk? I want to sit down, wherever it is. I don't know about you guys, but I've just had a tough two hours. For a while there I was wishing I was out on the mission field."

"We," George says firmly, with emphasis, "we've had a tough *five* hours. Almost six."

"Well, don't blame it on me," says the pilot. "I was only the pilot. I never claimed to be an electrical engineer. Besides, it was me who almost got tossed in with the sewage. Let's get away from here. This place gives me the creeps."

So we went over to George's place. Ethel fixed egg sandwiches and coffee for us. We didn't stay long, though—only about an hour. There wasn't much we could decide, what with Herm not being there and all.

But we did have some prayer about the situation before breaking up. And we remembered to pray for George and Ethel's next-door neighbors. Ethel suggested that we should.

Eight: Truth Is Organized

Herm got back the next day around noon. First thing he did after finding he'd backed into a hornet's nest was get together with the public relations fellow.

What they came up with wasn't what the rest of us expected, but you could see that it was only reasonable. Or at least we came to see that it was after they explained it to us. Our first reaction on seeing the evening newspapers, I'll admit, wasn't good.

What they did was this. The public relations man drew up a statement, which Herm signed, and copies were taken to all the papers and radio and television stations.

In this statement Herm first apologized to the public for the inconvenience caused by the "irresponsible actions" of International Gospel Blimps. He next expressed regret that he had been out of town on business the previous evening, when these irresponsible actions had come to such an unfortunate climax. Then he said how if he had been here, it would never have happened. (I never could understand that part of his statement. After all, Herm knows nothing about electronics.) But now that he was back again, he promised the public that he personally would see to it that there would be no repetition of the previous night's "fiasco." And, further, he wanted to assure our city that he would see to it that "any irresponsible element" in IGBI was dropped, and that this great community project would have "increasing civic conscious- ness." Finally, he appealed to the public for their sympathetic understanding of the tremendous pressures under which he had been working.

Well, that's about what Herm's statement said.

That night the board met in a special emergency session. All of us had read the statement in the papers, or heard it over television or radio. So we were sort of quiet when we came together down at IGBI headquarters.

"Hi, fellows," Herm says when he comes in with the public relations fel- low, about a half-hour late. "What's everyone so solemn for? You'd think you'd lost your best friends or something. Cheer up, everything's settled. We've got it made. Haven't we?" he asks, turning to the public relations fellow.

"Sure have, Commander," he replies.

I guess this was too much for George Griscom. So he begins, "About that statement you gave to the papers, Herm—"

"Oh, that. Just to quiet people down. Really nothing to it, nothing more than that. You know how it is. We've been in this thing from the beginning, and we've weathered a lot of storms together. Good ship. Good fellowship. Nothing to it."

"Commander, could I put in a word?" asks the public relations fellow.

"Sure thing. Only hurry—I want to get this meeting over with. Big day tomorrow."

"I'd like to explain why we issued that statement. You see, like I've told you before, it's hard to sell an idea. It's easier to sell a man. It's hard to sell a corporation, nonprofit or regular. It's much easier to sell an individual— especially a guy like the Commander. You all know that.

"Well, once you've sold people on somebody as representing the idea or the movement," he continues, "you have to see that they never lose confidence in him. They can lose confidence in the idea, they can lose confidence in the corporation. With all due respect to you men, they can even lose confidence in the members of the board.

"But there's one person," he concludes, pointing his finger at us, "they can't lose confidence in. That's the man you've built up as a symbol. In the case of IGBI, that's the Commander."

Everything's quiet for a minute or two. Then George Griscom asks, only he's not really asking, "So you decide to sell the rest of us down the river."

"Of course not," Herm interrupts before the public relations fellow has a chance to reply. "Of course not. That's not fair, George, if you don't mind my saying so. All it amounts to is this. Which is more important: you or the blimp? If you had to choose, which would it be: your membership on the board, or the success of this Gospel Blimp project? After all, George, you must remember that you have a great deal more at stake than many others. It's your next-door neighbors we've given special attention to. I've asked for no special thanks from you for all I've done. Fact is, I've sacrificed a great deal without much appreciation. But then when something like this comes along, you can hardly blame me for wanting to see just a bit of loyalty from you fellows."

George sort of has a hangdog expression.

"Actually, it was a godsend that the Commander was out of town last night during the television incident," the public relations man continues. "If he'd been here, everybody would have known that he could do no more than anyone else to correct the situation. And the net result would have been a loss of public confidence in him. That would have been disastrous. A man in his position, like I said, may have feet of clay, but we've got to hide them from the public.

"The question isn't whether the Commander could or couldn't have done anything about the mess if he'd been here at the time it happened. It's that we can't let people know he couldn't. We've got to preserve their image of the Commander as a man who is in complete control of every situation."

"Would you lie to do that?" George says it real soft.

"That's a nasty word," the Commander says, looking straight at George.

"And it's hardly a Christian attitude toward someone who's done as much for the Gospel Blimp as he has," putting his arm around the public relations fellow's shoulder.

"I guess there isn't much more to discuss, is there?" someone remarks, standing up.

"Just this," the Commander says. "Sit down a minute. Any of you guys don't like the way I'm running things, then, if you don't, why, for the sake of our harmony and testimony as a Christian organization, I think you ought to drop off the board. Nobody is indispensable."

"Except Herm," George murmurs close by my ear. "Nobody but Herm."

That was the last board meeting George ever attended. He just sort of dropped out. It made us all feel bad, but after all, there was a lot to be done. And personal feelings had to be subordinated to the Gospel Blimp. This was no time for discord. It was a time for pitching in, for rolling up our sleeves, for putting our heads to the grindstone.

The blimp weathered the storm with only one casualty: the PA system. We had to agree to drop that in order to satisfy the FCC, the City Council, and public opinion. Also, most of the Christians. Nobody wanted a repeat of the Maxie Belden incident.

So we settled down to the long haul. None of us on the IGBI board had quite the same feelings as we'd had earlier. But we decided that we'd put these things out of our mind for the blimp's sake.

Same way with Herm's family trouble. When we heard that he wasn't living at home any longer, and why he'd been taking those trips out of town, that really knocked us for a loop, temporarily. But after discussing it a long time (the meeting didn't end until 3 A.M.), with Herm not in on the discussion, we decided to give him the benefit of the doubt. Besides, as somebody said, Herm had really given himself to this project, right from the very start. Who else would have had the faith to take such a step as giving up his job at the meat packing plant?

After Marge actually filed for divorce, the issue became a lot bigger. For a while I thought it would split the board, but we were able to hold things together for the sake of the blimp. Our only loss was the blimp's pilot. He resigned after trying to get the board to do something about Herm. But there were plenty of Christian pilots around, and we got a good one.

As for Herm, he was spending more and more time in public relations work. By now he was in good with most of the civic and business leaders of our city. This brought in a fair amount of income, including grants from several foundations. (But it was still the thousands of little people, Christians, whose regular gifts paid the bills.)

Nine: Autumn Flight

One place that Herm cultivated these important people was at the country club. He liked to play golf and these executives seemed to like having him around.

The issue that really threatened to split our IGBI board began, innocently enough, on the golf course.

Herm had given orders to the blimp pilot that he wasn't to fly over the country club. The distraction bothered people who were playing, Herm said, and besides, since he—the Commander—was there so much, the blimp really wasn't needed. And, of course, the pilot obeyed his instructions.

This one day, though, the pilot must have forgotten. Or maybe, since it was a beautiful fall afternoon, he just decided to go for a drive in the country.

At any rate, the blimp drifted over the golf course, its sign trailing along behind. Herm and three other fellows were playing the ninth hole. (He gave us all this background information at the next board meeting.) Besides Herm, the group included the president of Dunlevy-Sanders Advertising Agency, the Chamber of Commerce executive director, and the treasurer of National Steel.

"Say," one of them said, "that's your blimp, isn't it, Herm?"

"Yes, it is. You're next, I believe."

"Looks beautiful up there. Wonderful idea. Every eye can see it. Outstanding example of institutional advertising."

"Yes," somebody agreed. (I think Herm said it was the head of Dunlevy-

Sanders.) "It's remarkable one other way, too. Almost any of the advertising media is limited to a particular class or income group. You choose the *Post,* and you reach the broad middle class. *Fortune* or the *Wall Street Journal* gets you a different group—quite selective. But that blimp up there—well, you can see that it gets through to us just as easily as it does to the day laborer."

"Ever think of broadening its appeal?" asks the Chamber of Commerce man.

"What do you mean?" Herm is interested.

Fortunately, they were the only ones on the course that afternoon, and nobody was pushing to play through. So they just stood there at the ninth hole talking and looking up at the Gospel Blimp. You have to see it to realize how beautiful that blimp is against a brilliant blue sky when the leaves are turning. Of course the same thing is true at other seasons of the year, but I always thought it looked best in the fall.

"I mean that your blimp is sort of limited to a religious message. Now if you'd just broaden it a bit, the impact would be tremendous. Real piggyback advertising value."

"I get your point," says the Dunlevy-Sanders president. "Just like those institutional ads by Continental Can—those classic Great Ideas of Western Man ads."

"Right. Only in this case it would be a much closer relationship. I mean, what connection do tin cans or plastic bags have with Western civilization? But Christianity and Western civilization have grown up together. They're natural. Pair them up and it does them both good. Piggyback."

"How would you do it?" Herm asks.

"Why, simply by carrying a second type of sign. Something like 'Free Enterprise Works.' Or 'Support People's Capitalism.' See what I mean? The potential would be tremendous. Tremendous."

"But," Herm objected, "what would that sort of an added emphasis do to the blimp's primary purpose? After all, the whole idea was a religious one. Now if we change that—"

"No need to change, Herm. Just add the other one on. As to what it will do to the religious impact, I have a hunch that it would increase it. Increase it. The new emphasis would bring a certain stability by tying your religious message into life today. That's my hunch, and my hunches have built up DS Advertising to a fifty million gross."

"I'm afraid it wouldn't work," Herm disagreed. "If for no other reason, we're dependent on a whole lot of religious people all over the country to support the Gospel Blimp. Costs close to eight thousand dollars a month. Monkey with the blimp's purpose, and that income could dry up overnight. It's hard enough getting money anyway today, without turning your supporters against you. No, I'm afraid the idea's out. Not that I don't think it's a good one, Mr. Sanders. I can see where the genius for your company's campaigns have come from. I'm not against the idea—it's brilliant."

"Ever think of new sources of income, Herm?" the National Steel treasurer asks.

"I dream about them every night!" Herm laughs. "But few of my dreams materialize."

"Ever think of tapping the big corporations? Of getting money from some of the leaders in industry who aren't particularly religious?"

Herm shook his head. "They'd never get interested in the Gospel Blimp."

"Probably not. But they might get very much interested in this new idea. I'm pretty sure my company would. And we're just one of many. Think it over, Herm. That's my advice. Take it up with your board. If they're big men, they'll not miss an opportunity like this. Neither will you. It could mean a great deal to you personally."

"Thank you, Sir. I'll certainly bring it up to my board."

And bring it up he did, at the next board meeting. It was on Friday night. Everybody was out, because Herm had passed the word around that something important was going to be presented. At Herm's request, the public relations fellow also was invited to sit in on the meeting.

Usually our board meetings were rather routine, mostly approving budgets and other business that Herm presented. For one thing, none of us had the time to put in on these things that Herm had, and so we just figured we had to have confidence in his recommendations.

Herm took devotions at the beginning of the meeting this particular night. He strung together a lot of different Bible passages, starting with the one about being wise as serpents and harmless as doves. Then he read a couple of parables: one about the men who were given the talents to invest, another about the tares growing among the wheat. He ended up with several verses about prayer being answered. Then he called on the public relations fellow to pray. (Usually we had a round of prayer, but not tonight.)

After we've disposed of a few other items of business, Herm says he has something new to present—something we may even be opposed to initially. But he wants us to listen with open heads before we come to any decision. And he'd like not to be interrupted with questions until he's given us the whole picture.

So he begins by giving a sort of summary of everything that's happened since that first summer night in George and Ethel's backyard (only he doesn't name them). He goes through all the developments, all the problems we've licked, all the things we've accomplished.

"If we're realistic," he says, "we've done a fair job of evangelizing our city. Maybe not perfect, but nothing human's perfect. At any rate, everybody's seen the Gospel Blimp. It's been a great testimony. Great.

"Now we've come to a possible major breakthrough. Up to this point we've been a rather small operation. Oh, I know it's seemed big—backbreaking at times. But is this our horizon? Have we reached the summit of Everest? Or is there more land to be possessed? I think there is. I think the past up to this moment is only introductory, that a step of faith at this point—well, I think you'll agree with me after I've told you what I have to propose."

So he tells us about what happened last week on the golf course, about Mr. Sanders' suggestion. Then he ends by giving us his opinion, which is that we ought to go along with the idea.

"I know that some people, perhaps even some of you fellows on the board, will think this is a compromise, that we ought to continue to be just what we've always been. But you've got to be realistic. If we're going to advance, if we're going to forge ahead, why, I think there's only one way. At least it's the only way I've heard up to the present time. If any of you fellows have anything else to suggest, why, I'll be glad to listen. Floor's open for discussion. Or a motion."

Several of us jump in at the same time.

One says that he feels when God has raised up something like the Gospel Blimp, we ought to be awful careful about changing it.

Herm replies that there is no question about a change. There would be no change in the ministry of the blimp. Absolutely no change. This would only mean that a new emphasis would be added.

But, another asks, wouldn't it mean less hours for the Gospel signs? How can you have both without the Gospel being affected?

Maybe, Herm suggests, we could combine the two types of signs. He's just thinking off the top of his head, he says, but it does seem like a distinct possibility.

We went on like that for a couple of hours, nobody really satisfied with Herm's plans for the blimp. Nobody that is, except the public relations fellow. He sided with Herm on every point.

Finally it came to a vote, or at least it would have come to that. But Herm saw which way the wind was blowing, so he suggested that instead of voting tonight, we appoint a committee to meet with Mr. Sanders and a few other men, business executives. Then the committee could report back and we'd be in a position to decide at our next meeting.

That sounded reasonable, so we tabled the matter and Herm appointed himself and two other board members, plus the public relations fellow, to the committee. Soon afterward we broke up for the night.

Ten: Those Worldly Griscoms

On the way home I passed by George Griscom's house. I hadn't seen him for weeks, and I didn't want him to think our friendship had been affected by his dropping off the blimp. So I decided to stop, even though it was getting a bit late.

Their place was sort of dark, only one light on downstairs. In a few minutes Ethel came to the door, her hair half up in curlers.

"Come on in," she says. "It's certainly been a long time since we've seen you. George will be so sorry he missed you."

"George away?" I ask. "I shouldn't really have stopped, it's so late. But you know how it is. I'm on my way home from the blimp board meeting, and I thought I'd just stop by to say hello."

"I'm certainly glad you did. We were talking about you and your family just the other day. George was saying we'd have to have you over for a lasagna supper or something. Yes, George is away until Sunday afternoon. He went to the shore with the man next door. You know, the one everybody's been praying for so long. He's got a small boat and they'll be doing some fishing out in the bay. Maybe the ocean, too, not far out. But George hopes it'll just be the bay," she ends with a little laugh. "He gets deathly sick in any sort of rough water. He turns positively green. You should see him."

"No, I won't come in tonight. It's too late, and besides, I mainly wanted to see George. Thought I'd bring him up-to-date on the Gospel Blimp. This guy next door—has he become a Christian?"

"Not yet. But we're praying for him."

"So are we. And the Commander's not forgetting, either."

"I know. The blimp comes over the neighborhood pretty often. And the bombs really clutter—I mean, there are a lot of them dropped. Just the other day George was mentioning it while he was cleaning out the downspout."

"Well, I'd better be getting home. Tomorrow I've got to do some painting and cleaning around the hangar. It's a full day's work, so I want to start early. So I'd better be getting home and to bed. Tell George I stopped, and tell him"—here I sort of laughed—"tell him I hope he's not falling into bad company since he got off the blimp board. What I mean is, we'd love to have him back. And you know how it is when you get away from Christian fellowship and with a beer-drinking, card-playing crowd. Not that I want to mind George's business, but you know how it is. But we'll be praying."

"Thanks. George'll be glad you stopped." She seemed to hesitate, then she said it real fast, so fast I almost missed it as I started down off the porch.

"It's easy to get out of the world on a blimp, isn't it?"

Out of the world on a blimp? I thought about it all the way home, but I couldn't quite figure out what she meant. Oh well. Ethel is probably just browned off about the blimp going so well and their not being involved in it any longer. I sure hope George hasn't started to drink or smoke. He's such a nice guy—it would be a shame to see him go down the river. But like they say, birds of a feather. I'll have to bring it up for prayer, I decide, at the blimp prayer meeting Sunday afternoon. And the women will have to remember Ethel, too. Her not seeming worried about George. That's something. Wonder if they ever were really one with us?

At any rate, I'm glad he's no longer on the board. It'd just take one guy who doesn't believe in the separated life to put the blimp on the skids. Really on the skids. But so far the Lord's been good to us. Taking George off, and keeping us from a split. Really good.

Eleven: Some Bright New Signs

A few weeks later the blimp started to carry the new type of signs. They were beautifully designed (DS Advertising had done them), and for the first few days, until we got fresh Gospel signs, there was quite a contrast. The Gospel ones had been out in all sorts of weather for over two years now. So they were sort of shabby and worn. You never realized it, though, until the new type were used.

Besides, there were a few changes that had to be made in the Gospel signs when the new emphasis was added. For instance, as Mr. Sanders pointed out to the board, it was sort of funny coupling "All Have Sinned" and "Free Enterprise, the Perfect System" together. They were, in his words, sort of incompatible. Same way with "I Am the Way" and "My Way's the American Way."

Since I was one of those on the board who questioned this new approach when Herm first brought it up, I suppose I ought to tell you that it really seemed to go over. For one thing, the fellows in the office where I work gradually seemed to change in their attitude toward the blimp. They now had sort of a respect for it, and you could have knocked me over with a feather when one day the boss called me into his office and gave me a check for IGBI.

Of course, the guys outside in the plant weren't too favorable toward the blimp, especially after the new emphasis was added. They'd make cracks whenever I had to go out there from the office for something. Cracks like, "The blimp's wearing a white collar now," and "Blimps and bosses are full of hot air."

The women on the subassembly line also really began to rib me. One of them would scream, "Save me, save me," whenever I poked my head in the door.

"I will save you," someone across the room shouts back.

"Who are you to save me?" the first girl yells.

"I'm the president of National Steel," she answers. "Come unto me and rust." Then they all go into gales of laughter.

Ignorant people. Members of unions. It's that sort of people who don't appreciate the free enterprise system. Blasphemous, almost, the way they'll pervert Scripture to their own ends sometimes. Like I just quoted, "Come unto me and rest." But then they don't know the Lord, so you can understand, sort of, their mixing Scripture up with their prejudices.

Financially God was pouring out His blessing upon the blimp. Some donors fell off, and we got a few letters disagreeing with the new emphasis. But in the main Christian people stood with us, especially after we told them of the ways these other Christians were disagreeing with us on the change. That seemed to make the Lord's people rally round the blimp, I guess to make up for the break in the ranks.

But the big financial boost came from all these important men and corporations and foundations. Only way I can explain it is a miracle, a miracle by which God worked in their hearts.

And we also got a whole lot of good advice and practical help as a result of the change. Herm saw to it that the board was enlarged so these big men could be included on it. One of the top lawyers in the city took care of changing the constitution, and he didn't even have to go to the capital. When I think of all we went through to get that constitution and the charter in the first place, it really seems wonderful we could get the change made so easily.

Everything was sort of like that. Expert advice, the very best that was available, on every question. When the next year's budget was discussed, the treasurer of National Steel had all sorts of charts prepared to show projected donations, business trends, and other factors, on the basis of which we could determine our rate of expansion.

I guess our choice of verses to carry on the blimp must have been pretty hit-or-miss before the new emphasis. About all we did was pray about it. But when these new men got on the board after its reorganization, especially Mr. Sanders, we sure weren't walking around in the dark any longer. His agency did marketing research on slogans and came up with answers in black and white. I tell you, he sure knew what he was doing. And he could make it all so plain to us through visual presentations.

Like I said, God really honored this new step of faith. It almost made you ashamed when you thought of how we floundered around in the early days of the blimp.

From then on the Gospel Blimp was really organized. You could feel it in every part of the work, from the spacious new offices with their modern furniture and illuminated map of the city, to the regular maintenance program on the blimp.

At long last we were in good with all, or almost all, the Protestant ministers in the city. Each Saturday we advertised a different church on the blimp. If any Sunday School had a contest, the winner was given a blimp ride. Most churches even had a special "Blimp Stewardship Sunday." We provided free church bulletins, with a photo of the blimp against a blue sky and a church steeple and an American flag on the front, and a low-key write-up about the blimp on the back. As a result, more and more churches put us in their budgets.

Same way with the city itself. Everyone was speaking well of us. This was partly due, I'm sure, to the caliber of new men who were on the IGBI board. But we were also doing little things to show our responsible community relations, things like running a sign "Don't Forget to Vote" on Election Day, taking part in parades, and other things like that.

Things had been going that way for several months, and it just made you thankful, also sort of proud, that you'd had a part in the original blimp vision. We often spoke of it at board meetings.

It hardly seemed possible that almost three years had passed since the idea first occurred to us. So one night I was surprised to get a phone call from George Griscom.

"Know what next Friday is?" George asks, after we've said hello, and how are you, and all the rest.

"Next Friday? No, can't say I do. Some sort of holiday?"

"No," he replies. "Something happened next Friday three years ago. Remember—you were over at our house for a picnic supper."

"Wait," I interrupted. "Now I know. That was the night we had our idea for the Gospel Blimp. A lot's happened since then."

"Sure has. Ethel and I were just talking, and we got to wondering if it wouldn't be a nice idea to invite everybody over next Friday who was here that night three years ago. Sort of a celebration, auld lang syne and all that."

"Sounds like a wonderful idea. I'm glad that you're still, well, I mean—"

"Still interested in IGBI and the blimp? Sure we are, though we haven't had much time to spend on it. And, of course, you know we haven't agreed with everything that's gone on. But Friday night we won't have to go into all that. We can just have a picnic supper, and remember the good old days."

"Well, count on us. I don't know about the rest, but we'll certainly be there. Anything we can bring—potato salad or ham or anything?"

"No, just your appetite," George says with a laugh. "Ethel will take care of everything."

I asked around and found that everyone had the same sort of phone call and invitation from George, only I didn't find out about Marge. And they all planned to be there except Herm. It seems he had a previous engagement.

Twelve: Fulfillment

Friday night came, a beautiful summer evening. We were the first ones there, and we found George in the yard, trying to hurry a charcoal fire along. "Welcome," he says. "You're just in time to help me get this fire going. Also to meet my friend and next-door neighbor."

This fellow I didn't know, but recognized, and was standing up by this time, having been kneeling next to the grill and blowing into it.

I was surprised, but I didn't say anything about it, even after I was alone with George. (The neighbor went into the house with my wife to help Ethel bring some things outside. I found out later that his wife was there, too.)

Seemed sort of funny to introduce somebody like this to the group. And I was sure that even if I was quiet about it, everybody else wouldn't be. Before the evening was over, somebody was sure to say something to George and Ethel.

Especially since the neighbor was smoking. I hasten to add that smoke doesn't particularly bother me, but there are some that it does. And even though it wasn't so bad out in the yard as it would have been indoors, there were some who would certainly not appreciate the introduction of this worldly element to our Christian circle.

As different people came, you could tell they were surprised and a little put out to find the next-door neighbors there. And smoking. It just sort of took the edge off the celebration. Not that anyone said anything to the neighbors—we were all nice enough to them. It was more the little remarks people made to each other. George and Ethel couldn't help seeing our reaction.

I must say that Ethel pulled out all the stops on that supper. She had everything, ending with ice-cold watermelon, the first of the season.

George had just collected the rinds in a bucket, and we were all sitting around on deck chairs and folding chairs. Somebody tried to strike up "I'm So Happy, and Here's the Reason Why," but everybody was too full to be much interested in singing. So she gave up after a few lines.

At this point George sets the bucket down and begins to talk to the group. He recalls how we were all here three years ago, and how it was a night just like tonight. Even an airplane going over like it's going over just now.

We all look up at the twinkling lights.

"That night," George says, "we had the idea of a Gospel Blimp for the first time. And that's the reason we're celebrating tonight—what brings us together. But that's not all. If you remember, the thing that got us thinking about evangelizing the city that night was my next-door neighbors. They were sitting on the porch, if you'll recall.

"And during the past three years there's been a lot of prayer that these neighbors would become Christians, that they'd put their trust in Jesus Christ.

"Tonight I invited them over to have supper with the group because—well, to cut it short, God has answered our praying. They've become Christians."

Well, you should have heard the group when George told us that. We were really excited. Everybody wanted to ask questions at the same time.

"Was it a verse on the blimp or a fire bomb?"

"Day or night? I mean, was the verse in electric lights?"

"It must have been while we were still using the PA system. Do you remember what Herm said in his message?"

"Did you both accept the same invitation—I mean, at the same time the invitation was given over the PA system?"

"What tract was in the fire bomb? And did you fill in the decision card?"

"Hey," George says, loud enough to be heard. "Hey, give them a break. One question at a time. And don't jump to any conclusions. Let them tell you."

So we finally quiet down, and the next-door neighbor begins to speak.

"Like George told you, we're Christians now. Both of us. But it wasn't the blimp."

"It wasn't?"

"You mean the blimp didn't save you, the Lord saved you? That's what you mean?"

"No, I mean God didn't use the blimp. Fact of the matter is, the blimp irritated me, to put it mildly. Always cruising over our place and bothering us with that PA system, and dropping trash—that's what I considered it then—dropping trash on our lawn and in the rain gutters."

"But we were praying you'd be saved through the blimp."

"Sure, and God answered. But not by the blimp."

"But by people connected with the blimp."

"Well, not exactly. At least not while they were spending all of their time on the blimp. I mean George and Ethel. We've already told them, so I can tell you that we thought they were lousy neighbors."

"Lousy neighbors? But they were awfully concerned for your soul's salvation. You should have heard them pray for you at the regular prayer meetings."

"I did. It was once when the women met over here, and I was working in my yard. I heard Ethel pray for us, that we'd be saved. But they were still lousy neighbors. Always busy working on blimp business, never time for us. We'd invited them over for an evening, or have tickets for the hockey game. Once it was the garden show. But no matter what it was, they didn't have time for us. They only seemed to have time for the blimp."

"Remember that night we were going over accounts and he stopped by?" George asks, turning to me. "That night he invited Ethel and me to go to the shore. But I turned him down—blimp meetings Saturday and Sunday. That's the way we were."

"Sorry, George. I didn't mean to make it so strong," the next-door neighbor says. "It's just that—"

"No," George interrupts, "don't back down on what you said. That's the way we were. Stinking neighbors. Ethel and me. But we're glad you're not just neighbors now, but friends. And a brother and sister in Christ. That's what counts. Really counts. Well, folks, guess maybe we'd better think about breaking up. We don't want to keep you too long. We did promise some of you we'd break up early."

"Wait a minute, George," the neighbor says. "I haven't told the people how we became Christians."

"Sure you have." You can tell George wants it to end there.

"Let him go on, George," I say. "It's not too late, and besides, anybody with a baby-sitter who has to get home can leave. Let's hear the rest. We've got plenty of time."

"It won't take more than a few minutes to tell you the rest," the next-door neighbor says. "I don't want to keep you. But the last thing in the world I'd want you to leave thinking is that we're criticizing George and Ethel. Why, they've been Christ Himself to us ever since that second time the wife went into the hospital."

"Ethel came to see me every day," his wife explained. "I was so terribly discouraged that I had to go back in. But Ethel would visit me, and bring some flowers from her garden and just sit and talk. She was always so cheery and understanding. She'd read to me and she'd talk about Jesus Christ. I'd never met anyone before to whom He was real. It seems strange, but I never had."

"I was awfully low, too," said her husband. "But George and Ethel had me over here for supper every night. And after supper George would read the Bible and pray at the table. He didn't read a lot, but what he read made sense. And I was struck with the same thing that struck the wife: Jesus was real to these people. They weren't putting on a show for our benefit.

"Like just before the wife came home from the hospital. Any of you guys ever spend two weeks keeping house with the wife away? You know what I mean—everything all crudded up. Not just egg stuck to the plates—egg stuck to the egg, which is stuck to the plates. Bed linens, towels. You know how it is. Well, Ethel came in the day before and gave that house the going-over of its life."

"Yes," his wife added, "and for a month after I got home she wouldn't let me do a stitch of washing or ironing. Took all our dirty clothes home and did them."

"That's about it," the next-door neighbor finished. "We could tell you more—like George going to the shore Saturdays to fish with me, even when he knew I had beer in the cooler. Sure, I knew how you felt about drinking, George—but you weren't a Holy Joe about it. If you had been, I'd probably never have been interested in doing anything with you. And we'd probably not have become Christians."

There is silence. Everyone's thinking.

"Well," I finally say, "that was interesting. But I've got a big day tomorrow—I'm planting some perennials out at the entrance to the hangar. So I guess I'd better call it a night. Yes, it's been quite a night. Always wonderful to find out that God has answered prayer. He never fails, does He?"

"Sure doesn't," someone agrees. "Maybe not the answer we thought, but He always answers."

A sudden thought strikes me. "Hey," I say to the next-door neighbor, "how about coming out to the hangar with me tomorrow and working on the blimp? You'd enjoy it."

"Sorry," he says. "George and I are going bowling with the guy across the street."

For decades Joe Bayly team taught one of the larger Sunday School classes in his home church. The class had all ages including older adults, graduate, college, and high school students. Those who sat under his teaching would affirm his own statement of the high calling of Sunday School teachers: "God can't call a person to a more important—and often more difficult—task than teaching others about Him and modeling before students what it means to be a Christian."

I Love to Tell the Story

September

It's fun to teach. I know it's a heavy responsibility, it takes time for preparation, it ties me down, it's draining, it's hard to get through the lessons when I have a headache—but it's fun.

To see comprehension replace puzzlement on a student's face, to hear words of certainty from one who not long ago was filled with doubt, to follow another into the joy of discovery, share a smile or laugh, be aware of quiet trust and expectant waiting, feel warmth and respect and love—it's fun to teach.

It's awesome to teach.

To speak for God, to explain His Word, point out the way, share with others the lessons His Spirit is teaching me—it's awesome to teach.

I teach with fear and trembling, fear lest I obscure the way rather than reveal its radiant track, trembling lest I be a hypocrite, castaway.

Yet I teach. With faith in God, by faith in God, I teach . . . the God, who "is able to keep you from falling, and to present you faultless before the presence of His glory with exceeding joy . . ."

And teaching, I am taught. My teachers are God and my class. Each teaches me of the other, each brings me closer to the other.

Tomorrow is the beginning of a new teaching period, the fall quarter. Vacations are over; children have returned to school; the church program is back to normal.

Yesterday I was reading about England in 1780, when the first Sunday School was organized.

England had just lost an unpopular war with the small American colonies. A spirit of revolution was in the air. France's devastating revolution was only nine years in the future.

Children in England were being exploited as a cheap source of labor. Boys and girls as young as seven and eight were forced to work fifty to sixty hours a week—every day except Sunday—in mines, sweatshops, and factories.

At this low point in British history a publisher, Robert Raikes of Gloucester, started the first Sunday School. He seems to have gotten the idea for such a school from the wife of Samuel Bradburn, one of John Wesley's most noted preachers.

"Raikes' Ragged School" was what people, including many church people, jeeringly called it, when the publisher gathered children from the lower classes on Sunday afternoons to teach them how to read and write.

The Bible was his textbook. As a result, those poor exploited children were not merely freed from the bondage of illiteracy, they were also freed from the bondage of sin. As the prototypes of tens of millions during the next two hundred years, those children discovered in Sunday School the glorious freedom of becoming sons and daughters of God.

Nobody in 1780 could have foreseen the long-range effects of that Christian act of Robert Raikes: to teach children on Sunday afternoon. Raikes simply did it as his Christian duty.

Historians tell us that the Wesleyan Revival and the Sunday School, which spread from Gloucester throughout the British Isles, kept England from a disastrous revolution such as the French experienced.

The thing that impresses me—especially today, when so many people are saying Sunday School is on its way out because of the critical, godless days we're living in—is that Sunday School was born in crisis and has been strongest in times of crisis . . . for two hundred years.

Who knows what the effects of the Sunday School in our church may be? After all, God is the same in the United States and Canada today as He was in England in 1780.

What kind of teacher do I want to be? How would I describe myself if I were writing a letter to the class during a period of prolonged absence? What would I say first?

Those questions occurred to me when I read 1 Thessalonians 2:4-13 this morning, because Saint Paul wrote about that very matter in this passage.

"I didn't flatter you; I didn't covet anything from you, I didn't look for praise or glory from you," the apostle said.

"Instead, I treated you gently, as a nursing mother treats her child. I comforted you and commanded you, as a father does his children."

"I was filled with affection for you, willing to share not only the Gospel with you, but my very life. This was because you were dear to me."

Gentle as a nursing mother, dependable and comforting as a father, filled with feelings of affection, sharing the Word of God—but also my very life . . . *God, make me that sort of teacher.*

I think one difference between teaching a Sunday School class today and the teaching Jesus did is that Jesus usually taught out-of-doors, where there was always something to tie His lessons to.

I teach in a bare room. (Idea: Next Sunday, be sure to take the Hook teaching picture of Jesus' conversation with Nicodemus, and tape it up on the wall, since we'll be studying that chapter.)

What I mean is, Jesus could say, "The fields are ready to be harvested," because He was walking through them with His class. Or "Behold the birds of the air," or "the lilies of the field," because the members of His class could see them or smell them.

I can't do that. I wish I could. Maybe Sunday School should be held in the park, when the weather's good enough.

But wait a minute. I think there's something more important about

Jesus' teaching than having the whole outdoors for His illustrations.

He started His lesson with where people were. He wasn't in the market-place when He spoke about the poor woman counting her money to see if she had enough to take two sparrows home for supper or not. He wasn't at the tower that fell and killed people when He used that incident to raise the question of evil and God's judgment.

But He was talking to people who knew about poverty and catastrophe. So He began His lesson where the people were, the people He was teaching.

And I can, too. I don't need the out-of-doors; I do need to understand the hopes and fears, joys and sorrows, doubts and perplexities of my class.

October

Why do I teach Sunday School? The question sometimes comes to me.

Because they needed a teacher; because someone asked me to; because I like people; because teaching forces me to study the Bible; because I want to help influence the next generation for God; because I have at least a small gift for getting through to adults—helping them think and discuss—and I feel responsible to use it. All good reasons, I guess. But not the key one, the best one, perhaps—the one that will hold me when all else fails.

I teach because the last words Jesus spoke before He ascended to heaven were these: "Go ye therefore, and teach . . ." (Matthew 28:19). I teach my Sunday School class because Jesus commanded His followers—and I believe that includes me—to teach His Word.

During this century, we've put a lot of emphasis on the word "Go"—this is a strong basis for foreign missions. But the real emphasis in this verse is on "Teach": "While you are going, teach."

My pattern of life is to teach others, especially my Sunday School class, the things Jesus teaches me.

I've been reading about the early church in the Book of Acts. (Doesn't it seem as if it should be "The Acts of the Holy Spirit" instead of "The Acts of the

Apostles"? No, I guess it should be both, since the Spirit works through men.)

This reading in Acts has impressed me with some similarities between my Sunday School class and the early church. The early church met regularly; so does my class. The early church met around the Word, the Bible was central: it's central in my class, too. Jesus promised to be in their midst, even if they only numbered two or three: we've never gotten that few in number, although we approached it several years ago, the Sunday of the big snow-storm. And the men and women in the early church had fellowship with each other, they cared for each other: so do the members of my class.

It's easier to share needs in the smaller, less formal room where our class meets than it is in the church worship service. The smaller size of the group helps, too.

In a way, we're a church within a church.

Since this is so, I have to be careful as the teacher that we never discuss the affairs of the church itself, that we never criticize the leadership, that we always are loving toward those who are not in the class.

I want the pastor to know that he can count on us to stand with him in building a strong church, for God's glory.

I was going through some old papers last night and came upon these pages of lined paper, in my great-grandmother's handwriting. I've often read them, to remind me of my Christian heritage.

During the War Between the States, my great-grandparents lived on a farm outside Gettysburg, Pennsylvania. Their fields were part of the tragic battlefield, their barn was taken over and used as a hospital.

"On Sunday afternoon," Great-grandmother Bayly wrote, "as was our custom, my husband Joseph and I walked to the schoolhouse to hold Sunday School. However, the noise of troop movements and cannon in the distance was so great that we could not hold the children's attention. Therefore we dismissed the school early."

Another crisis in our history, another time when Sunday School helped preserve stability and spiritual values.

I'm glad my great-grandparents were involved in teaching Sunday

School. And I'm glad they had the common sense not to try to compete with a war. (Some teachers I know would say, "Battle or no battle, you remain in your seats until the hour is over.")

November

I have to be a Christian person if I'm to teach others how to be Christian persons. I have to know Jesus Christ by faith if I'm to teach others how to know Him.

Otherwise, in those words of Charles Haddon Spurgeon, the nineteenth-century Bible teacher, I'm "a blind man elevated to the chair of optics in a university, a deaf man appointed to lead a symphony orchestra, a toad trying to teach eaglets to fly."

The place where I have to begin as a teacher is to be sure that I know "the old, old story of Jesus and His love."

"For God so loved the world, that he gave his only begotten Son, that whosoever believeth in him should not perish, but have everlasting life" (John 3:16).

I believe those words, that promise. So I can share my faith—small though it is—with my class tomorrow morning.

I spoke at a Sunday School convention in New Hampshire last week.

During a workshop, I asked the people if there was one Sunday School teacher from their own childhood they remembered above the rest. About half of them answered yes, there was. So I asked why, and they had some interesting answers.

"I was special to her. I could tell she was pleased that I was in the class."

"He came over to the schoolyard during the week to play ball with us."

"She told me my dress was pretty. We were poor, and my own mother and father were so busy they probably didn't have time to notice me or compliment me. But my Sunday School teacher did."

One woman said, "My mother died when I was eight years old. My Sunday

School teacher literally carried me through the next two years by her love for me."

What always strikes me when I ask that question, "Why was the teacher special?" is how it's the caring that people remember, the love, the affirmation those teachers gave to their students by their words and actions.

I'm pretty sure they must have known the Bible, must have prepared carefully. But that's not what these grown-up men and women remember years later . . . when they have picked up the responsibility for teaching and caring.

A Sunday School teacher doesn't just teach the lesson; the teacher is the lesson.

This morning I tried role play, a teaching technique I've seldom used. (Maybe I don't try different ways of teaching because I'm afraid they might fail.)

But this role play really succeeded, both in holding the class' interest and—more important—in advancing what we were studying.

We'd been thinking about the Christian person's attitude toward death, especially in the light of the ethics of the right to die. So I read a case study of a teenage girl who suffered kidney failure and was on dialysis.

I asked different people in the class to take the parts of the girl, her parents, her younger sister, her physician, and her pastor. The girl had separate conversations with each of these people about her desire to go off dialysis and be permitted to die.

Most of the people who played the roles matched the sexes and ages. But when it came to the girl's conversation with her doctor, I asked a physician who is part of the class and a young woman to take the parts—then switched the roles. (The real-life physician played the teenage girl, the young woman played the physician.)

The high point was a conversation between the teenager and her younger sister. The two young women (college students) actually seemed to become the persons whose roles they had assumed. Mine weren't the only moist eyes after that particular role play.

We were as close as we could possibly come to such a heartrending problem without actually experiencing it. And we understood the difficult emotional, relational, and ethical considerations in far greater depth than would have been the case if I'd merely lectured.

One of the sharpest impressions I receive of Jesus as I read the accounts of His life and ministry in the Gospels is of His sensitivity. It is said that He fulfilled an Old Testament prophecy: "A bruised reed shall he not break, and smoking flax shall he not quench . . ." (Matthew 12:20).

He is my model as a teacher. Therefore I must be sensitive to my students. I must perceive the reed that's bruised and not break it, the flax that's smoldering and not quench it.

Some students have the mere beginning of spiritual interest, even of Bible knowledge. I must be careful not to embarrass them by pushing them into discussions beyond their depth, by asking questions they cannot answer.

Other students hesitate to ask the question that's on their minds. How beautifully Jesus dealt with such people; He answered the unasked question —sometimes later—and didn't say, "What you really want to know is . . ." or "Don't you really mean . . ."

A pastor was discussing a problem involving the high school class in his church with me at a Sunday School convention.

"We've got the best possible man to teach those kids," he said. And when he explained the teacher's background, work, family, and interests, I had to agree. "Yet we keep losing students from the class. It's about half the size it was when he took it over."

"Tell me more about the man," I said. "What's he like as a teacher? Have you seen him in action, if not in the teaching situation, then on the church board or somewhere else? What's your first impression of him?"

The pastor was silent for several moments. Then he said, "I know the answer to the problem with his class. He's sarcastic. He can make you feel that big"—here he spreads his thumb and index finger about an inch apart—"if you disagree with him or don't quite see things his way."

Teenagers are tender plants, easily wilted by a strong wind. A tender touch, a tender teacher is needed.

For adults too. And children.

Jim makes things interesting in class. He gets us to think, although I'm not sure that's his motive for what he does.

What he does is ask questions, sometimes shockers. Like today. We were studying the account of Jesus walking on the water, and Jim said, "Did Jesus really have to walk on the water? Couldn't that have been an optical illusion?"

After a moment, from the other side of the room, Evelyn spoke up: "Why, that's heresy!" (A good discussion-stopper if there ever was one.)

I tried to redeem the situation, saying something like, "Now that you've named it, let's discuss it."

And we did. I've never been in such a good discussion of miracles. The thinking of all of us was sharpened, because Jim asked the question in the first place.

Jim is a scientist. He finds it hard to believe. I can't help wishing he'd spend a tenth of the time studying the Bible and Christian books that he spends studying the books and journals of his field of specialization.

Maybe someday he will. But meanwhile, I'm glad he feels safe with the class, safe enough to bring up his doubts and problems. I'll have to talk to Evelyn—I'd hate for her to squelch him.

December

This has been a busy week for me. I've been on the road most of the week, and also had some difficult decisions to make at the office. It's hard to get my mind settled on the class tomorrow.

But I guess I don't have it quite so bad as Dwight L. Moody did a century ago, when he was on the road all week and still taught Sunday School on Sunday morning.

Moody traveled throughout the Middle West, selling shoes. (Come to think of it, there were no airplanes then, only slow, dirty trains and horse-drawn wagons. I guess some stagecoaches, too.)

But he always returned to Chicago by Saturday night, because he had established a Sunday School on the near north side of the river, an area of high crime and juvenile delinquency.

His evangelistic concern for the poor children and young people, who would not go into a church, led him to locate his Sunday School in a public hall above a city market.

"Sunday was a busy day for me then," Moody later recalled. "During the week I would be out of town as a commercial traveler, selling boots and shoes, but I would always manage to be back by Saturday night. Often it was late when I got to my room, but I would have to be up by six to get the hall ready for Sunday School. Every Saturday night a German society held a dance there, and I had to roll out beer kegs, sweep up sawdust, clean up generally, and arrange the chairs. I did not think it was right to hire this on Sunday, so sometimes with the assistance of a scholar, and often without any, I would do it myself.

"This usually took most of the morning, and when it was done, I would have to drum up the scholars and new boys and girls." (One scholar later recalled: "My first recollection of Mr. Moody was peeping around the corner of the building in order to have him chase me and bring me into the school.")

"By the time two o'clock came," continued Moody, "we would have the hall full, and then I had to keep order while the speaker of the day led the exercise. We had to keep things going to keep up the children's interest. When school was over I visited absent scholars and found out why they were not at Sunday School, called on the sick, and invited the parents to attend the evening service." (*Chicago Tribune*)

If Moody could make it in those circumstances, so can I. In spite of the week I've been through.

I failed today. The lesson didn't come off. I know it and the class knows it.

First, there was that tangent. I should have stuck to the lesson when Matt raised the question; I should have said, "Matt, if you want to, we can discuss that after class. Or sometime during the week. I want to get through the lesson, and I don't think enough people are bothered by that to justify taking the time to discuss it now."

I know, and Matt knows, that there are some questions that bother so many people that it's necessary to consider them in class, even if you never get back to the lesson. But this wasn't one of them.

So we wasted fifteen minutes. I mean, I wasted fifteen minutes.

Then I tried to cover everything in the lesson in the time that remained. I rushed through the material; I even said, "There's no time for questions" when Grace raised her hand.

I know I should have settled for getting the main point across. But I didn't. I had to dump the whole load because I'd prepared it.

Then the culmination of that miserable class session was when Frank disagreed with me and I cut him off. I could see people's heads jerk back.

I'll have to tell them I'm sorry next week. I hope they'll forgive me.

I hope You'll forgive me, Lord. Thanks.

I think Christmas Sunday should be a special time. And it was special in the class this morning.

First, we had steaming coffee and Danish strudel, brought by Marge and Al, ready for us when we arrived. A Christmas tablecloth, plates, cups, and napkins brightened the room and gave it a festive air.

Then we sang carols, several of them. Most of us don't get enough carol singing during the Christmas holidays, I've found.

We prayed specially for missionaries who have been part of the class and are now serving in various parts of the world. Somehow this brought them closer to us. We also had special prayer for our children, and welcomed students who were home for the holidays.

For the lesson time, I interrupted the series I've been teaching, since today's lesson would have been unrelated to Christmas. I don't hesitate to make such changes, because it's easy to get into a rut.

We read the Luke 2 Christmas passage. This is a supremely familiar chapter, yet I was interested—as I almost always am when we are in such a passage—at the fresh insight people had, the way the Holy Spirit got through to us in a new way.

I often ask the class, "What impresses you about this passage? How do you feel at this point in your life as you read it?" Their replies never fail to interest me, and enlighten all of us.

The written Word, like the Living Word who became flesh today, is of such depth that we can never exhaust its meaning. It is like an ocean, and we are always taking out fresh water in our sand pails.

When we left the building where our class meets, to cross the street for the worship service in the main church building, it had begun to snow. The ground was already white.

"Looks like we'll have a white Christmas after all," someone said.

Suddenly a small snowball hit me, and I saw our son, who had been waiting to go into the service with us, put his gloves back on.

"Merry Christmas!" he called with a big grin.

I just smiled.

Later, when we got home, I smeared him with a big snowball. All in the spirit of the holiday, of course.

January

When I was a boy, maybe nine or ten years old, I remember how my father helped me make a model of a house during Jesus' time for Sunday School. We spent hours planning the project, getting the wood, sawing it and nailing it together, sanding and painting it (gray, with black lines tracing the outlines of stones). We even had a little opening in the roof of the house, like the one through which his friends lowered the man when they brought him to Jesus for healing.

I had a lot of fun with Dad, and learned through the project; the whole class benefited from it.

Sometimes I assign projects to members of the class I'm teaching now. Not construction projects, although that might not be a bad idea. Things like reports on books, what the Bible says about a certain subject.

When we studied Amos, which speaks of God's judgment on a nation that forgets the poor, I asked one man, a sociologist, to prepare a report on poverty in the United States. (When he gave the report, we discovered he'd concentrated on poverty in DuPage County, the county in which we live. That brought it home to all of us in a way that the whole country wouldn't.)

At the end of that series of lessons, I assigned a project to each member of the class: Bring in a project you intend to do personally, or as a family, to help poor people. It was exciting to see how creative and yet down-to-earth the projects were.

(Mary Lou, my wife, has our family on what seems to be a rather permanent extension of this project and one of the pastor's sermons: a "Third World Meal" each Wednesday night. That means a dinner of rice only. We're giving the money we save to a relief organization. I can't say our two teen-age boys are wildly enthusiastic about the idea.)

I'll have to think up more projects related to lessons. This takes time, which may be why I don't do it very often. But the results far exceed the investment of time, like a lot of things related to teaching a Sunday School class.

Frank, who's in my class, told me about his daughter Yvonne today. She's home for the Christmas holidays, with her husband and little boy.

Their family was pretty strong from a Christian standpoint while she was growing up, and so was the church. But she's gone through a period of doubt and rebelling.

Now she's on her way back, according to Frank.

He says that he came into the living room a couple of days ago and found her sitting alone, just sitting and rocking in a chair.

"What are you doing?" he asked.

"I'm forgiving people," his daughter replied. "I've learned that it's necessary for me to be healed of my memories, and forgiving people is a very important part of it."

"Such as, forgiving whom?" her father asked.

"Well, I've just been forgiving a Sunday School teacher I had as a child."

"Why do you feel that you have to forgive her?"

"Because she forced a stupid curriculum on me and never hugged me."

That was twenty years ago, and I think there's been a big improvement in Sunday School curriculum materials since then—especially the ones we publish at David C. Cook. (Of course, I'm most concerned about them and familiar with them.) We know a lot more about how children learn what parts of the Bible are most relevant to their daily needs, how to explain spiritual things through their daily experiences.

But they still need attention from the teacher, the sort of attention that says, "I like you. I don't just teach because I have to, I teach you because I like you." And if you like someone, you'll give them a hug once in a while.

I hope nobody has to sit and forgive me, or the way I teach, sometime in the future.

It must have been a year ago that John and Kathleen asked to say something to the class.

I had a hunch that they were going to tell about their daughter, Becky. I was right.

John was the one who told the story, one that I knew already, along with the pastor and a few others. But the class—and the church itself—had not previously been aware of the serious problem.

In a simple, straightforward way, John told how, nine months before, their fifteen-year-old daughter had run away from home. They notified the police and searched for her everywhere, without success.

Then, about a month ago, the police found her: living with prostitutes, addicted to hard drugs, in an evil part of Chicago.

Becky was really spaced out when they found her, but it was only after examination by a team of psychiatrists that John and Kathleen realized how seriously she had been damaged.

"They tell us she has to be put in a mental institution," John said, struggling for control. "She's so sick that they don't think she'll ever be able to leave. One of them even said it would be no help to visit her there—that perhaps we'd better just forget we ever had a daughter."

Then, after a moment of silence, John concluded: "We wanted to tell you about this so you'd pray with us. Becky's in the institution now, but we know God can do anything. He can heal her, and we hope you'll pray with us that He will—in spite of what the doctors told us." John and Kathleen sat down.

The class was deeply moved. Someone stood up to pray; then others prayed too.

Like I said, that was about a year ago. And we've been praying ever since.

This morning John and Kathleen asked to say something again. Only this time the two of them were radiantly happy when John spoke.

"We want you to know that Becky came back home last week. They've discharged her from the state hospital as cured. And she really is. She's already back in school, and she'll even be getting a job. I think you can guess how we feel. We want to thank you for sharing our heavy burden, for praying for Becky."

Again people prayed, this time praising and thanking God.

And in my heart I thanked Him for a class that cares, a group of Christians with whom John and Kathleen felt safe in sharing such a heavy concern—safe from a judgmental attitude toward them, or Becky, or how they had raised Becky.

I had one other thought: "Ye have not because ye ask not."

I wonder if I really got through to the class with Jeremiah this morning. It's hard to know for sure.

Maybe I need to remind myself again of that story Donald Grey Barnhouse told. (What an outstanding Bible teacher he was—he had the gift, like C.S. Lewis, of creating fresh windows through which you could see the truth.)

According to Dr. Barnhouse, he was riding in a car with a friend when the subject of music came up.

"What's your favorite symphony?" the friend asked.

"Brahms' First" was Dr. Barnhouse's reply.

"How does it go?"

Dr. Barnhouse began to whistle the main theme of the symphony.

"Then suddenly," he recalled, "I was overcome with how ridiculous it was that I should be trying to communicate that great musical composition with my weak whistle.

"But by the wonder of the human brain, my weak whistle was changed in my friend's mind into the strings and percussion and brass of the full symphony orchestra."

Then he applied the experience to his teaching. "Every time I stand up to teach the Bible, I'm overcome with how ridiculous it is that I should be trying to communicate God's Word to the class.

"It would be hopeless, except for one thing: The Holy Spirit is in me, teaching through me; and He is also in the men and women in my class who listen. So He turned my weak little whistle into the full symphony of God's revelation in their minds and lives."

I guess I have to learn more about trusting the Holy Spirit to teach through me, and to receive and confirm the Word of God in my students. Including the Book of Jeremiah.

Late this afternoon I sat at my office desk and thought about the members of my class. The day was dull gray; snow was starting to fall in the little avenue outside my window.

I'd finished all my correspondence and the reports of the day; I'd seen my last associate. In less than an hour I'd be leaving for home.

My desk was clean, except for the small lamp.

So I imagined the members of my class, some of them, walking across the desk. In my imagination they were little people; they took little steps, so it took each a half-minute or so to move from one side to the other.

There's Norm, alone. I wish Dorothy were with him; they're living mostly apart, she at some distance. They're both such great people; they'll need each other more and more as they get older. *Lord, help them to give in to each other, to find the joy of living together, doing Your things together rather than their own thing apart.*

Bart and Elsie. So concerned about their grown kids, living at such a distance from the Lord—and from them. How can kids be so cruel? Why did their Christian upbringing have so little effect? *Lord, I don't have to understand, to diagnose the situation. I want to bring Bart and Elsie with their hurt to You, and I want to bring their children to You.*

Dear Jenny. So faithful to the Lord and to all her responsibilities as a schoolteacher. And so alone, with her family a thousand miles away. We'll have to see if she can come over for the afternoon some Sunday soon. *Thank You for such a consistent Christian and interesting person, Lord.*

Here comes Martha. Last Sunday she asked us to pray for her; she's taking the exams for her registered nurse qualification this week. And I forgot. *Lord, help Martha have a clear mind so she'll remember what she's studied during the past several years. Give her the assurance of your presence now and your concern for her future plans.*

Florence. How she must miss Arthur. It's about a year since his sudden, unexpected death. She's had so many loose ends to gather together and she's done it so well. Help Florence in her loneliness, Lord. You've promised to be a husband to the widow and a father to the fatherless. *Carry out your promise to her and to Art. He's just entering adolescence, she's raising him alone, and she needs your help.*

I turned around to look out the window. The snow was falling much harder. I thought I'd better leave if I was going to get home—the hill by Villa Olivia would really be crowded with cars and semis, and some would probably be stuck.

February

Martha passed her exams and will soon be an RN. She could hardly wait until we had sung the hymns and the leader asked for any prayer requests or praise items, to speak up and tell us.

We were all excited along with her. After all, we had prayed her through those exams.

"You're like my extended family," she said.

An extended family: that's what our class is all about. A safe place for

Martha and the rest of us. And God's the head of the family.

At the Boise, Idaho Sunday School convention last week, a teacher asked me, "What do you do when you ask a question and nobody answers?"

My first suggestion was that after giving the class time to respond, I go on with the lesson, leaving the question unanswered. The minute you begin answering your own questions, I told her, you're lost. After a few times, the class never will respond. They'll think all your questions are rhetorical, that you don't expect answers. On the other hand, if you just go on with your teaching, leaving the question unanswered, they'll know you mean business.

Of course, I said, you have to be sure that the questions you ask aren't too easy, the answers too obvious. Children will answer such questions, but teenagers won't.

An occasional teenage class—not adults—usually will refuse to respond to questions or participate in discussion, regardless of what you do. I once had such a class of senior highs and was quite discouraged by my inability to break through to them.

I talked the problem over with a skilled professional schoolteacher whose answer made me feel better: "The same thing happens to us who teach all the time. The first period of the day, you'll have a class that is fairly bursting with responses. You can hardly keep them quiet. Then along comes the second-period class. There's no perceptible difference in size or makeup of class from the first-period one, and they sit on their hands. You can't get any response at all. It's one of the mysteries of teaching."

Her answer comforted me. But I did one thing that finally worked with that class: I told them that I was setting aside the last ten minutes of class for any questions that they might want to ask. The questions might arise out of what we had studied, but they didn't have to.

That idea really worked. My silent class began to talk, and I was no longer in the dark about their understanding of the lessons, or their needs.

But they never did answer questions or discuss things in the main class period.

I've been thinking about how Jesus worked as a carpenter from the time

He was a child until the age of thirty, when He entered upon His "mission," His public ministry.

Almost half of His parables were about business and ordinary work, about the "life that is so daily."

When He called men to be His disciples, He didn't call them from religious vocations. Instead, He called fishermen, tradesmen, government employees. And He told them to teach people what He had taught them.

He still calls business people and homemakers, doctors, nurses and lawyers, government employees, schoolteachers and fishermen, farmers and welders and scientists and construction workers, and tells us to teach boys and girls, teens and adults what He has taught us.

We can't turn Him down (or turn down the Sunday School superintendent, pastor, or director of Christian education who confronts us with His call) with the excuse that we haven't had formal religious training. If we do, we'll miss out as surely as Peter, John, and Matthew would have missed out if they had refused His call.

I must teach tomorrow morning, and I've left my preparation until tonight. It's already after eleven o'clock; maybe I should go to bed and set the alarm so I'll get up early. Then I can study with a fresher mind.

This has been a busy week. A lot of unexpected things came up at the office and here at home. These and other rationalizations fill my mind.

But I got the other things done; why did I put off preparing the Sunday School lesson I'll have to teach tomorrow morning?

It mustn't have seemed as important as the other things. I know enough about the Bible that maybe I felt I could get by without the preparation I needed for the other things.

Whatever the reason, I'm stuck. I can't even pray for God's help with a clear conscience, because it's my fault I'm stuck.

I'll set the alarm.

Maybe you'd better set it tomorrow night.

Why? The class is tomorrow morning; it will be all over tomorrow night.

Set the alarm to remind you to begin studying for the following Sunday.

But that's a whole week away.

Ten minutes each day is a lot better than sixty minutes on Saturday night or Sunday morning.

I guess that's right. But what should I do each day?

Read the Bible passage you'll be teaching. Read it through once or twice each day. Pray that you'll understand it.

That sounds like something I read about called unconscious learning.

And that's what it is. You'll be thinking about those verses and your class all week; you'll be steeped in them by the time Sunday comes.

Right. What else should I do?

Read the teacher's guide. Mark it. See if there are any illustrations or applications that should be changed for your class. Your class is unique, you know.

Don't I know it.

So is every class. The editor can't possibly know all these classes the way their teachers know them. So teachers have to tailor-make the lesson for the class.

What else should I do?

Set your alarm for six o'clock tomorrow morning.

I don't need that much time to prepare. I don't need to get up that early.

Have you prayed for your class this week?

Well . . .

Set your alarm. Now. And pray to be forgiven for taking your teaching responsibilities so lightly, for failing to set the right priorities.

March

I taught a series of lessons on death and the Christian a few months ago.

Today Bruce came up to me after class and said, "I want you to know that those lessons on death you taught some time ago have changed my whole attitude.

"I've had a series of tests at the hospital this past week, tests that could reveal something pretty serious.

"I don't know the results yet, but the surprising thing is that I'm at peace.

I've found I can really trust God. So I wanted to thank you."

A young woman who's working on her doctorate in psychology recently told me about her research project.

She's investigating the importance of eye contact, looking directly into a person's eyes when talking or listening to him or her.

Somehow, she said, this communicates a number of different impressions: concern, interest, attention, acceptance, sometimes affection.

I've thought about this young psychologist's words in connection with teaching. I've come to several conclusions.

One is that I must know the lesson well enough to look at people while I'm teaching, instead of having my eyes mainly looking downward at a book or notes.

Another is that I must look directly into the eyes of a student who's responding, give him or her my undivided attention. This says, "You're important; you're why I'm teaching."

Still another is that if I ask a question and no one answers, I must look at the class rather than look down or away in embarrassment at the silence. Looking into their eyes will indicate that I expect an answer, that I'm not uptight over the period of silence.

As the teacher, I set the tone for the class. In this, as in other situations, if I'm not embarrassed or uptight, the class won't be either. If I am, they'll be.

Men, women, children, important people, little people, traitors, sinners: Everybody felt at home with Jesus because He never put them down; He gave Himself totally to each individual. He sincerely wanted each one to realize the potential of his or her life.

Someone passed the following quotation on to me, from a graffiti wall at St. John's University in Minnesota:

"Jesus said to them, 'Who do you say that I am?'"

"And they replied, 'You are the eschatological manifestation of the ground of our being, the kerygma in which we find the ultimate meaning of our interpersonal relationships.'"

"And Jesus said, 'What?'"

I like that.

I like it because it sets the simplicity of our Lord's words and teaching over against the complexity of some technical expressions of truth.

Not that theology is wrong. We need deep thinkers who can explain the ramifications of our faith.

But such complexity of ideas belongs in a seminary classroom, not on the hillside where Jesus taught multitudes, or in the room where I teach my Sunday School class.

Jesus was profound, but simple in expression. Ordinary people heard Him gladly, eagerly.

To use an old but true way of expressing it, He put the cookies—or the bread of life—on the lowest shelf, where anyone could reach it.

And so must I.

I cannot show off my knowledge (the little that I have) or my vocabulary and still teach as Jesus taught. Nor get through to people as He got through to them.

What expression of truth could be more simple than that contrast at the conclusion of the Sermon on the Mount between the man who built his house on the rock and the man who built his house on the sand.

I have a few professors and medical doctors in my class. I could become threatened by their presence, overwhelmed by the impossibility of my measuring up to their standards of scholarly teaching.

That I'm neither threatened nor overwhelmed is the result of knowing that Ph.D.'s and M.D.'s have the same feelings I have: they bleed when they're cut; they grieve when their children go into a far country, away from parents and the Lord. And they have the same God, the same Bible, the same life in Christ.

One more thing gives me confidence as I teach. I believe these learned people come to Sunday School for the same reason as the rest of us: to learn about God and have fellowship with His people, our brothers and sisters in Christ. They appreciate simple truth.

But when I run into a question I can't answer, it's great to have such resource people around.

The young adult (singles) group had their Easter sunrise service at our home this morning. This is the third year they've been here, and we hope they'll make it a tradition.

Actually, "sunrise" is wishful thinking, since the sun was well up when they got here.

Last year Easter was later and they could meet outside, sitting on blankets. Today there is still snow on the ground, so they crowded into our living room and country kitchen.

They sang Easter songs and laughed happily and read the Bible and prayed and talked about the meaning of Easter to them and laughed happily and sang some more, while Mary Lou and I did the final work on the breakfast in the kitchen. We could hear everything and see part of the group.

I don't know whether the smell of coffee perking and sausage frying had any effect or not, but their service didn't last long. Soon the happy group had overflowed into the kitchen and they were helping take the egg-and-cheese soufflé and coffee cakes out of the oven, and everyone was filling cups and plates. The coffee cakes were brought by the young adults, some of whom had made them. One of the most delicious was made by a young man; I wonder, will he ever get married?

Martha shared the secret of her impending engagement with Mary Lou and me before she left. We're so glad for her.

Believe it or not, we got the dishes finished and the place straightened up before we left for Sunday School. Our own class was sort of an anticlimax, and a sleepy one at that.

Phil took his own life this week.

Nineteen years old, studying music at the state university, an accomplished cellist, a warm human being who was liked by everybody who knew him: Phil stepped in front of a freight train last Wednesday night.

His parents are in my class. So was Phil, when he was home from school.

Why didn't I see that something was wrong? Why didn't I arrange to spend time with Phil outside of class?

Did I look at him as an extension of his parents instead of a person with his own independent life and tremendous needs?

The funeral will be hard. So will class next Sunday morning. Everybody is hurting. We look at each other, our eyes forming questions.

I hope we hurt enough to change, to really care for each other—especially the lonely ones—as Jesus cares.

April

Phil's parents seemed to be absent from class this morning. Actually, his mother was there, although she was sitting behind someone and I didn't see her.

So thinking neither one was there, I suggested that we pray for them and their other children before I started to teach. It was a time of warm, specific praying.

Afterward, when I was about ten minutes into the lesson, I saw her. My mind formed one of those flashes of prayer while someone else was talking. "Lord, help Betty to understand our love for them and not be hurt by being singled out in that prayer."

The class was subdued for the whole teaching time. I'm sure Phil was on all our minds—beautiful, outgoing, seemingly happy Phil. The seat he'd never fill again.

About fifteen minutes before I was finished teaching, Betty quietly left the room. This really troubled me. Had the prayer, the atmosphere of the class, been too much for her? Again I prayed, "Lord, be with Betty. Help her know we love her."

I was under the burden right through the church worship service that followed.

After the service, Betty came up to me.

"I'm sorry I had to leave the class early. I'd promised to help with the nursery, and I felt I should go through with it . . . in spite of what happened last week. And thank you for praying for us at the beginning of class. It means so much to know that the class is standing with us."

My heart sang. Not like a dove on a summer night; more like a sparrow on a cold, snowy day in the dead of winter.

How easy it is to misunderstand, to come to wrong conclusions.

I have to remember that I'm an authority figure to the class. I may try to preserve a low profile, ask others for their opinions, be tentative rather than "Now hear this," but I can't really escape it.

I may not escape it, but I can try not to foster it.

The authority in any Sunday School class, including mine, is the Bible—not the teacher. I have to turn people to the Word of God rather than to my personal opinions.

I do have opinions that I occasionally share with the class. But I try to remember to say immediately afterward, "If you disagree with me, the Lord bless you. You may be right and I may be wrong."

On the other hand, when I have a "Thus saith the Lord"—something the Bible clearly says—I indicate its authority, to which both I as teacher and the class must submit.

The trouble comes, it seems to me, when a teacher confuses his or her own opinions with the Word of God, and teaches both with equal authority.

In later years (and this is a special danger when teaching teens and young adults), if members of the class discover that the teacher was wrong in the personal opinions he taught with such authority, they are likely to discard the Bible he taught as well.

I also think we teachers should be careful to teach from the Bible, not from a teacher's guide, or at least read the Bible passage directly from the Bible and have it open throughout the class session. This makes the Bible's authority clear to the class.

I often outline what the teacher's guide says, and put the outline alongside my Bible, to reinforce this. An added advantage is that I am forced to express the lesson in my own words, and am not tempted just to read from the teacher's guide.

But because I can't escape the authority of my position as teacher, I must be sensitive to what people say and how I respond.

Like last Sunday, when Ron, who hasn't come very often, gave that far-out opinion during the discussion. I knew that he'd feel it pretty keenly if I told him he was wrong. So instead I said to the class, "How do the rest of you feel? Do you agree with Ron?" And they handled it.

Of course I could have asked Ron, "Where do you find that in the passage we're studying?" and it wouldn't have been quite so bad as telling him he was wrong in front of everybody. But I still think it was better to let the class respond. They're his peers—I, the teacher, am not, even though I try not to be authoritarian.

We had a great time of sharing concerns and praying for each other at the beginning of class this morning.

I think the class would continue to meet even if there were no lesson. We've found out that we can depend on each other, that we can trust each other, that we can be open with each other.

I guess one thing we've found out is that we're not alone with our problems. Other Christians have the same ones, whether it's older children who have gotten away from the Lord, relatives who are seriously ill, loss of employment, final exams, important decisions, personal or family crises of various kinds.

This week I had a letter from a woman in another part of the country. That letter made me realize what a priceless treasure we have in our class' warm fellowship.

"Last year I passed through a severe depression and felt so strongly the need to be able to discuss my problem with people who could 'really' pray for me and with me—people who cared enough to share my agony. I think of my church as being a friendly place and it is really my family, since I have no Christian relatives. . . . Now that God has supplied a victory over this, I can share it to a certain extent; but even now, I feel embarrassment on the part of listeners. I'm certain that shared prayer would have helped me through this time much faster.

"During my own infirmity, a young couple of the church separated— the wife left her husband to return to her parents in another state. The young man broke down in a Wednesday night prayer meeting and asked for prayer, saying that he had examined himself before God and thought that he was doing everything he knew to make things right with her. But he wanted the people to pray for their reunion. Again, I felt strong embarrassment on the part of the congregation and lack of deep caring. The church is his only family, too. My distress for him was made worse when the only comments I heard later were that he should have known better than to speak of such a private affair in a public service."

Thank God we can speak of "private affairs" in our Sunday School class. I think every church needs such safe places, places of refuge and Christian concern and support.

I can't explain it. Sometimes there are three or four hands in the air at once. (My class is too large for students just to speak out.) Then I'm pretty sure the lesson is making people think and respond.

Other times there are no hands. I ask a question and nobody answers.

Of course it may be the question I've asked. Teens and adults won't usually respond to "where" or "who" or "what" questions: Where did Moses go when he left Egypt?

Who sentenced Shadrach, Meshach, and Abednego to the fiery furnace? What verse in today's text tells us not to worry?

The answer is there in the Bible in front of everybody, so why should anyone bother to respond?

I have to admit that when I've booby-trapped myself with such a question, a dear older person often rescues me by answering. But it's obvious to the class that I'm the recipient of an act of Christian charity.

I've found that the questions that get results start with "how" and "why."

Like, "How do you think Moses felt when his own people turned on him and refused his help?" Or, "Why shouldn't we worry about the future?"

When I ask that sort of question, I'm making people think, expecting them to think. I'm letting them put things together in their own heads.

In my opinion, people of all ages (not just adults) like to discover things for themselves, rather than be limited to what the teacher says. When I ask a "how" or "why" question, I open up this possibility to my class.

There's another question I like to ask. It's this: "Have any of you had a similar experience?" For instance, "to what Moses had when his own people rejected him?"

Why should the class be limited to my perceptions, my feelings, my experiences, when they have equally authentic ones to share? And when someone does share, his or her experience will probably speak to members of the class who can't relate as well to my age or lifestyle or background.

Today I asked the right kind of questions and the class still sat on their hands. I gave them the opportunity to share their own thoughts and experiences, and only one or two responded.

Maybe it was the rainy Sunday doldrums. It's a miserably gray day.

Or am I rationalizing?

In its beginnings two centuries ago, and for more than half of its history, Sunday School was primarily evangelistic.

That's why it was held on Sunday afternoon, rather than—as in this century—before church on Sunday morning.

Children whose own parents did not attend church were thus attracted, and many put their trust in Jesus Christ. Most children of church people, on the other hand, did not attend. Instead they went with their parents to the morning worship service.

A great change took place early in the present century, when Sunday School was moved to the morning hour and children from church homes began to attend.

This changed the nature of Sunday School from an instrument of evangelism to one of Christian education. It did something else: Parents who had previously taught their children the Bible and Christian doctrine (often through the catechism) at home turned this responsibility over to the Sunday School. Family altar (Bible reading and prayer) was dropped in most church homes.

I think we have to be aware of this bit of history if we are to understand two urgent needs in the Sunday School's ministry today.

The first is the need for a fresh emphasis on evangelism. Christian education begins with Christian people, whether children, teenagers, or adults, who have trusted Jesus Christ and committed their lives to Him.

The bus ministry of many churches is similar to the original evangelistic emphasis of Sunday School.

But we also need fresh attention to evangelizing children from church homes. Without family Bible reading and prayer, their need for a clear explanation of the Gospel and opportunity to respond cannot be forgotten. But it often is.

I know a teacher of junior boys whom I admire because he is aware of this need and is doing something about it.

Each fall, when he gets a new class, this young man takes the boys—one at a time—for Saturday morning breakfast at a pancake house. Over this breakfast, he tries to find out the boy's relationship to God and to lead him to faith in Christ if he is uncertain.

I need to have this same concern for my class.

The second urgent need of today's Sunday School is to impress upon church parents the need for Christian education in the home, and to train them to provide this education. God gave Christian parents primary responsibility for their own children's spiritual training, not the church or Sunday School.

The Christian home and Sunday School make a great team.

May

We got into a discussion of Christian business ethics in class today. I was reminded of something that happened ten years or so ago at a small college in Virginia, when I was invited to speak at religious emphasis week (which the students irreverently but accurately called "Let's be kind to God week").

I was at a fraternity house for dinner, with a voluntary attendance discussion on religion in the lounge afterward. Most of the men stayed for the discussion, and there was a lot of interest in the Christian Gospel.

After about two hours, they thanked me, said good-bye, and went back to their studies—all except a rather intense young man. He was one of the few who hadn't said anything earlier.

When we were alone, he introduced himself and said, "I used to believe everything you told us tonight. I could have presented my faith as clearly as you did. But all that ended the summer after my senior year in high school."

"What happened then?" I asked.

"I had this Sunday School teacher my senior year. He was a really good teacher, and we learned a lot from him. He was a leader in the church.

"That summer, before I entered school here, I got a job in our small city. On that job I learned that this great Sunday School teacher was despised by the business community for his ethics. He was in on all the shady deals, it seemed.

"Well, I decided if that's the way Christians lived, I didn't want any of it. If he could talk so great in Sunday School and live so lousy during the week, his religion wasn't for me."

I reasoned with him: his faith should rest in Jesus Christ, the perfect Lord and Savior, not in any businessman or Sunday School teacher. I told him about Christian leaders I had known who were exemplary businessmen: H. J. Taylor of Club Aluminum, Dave Weyerhaeuser of the West Coast lumber company, Bob Swanson of New York's Thomas Bread Company.

To no avail.

He left, and although I saw him again toward the end of the week, he gave no indication of any change of mind.

It's not enough for me to claim to be a Christian, to be able to give a clear statement of my faith.

I must be trying to live up to my high calling as a Christian in Christ Jesus. And that includes my ethics as a businessman.

There's a danger in "talking further down the road than you've walked," as Vance Havner put it. It's dangerous for me, and it's dangerous for my students.

"If any man's life at home is unworthy," Charles Haddon Spurgeon said before the introduction of the automobile, "let him go ten miles away from home before he stands up to teach." Today he'd say a couple of hundred miles.

"Then, when he stands up," Spurgeon concluded, "let him say nothing."

I've been sitting here thinking about Bruce's encouraging words one Sunday about the lessons on death. Actually, his phone call telling me that everything's okay started me thinking.

Teaching adults has one distinct advantage over teaching other age groups—that members of your class occasionally mention help they've received from the lesson. Not just Bruce, but others. Steven is such an encouragement to me—he's a good Bible teacher, but so often he expresses appreciation for things I've said in class.

I remember teaching junior and senior highs. They never said anything; I was forced to operate in the dark.

In the dark? No, I guess I mean, by faith. Faith that God was using my teaching even though I had no feedback from the class.

I like feedback, especially when it's complimentary. But I have to remember that this isn't the primary indication that God is working.

I also have to remember that sometimes God's Word hurts. As that great missionary to India, Amy Carmichael, put it, "If you have never been hurt by a word from God, it is probably that you have never heard God speak."

At regular intervals I pick up a newspaper or magazine and read an obituary of the Sunday School.

In ten years, says the spokesman for a major church body in a typical interview, projecting present losses of students, the Sunday School will be dead, an extinct species.

These articles depress me until I go to Sunday School and see the interest people still have in studying the Bible; or to a Sunday School convention and see the interest other people have in becoming better prepared to teach the Bible. (Such conventions have greatly increased in number and size in recent years.)

Studying the Bible and teaching the Bible: there's the key, in my opinion. Sunday Schools that are centered in the Word of God are seldom losing students; many of them are growing dramatically. On the other hand, it's not surprising that schools that have turned from the Bible and are concentrating on psychological and sociological studies are losing ground.

People want bread, not a stone. They want to hear about Jesus. And they want their children to find the road that leads to life—especially in these years when there are so many other roads that lead to frustration and death.

I can't believe that an institution that has forty-six million students and four million teachers is dying. Rather, it seems to be one of the few hopeful signs on the horizon in the United States and Canada.

"When the enemy shall come in like a flood, the Spirit of the Lord shall lift up a standard against him" (Isaiah 59:19). This seems to be a principle illustrated in Western civilization during the past two centuries by the Sunday School.

Whether in late eighteenth-century England with all its immorality and callousness toward children, when Robert Raikes started the first Sunday School; in nineteenth-century America, when the period of westward expansion was at its height—and Sunday Schools were being founded in new communities from the Mississippi to the Pacific, schools that later grew into churches; in the crisis of the War Between the States; in Chicago after the great fire, when Dwight L. Moody and David C. Cook were establishing Sunday Schools in that devastated city: Sunday School has always proved to be a standard raised by the Spirit of God in periods of crisis.

Can it be different today, where an Enemy of our souls and the souls of our children has come in like a new and terrible flood, with waves of materialism, of anarchy, of moral relativism?

I think not.

At the time of the Communist takeover in China, when Christians were going through a period of severe testing and imprisonment—another kind of satanic flood—someone made the statement, "Christians are like tea. It takes hot water to bring out the best in them."

I think Sunday School is like that too.

Last Thursday night, Mary Lou and I attended an appreciation dinner put on by our church for the Sunday School staff. It was a nice evening; the food was especially good. (At potluck suppers, I think it would be good idea to have a card in front of each dish: "Prepared by—or created by—" followed by the name of the person. Then you could express your appreciation to the right person for that extra-special salad mold. Also, it would probably upgrade the food.)

The speaker was good too. But one question he asked bothered me. It was, "Do you ever get impatient with the stupid questions people ask during class?"

After we got home, I said to Mary Lou, "You know, I can't recall ever being asked a stupid question in class."

She couldn't either, from her experience teaching children.

"I've heard some stupid answers," I told her, "and given some. But no stupid questions."

It's such a delight to have a student ask you to clarify something he doesn't understand, even though the rest of the class does understand it. Or to express a doubt that you—and the class—can help resolve, because she had the courage to bring it out into the open. Or to ask how to deal with some problem of Christian lifestyle.

If I respect the students I teach, I'll respect their questions.

"I hear, I forget; I see, I remember; I do, I understand." I don't know who said that, but whoever it was, that person knew a lot about teaching.

It's so easy for me to limit myself to lecturing when I teach, to aim the lesson at ear-gate alone.

Jesus didn't make this mistake. He did lecture—the Sermon on the Mount is a beautiful example of this. But He used other teaching methods as well.

He told stories that were aimed at the heart. Who can forget the Prodigal Son (and his older brother), the lost sheep, the Good Samaritan, the poor widow, and an unjust judge?

And sometimes He left those stories open-ended. He didn't explain what they meant, but left the members of His class to figure them out for themselves.

I think we'd be better teachers today if we left some things open-ended, if we confronted our students with the nagging attempt to discover elusive truth. Why do we have to hit people over the head with the truth every time? There's joy in personal discovery.

He also wrote in the sand on at least one occasion. I guess that's next best to a chalkboard or overhead projector. Such an extension of teaching certainly makes more of an impression than spoken words alone.

Jesus used object lessons. It almost seems sacrilegious to refer to the Lord's Supper as an object lesson, but that's what it was, and still is.

He took the elements of an ordinary meal—bread and wine—and used them to impress the truth of His death for our sins indelibly upon our minds.

Could the disciples ever forget the lesson of their Lord, kneeling before them to wash their feet, the night He was betrayed?

He also carried on dialogues with individuals, both to teach the one with whom He spoke and also to teach the larger group who listened in. And the larger group did not merely learn from Jesus' words; they also learned from His attitude toward the other person. Love and respect and acceptance were doubtless communicated in this way.

How did the disciples know that Jesus loved the rich young ruler (Mark 10:21)? He didn't say He did; in fact, what He said to the young man resulted in his turning away from following Jesus.

I think it was Jesus' attitude toward him that convinced the disciples.

And the class observes my attitude toward the people with whom I carry on a dialogue, especially if they don't automatically follow what I say.

June

"I do, I understand." When people actually do something, the lesson is grasped.

Hearing and seeing are essential to learning, but doing seems to be the test. "If you know these things," Jesus said, "happy are you if you do them."

And for three years Jesus was involved with His disciples in the doing.

He didn't just teach them the elements of prayer; He prayed with them. He didn't give them principles of witnessing; they listened as He confronted men and women with the necessity to believe. He didn't just tell them they ought to be compassionate; they observed His compassion.

And then He sent them out, two by two, to do it on their own.

When I was a high school student, I had a Sunday School teacher who taught us the Bible on Sunday morning, but also taught us how to do it other nights of the week.

This teacher was a busy medical doctor, but he and his wife (they had no children at the time) took the class to New York City rescue missions to hold meetings. We learned that the Spirit of God was able to use even our weak words to deliver hopeless alcoholics. They took us to busy corners to hold street meetings, where we learned boldness in giving a Christian testimony to those who often opposed us or belittled us.

Today, more than forty years later, I continue to benefit from those lessons in doing.

It's harder to involve adults in doing, but it's possible. Maybe Sunday School classes should be the center for doing in the church, rather than a lot of other isolated interest groups. This would certainly provide for natural follow-through and prayer support.

Two weeks ago we had an example of doing. And Ray told us of the results in class today.

Ray heads up an organization that provides assistance to medical missionaries overseas. He told us during the prayer time in that earlier class session about one of India's outstanding evangelists who needs a kidney transplant if he's to continue to live. The kidney is available, he said; the money for medical expenses is not. He wanted the class to pray about this need.

We did pray. Then, when I got up to teach, I said, "Do you think that God may be speaking to us about meeting this need? If you do, and if you want to help without affecting your regular giving to the church or the church's missionary budget, leave money or a check with Doug (one of the class members) before you leave."

Today Ray told us how much has come in from the class during the past couple of weeks: two thousand dollars. Almost enough, he says, for the life-extending surgery on this man of God in India.

It's exciting to do things together . . . for the glory of God.

When I stop to think about it, one of the most exciting things about teaching Sunday School is that I'm building the church: the church of which I'm a part today, and the church of my children and grandchildren tomorrow.

Without men and women grounded in the Word of God and in Christian doctrine, the church would fall apart—or, perhaps worse, become a shadow of what our Lord intended, even a caricature.

Where do these men and women become thus grounded? In Sunday School, usually from the time they are little children.

"Whom shall he teach knowledge? And whom shall he make to understand doctrine? Them that are weaned from the milk, and drawn from the breasts. For precept must be upon precept, precept upon precept; line upon line, line upon line; here a little, and there a little" (Isaiah 28:9-10). This is the Bible's own description of the process, which begins with preschoolers and continues to old age.

And my class is part of the process. I'm part of it.

In the pre-lesson part of our class (I dislike the term "opening exercises"—it sounds like doing the knee bends), the leader asks anyone who has a first-time guest to introduce him or her, or if a person has come without being brought by a regular attender, to introduce himself or herself. (Even in the latter instance someone sitting next to the newcomer often has found out who the person is and makes the introduction.)

These introductions are brief and low-key. The person doesn't stand up, and isn't embarrassed or put on the spot too much.

If they're newcomers to the community, George (our class president, who has a friendly manner that puts people at ease, despite the fact he is a lawyer) may ask where they live or work—then mention someone else in the class who lives or works in the same place.

There's a family feeling in class. At times someone needs special affirmation—and receives it. Or someone has done something special, or the child of a class member has achieved some honor or goal. Then there is recognition, and the whole class rejoices. If someone has been away, he is usually welcomed back. This includes children who come home from college or the service.

We have some Christian workers in the class. Two sisters went to the Far East to teach, and we prayed for them at home each morning (at least the ones we remembered) when we put on our shoes.

Requests for prayer aren't just remembered in class; they become part of many members' prayer lists of the next week or longer.

We're like a family, the family of God in this place.

This morning Herb had too much to say again. I tried to overlook him when he raised his hand repeatedly to answer questions, or to volunteer insights.

His contributions are usually good, because he really knows the Bible. I wish I knew as much of it by memory as he does! (Maybe I'd better get started on a Bible memory plan, if for no other reason, to prove I still can learn.)

And Herb is eager for the return of our Lord Christ. His gaze is fixed on that happy hope—and he frequently reminds us of it. I like that. It brings us back to Christian reality.

But sometimes Herb's a problem, like this morning. Most of the people in the class know about the automobile accident he had a few years ago, that cut his brilliant career in engineering short. We all love Herb and his wife, Elaine.

But it's not good for the class when one person tends to monopolize things. And I don't think it's good for Herb, either.

I've tried to do something about it. A couple of times I've said, after class when we were alone, "Herb, you and I know a lot about the Bible. We have to be quiet sometimes and give other people a chance to respond to questions."

And I've tried to let Elaine know that I'm not uptight about it, and that I'm sure the class isn't, either.

Maybe that's all I can do. Maybe the class needs the example of my loving acceptance of Herb and respect for his ideas more than it needs opportunities for more people to answer questions.

July

Vacation time. People are away, the class was smaller than usual.

And the room was stuffy, in spite of the fan I brought along this morning.

I hope something got through to the class. They must have had a hard time concentrating on the lesson; I know I would have, if I hadn't been teaching.

What was the lesson about this morning? Nothing new to that group of people, or to me either, for that matter.

I remember, years ago, reading about an older woman—a Christian of many years—who thanked her pastor for what his recent sermons had meant to her, one Sunday as she left the service.

She said it quickly, and was about to move away after shaking his hand.

"Thank you," the pastor said. "What did you find helpful in last Sunday's message?"

"I don't remember," the woman said.

Somewhat crestfallen, the pastor said, "How about the week before that?"

Again, "I don't remember." Then, as the pastor was turning from her, she said, "You know, Pastor, it's like putting a colander under the water to wash it when it's dirty. The colander doesn't retain the water, but it gets cleansed in the process. When you teach me God's Word, I may not remember what you said, but I get cleansed and renewed by it."

Thank you, God, that even when the lesson isn't exciting, even when the students can't remember what I said, Your Holy Spirit can use it in their lives. Just let me teach Your Word and have faith in You. Amen.

I'm glad Kenny is in the class. He's God's special gift to all of us.

His bright smile and "Hi, Joe," as he hands me a hymnbook at the door, start the hour off just right.

How much does he understand of the complicated ideas we pass back and forth, teacher to student, student to teacher, student to student?

Very little, I'm sure.

But he understands that Jesus loves him, that his parents, brothers, and sisters love him (they have for more than thirty years), and the class loves him.

I remember the Sunday we sang "Happy Birthday to Kenny": his smile almost exploded off his face.

Sometimes when I speak to him after class, he points to some article of clothing, letting me know it's new.

By his faithful attention to giving out the hymnbooks before class, and turning out the lights afterward, Kenny teaches the teacher.

But he teaches me something more. Sometimes when I'm teaching, my eyes light upon Kenny, sitting there in the first row, taking notes (regular up and down lines in a notebook).

Then I think, "God, help me and the whole class to see You with Kenny's simple faith and love. Move us beyond the clutter of complicated ideas to Yourself."

"The last shall be first," Jesus said. Maybe in heaven I'll be studying under Kenny's teaching.

Alfred North Whitehead, the great educator, described enthusiasm as "the extra spurt of energy that drives a buzz saw through the knots in a log."

I find that I must be enthusiastic if I'm to carry the class along with me through the lesson. They seem to know when I enjoy teaching; then they enjoy learning. When I don't, they don't.

This morning I was teaching a lesson that I wasn't particularly enthusiastic about. Maybe I should have substituted something else, but I don't like to break the continuity.

I prayed that I'd have enthusiasm anyway.

Then I stood up to teach (sometimes I sit down; the desk has a lectern on it, so I can choose), and I suddenly realized that these people were waiting to hear the Word of God. They had come to Sunday School to hear God's voice, not mine.

Suddenly I felt enthusiastic—not for the lesson, but for those people in my class. And above all, for the awesome privilege that was mine to teach them God's Word.

It was a good lesson.

I've found that sometimes a student rescues the situation with his or her enthusiasm. This seems to occur most frequently with those who have recently come to faith in Jesus Christ, to knowledge of the freedom He brings to living.

You can't manufacture enthusiasm. But you can pray that God will give it—through the teacher or through a student.

August

It's late. The class went to Hansens' for a "sing" tonight, after church.

Their apartment is eighteen floors up, and in the middle of the sing, a sudden, violent storm arose to the northeast.

The lights went out for a brief time, and we crowded the windows and small balcony to observe the lightning flashes and hear the thunderclaps.

The power of God is so obvious during a storm, whether it's over the ocean or over the prairie.

Then the lights went back on and—as suddenly as it had begun—the storm ended and a heavy rain began.

We found our seats again, and Bob finally got the group quiet.

"Tonight we're saying good-bye to Eileen," he said. "She'll be returning to her teaching in Singapore. We'll miss her from the class, but we'll look forward to her letters back to us. And of course, we'll look forward to welcoming her when she has her next furlough.

"We promise to pray for you," Bob continued, turning to face Eileen. "Now let's pray, committing her to the Lord's care and a fruitful ministry."

There's a power beyond the power of any storm, or any nation, or Satan himself. "All power is given unto me," Jesus said. "Go and teach."

Eileen will be going in that power to teach in Singapore . . . an extension of our class.

I'm not different from most other teachers in wanting to see immediate results, sudden changes in the people I teach. This seldom happens; I must admit that my own life is an example of the time it takes to change, or be changed.

I find some comfort in the fact that when Saint Paul said, "I have learned, in whatsoever state I am, therewith to be content" (Philippians 4:11), he was an old man. How long did it take the great apostle to learn the lesson of contentment in adverse circumstances?

My responsibility is to teach God's Word; His is to change people. I have to learn to teach by faith—just as I'm to do everything else in my life by faith—rather than by sight. I must trust God for results, for change. I must believe that His Word will not return to Him void; it will accomplish His purpose.

The accomplishing may take years. Meanwhile, I planted a bomb in people's lives this morning, a delayed-action bomb that will go off at some future date. My responsibility is to plant the bomb. God's responsibility is to detonate it.

I hope I'm around to see it go off.

A modern Christmas story set in Wheaton, evangelicalism's Bethlehem.

How Silently, How Silently

HE ARRIVED AT Chicago's O'Hare airport on TWA flight 801 from Israel. The plane was two hours late, but the delay made little difference, since there was no one to meet him.

It was December 23, a Friday afternoon. The terminal building pulsed with people coming home for Christmas, relatives meeting people coming home, businessmen and students trying to get on flights for Cleveland and New York, Seattle and Atlanta, so they could be home for the holidays.

The Israeli had gone through immigration and customs in New York. He had no baggage, only a small airline bag with a broken zipper.

Christmas carols issued from concealed speakers the length of a long corridor into the main building, interrupted only by announcements of arriving flights, departing flights, boarding areas now open, passengers being paged. He walked down the corridor listening, watching people.

In the main terminal building a massive, white-flocked Christmas tree, decorated with golden balls, stood in a corner beyond the telephone booths and rows of seats. He turned aside to examine the tree, then stepped onto an escalator marked "Down to Baggage and Ground Transportation."

"Excuse me," he said to a pretty girl at the Avis counter, "can you tell me how to get to Wheaton, Illinois?"

"Easiest way is to rent an Avis car and drive there," she replied. "Only thing, we don't have any available. I'm sorry. Unless you have a reservation, that is. If you don't, you might try Number One over there."

"Thank you, but I don't drive. Is there a bus?"

"I don't think so. You'll have to take a cab."

He repeated his question to a man in uniform who stood near the door of the terminal, explaining that he didn't think he had enough money for a cab.

"Take the bus to the Loop," the man said. "Get off at the Palmer House, walk back to State Street, down State to Madison—get that? On Madison, get a bus to the Chicago and Northwestern Station. You can get a train there for Wheaton. Bus is loading now."

The young Israeli murmured his thanks and walked outside the terminal building. He shivered as the sharp wind whipped through his light topcoat. It was snowing.

"Please tell me when we get to the Palmer House," he asked the bus driver.

"First stop," the driver said.

The bus cruised down the expressway. Lights and signs and thousands of cars. Trucks and shopping centers and Christmas trees and lights. Signboards in green and red, "Merry Christmas" in letters two feet high.

"Palmer House," the driver called.

The Israeli left the warm bus. A blast of cold air off the lake hit him as he stepped down to the sidewalk. His teeth chattered; he turned the ineffectual collar of his coat up around his neck.

At the corner he hesitated, then stopped to look at the jewels and expensive ornaments in Peacock's window. Then he hurried on, after asking a policeman which direction Madison Street was.

Almost running because of the cold wind and driving snow, he covered the three blocks to the other bus quickly. It was crowded; he stood between an elderly woman who kept sneezing into the elbow of her ragged coat, and a teenage boy, his arms full of packages.

At the Chicago and Northwestern Station he bought a ticket to Wheaton, then sat in the waiting room for half an hour. Once he went over to the newsstand to buy a paper. The front page had stories about war, politics, and crime; a photograph of a wan child with leukemia, slumped in a wheelchair beside a smiling actress and a Christmas tree at Children's Hospital; a reminder of "One Shopping Day Left Before Christmas."

Finally he boarded the train. It was so hot inside, and he was so tired from his trip, which had started the previous day in the Middle East, that he fell asleep.

About an hour later the conductor shook him awake. "You want to get off at Wheaton, this is it."

The young Israeli stepped down onto the snow-covered station platform. He almost fell as his foot slipped on the smooth surface.

"Careful there, young fellow." The conductor clutched his arm.

He crossed the tracks to the sidewalk. As he looked uncertainly in both directions, a young woman smiled at him. She was leaning against a green Vega.

"Hi," she called.

"Hello," he answered. "So this is Wheaton."

"It is, for better or for worse."

"Is there any worse?"

"Yes. Me, for instance. You look cold. Where are you going?"

"I'm not sure."

"It's darned cold talking out here. How about coming up to my apartment? It's only a few blocks over—I'll drive you."

"Thank you. Do you live with your mother or someone?"

"No, I live alone. Say, are you from around here? Or maybe Glen Ellyn? I saw you get off the train."

"I'm from Israel."

"You're Jewish, aren't you?"

"Yes, I'm Jewish. And you're Mary."

"How did you know? Did someone tell you about me?" An edge of belligerence showed in her voice.

"You had to be Mary."

"What do you mean, I had to be Mary? Why couldn't I be Judy or Jean or Connie?"

"Because you're Mary."

"If you're from Israel, you're a long way from home. Do you have any friends here? I mean, is anyone expecting you?"

"Nobody's expecting me. And I haven't a place to stay, so I'm in the market for one."

"You can stay with me for a few days."

"Thank you, Mary. Any other suggestions?"

"I mean it. It'll be nice having company over for Christmas. You won't put me out."

"Mary, I do appreciate your invitation, I do. But are there any other possibilities?"

"Well, there's a house over near my apartment building, where the lady takes roomers. She's really old—and safe. Maybe she'd have a room for you."

"Would you drive me there so I can find out?"

"Sure. Get in the car—you must be freezing."

"I am. This coat was made for Jerusalem, not Chicago."

"Or Wheaton. This is a cold place too."

The elderly lady had a room, which the Israeli took. He had barely enough money for one week's rent.

Mary saw him count out the bills, and saw how little was left in his wallet.

"Look," she said, "I just got paid. Let me give you something to tide you over."

"Mary, you're generous. I don't think I'll need it, though. After all, I'll only be here over Christmas."

"Well, as long as you don't forget that I'm ready to help you—no strings attached."

"No strings attached."

"Hey, it's almost seven o'clock and I haven't eaten yet."

"We had a big meal on the plane from New York, so I'm not hungry."

"Good. In that case I know where we can get enough to eat without having to pay for it. This Christian publishing company is having a sort of Christmas open house this evening. The public's invited to see their new building. We can go and fill up on cookies and punch."

"Sounds interesting. Let's go."

Mary drove several miles, then parked her car in the parking lot of a rather imposing one-story building.

"Look here," she said as they closed the car doors, "we don't have to stay very long."

"All right, Mary. By the way, what are those other buildings?"

"That one's Christian Youth headquarters, the next one's Sunday School, the one down the road there is Congo Missions. Let's go in out of the cold."

Inside the building, a table was placed in front of a Christmas tree. The tree was decorated with hundreds of little Bibles, about the size of a child's hand, hanging from the branches.

The table was covered with a white cloth and decorated with holly. A poinsettia plant in the center was surrounded by sandwiches, Christmas cookies, a silver coffee service, plates, cups, napkins, and spoons. An empty punch bowl stood at one end of the table.

"I'm sorry we've run out of punch," said the lady seated at the other end of the table. "May I pour you some coffee?"

"Yes, please." Mary extended her hand for the cup.

"Could you get me some water, please?" asked the young Israeli. "Maybe just fill up the punch bowl."

"Oh, we won't need to do that," the lady replied. "That many people won't be wanting water tonight."

"Why don't you do like he says?" Mary asked. "Maybe he's really thirsty. Or maybe some other people will be. It's hot in here, you know. Or hadn't you noticed?"

"Certainly," the lady said. "Bob, could you come here a moment? Will you please fill the punch bowl up with water?"

Bob returned after several minutes, carrying the large bowl awkwardly because of its weight.

"Strangest thing happened," he said in an excited voice. "When I took it out in the kitchen it was empty, except for some ice. But when I turned the faucet on, and began filling the bowl, it wasn't like water at all. Look, it's dark red."

"Let's have a taste."

"I can't believe it. I really can't. There's—yes, I'm sure it's wine in that punch bowl. Bob, tell us the truth. What really happened?"

"Just like I said. When the water from the kitchen faucet ran into the punch bowl, it turned to what's in there now. Honest it did."

"I haven't tasted that stuff in fifteen years, not since I was saved. But there's no doubt about it—that's wine, and it's the best."

"Bob, will you please take it back out in the kitchen and pour it down the drain? We can't have word get around that we served an alcoholic beverage here at our open house.

"I'm sorry about what's happened, Sir," she said to the Israeli. "Would you like some coffee?"

"No, thank you. I'll just have some of these sandwiches and cookies."

A few minutes later, Mary suggested they leave. And they did.

"That was great," she said as they drove away in her car. "I don't know how you did it, but it was just great."

"I'm tired—I guess it must be the time change form Israel to here. You won't mind driving me back to my room now?"

"Of course not. And I won't even try to get you to stop at my apartment first."

Next morning the young Israeli slept late. When he left the house, he saw Mary waiting in her car at the corner. It had snowed all night, and the heavy flakes were still coming down.

"How long have you been waiting here?" he asked as he opened the car door.

"Oh, ten—maybe fifteen minutes. That's all."

"It would have taken a lot longer than that for the windshield to get this covered with snow." As he sat down in the warm car, he brushed the snow from his thin topcoat.

"Hey, I have something for you," she said.

"What is it, Mary? Say, will you please turn that radio down? I can hardly hear you, and I feel as if I have to shout to make myself heard."

"Sure. That's WLS, by the way. Here's what I got for you."

"A heavy coat and earmuffs! Mary, Mary. You knew how cold I was, and you bought me some warm clothes. Do you mind if I put them on right now?"

"I'll mind if you don't."

As they sat at breakfast in a small restaurant, Mary and the Israeli were silent for a long time. Finally the Israeli spoke.

"Mary, you're sick of it, aren't you?"

"Up to here." She put her hand to her mouth.

"Things will be different."

"They already are. I know you now. Please stay for a while."

"Not for long."

"Long enough to make sure the change is permanent?"

"It will be. I don't need to stay around here for that, Mary."

"Long enough to change this town?"

"No, I can't stay that long. Just until tomorrow night."

"Christmas night."

"Christmas night. Then I must leave."

"It's funny, having you here in Wheaton for Christmas. And funnier that I'm the only one who knows you're here."

"You were there at the Northwestern station to meet me."

"Am I glad I was!"

"Let's finish our coffee and leave."

"Look, I have to work this afternoon. You take my car. You can drop me off, and maybe pick me up around six o'clock. Or I can walk home. It's not far. But you can use my car to get around in today."

"I don't drive. Thanks anyway, Mary. But I'll manage without transportation today. Especially with this warm coat." He smiled at her.

"Do you like it? I hoped you would. Now I'll have to get to work. How about meeting me for supper tonight? I'll stop by your house for you at six-thirty or seven. Then later we can go to the Christmas Eve service at church. I haven't been there for a while, but I'd like to go again."

"Fine, Mary. I'll be looking for you around six-thirty."

He walked all over town that afternoon, stopping at the county jail, a convalescent home, and the church parsonage.

A middle-aged, worried-looking woman answered the door at the parsonage.

"Yes?" she said.

"I'm a stranger here, from Israel. I thought I'd stop by to meet the pastor."

"He's very busy today—the day before Christmas, you know, and Christmas on a Sunday this year. But step inside. I'll call him."

He waited inside the door for several minutes. Then the pastor came downstairs with his wife.

"James, this is a man from Israel who wants to meet you. I told him how busy you are this afternoon."

"Never too busy to meet one of the Lord's people. Welcome!" He gripped the younger man's hand. "Are you here for long?"

"Just through Christmas. I'll leave tomorrow night."

"Well, it's great to meet you. Will you be in church tomorrow? We're especially interested in Israel—our church supports two missionaries there. Israel General Mission. Know it?"

"I've heard of it."

"'To the Jew first,' I always say. Maybe you'd share something with us at our morning service tomorrow. Our missionary conference is coming up in February and it won't hurt a bit to have a word about Israel and missions on Christmas Sunday morning."

"I'll be glad to speak."

"Just briefly, you understand. Five minutes at the most. We'll really be pushed for time tomorrow—special music, you know. Probably you have the same problem with time back home in Israel."

"Perhaps things are a little more simple there. Yes, I'll stick to the five minutes."

"Good. The Lord bless you. Is it still snowing out? I'll see you tomorrow—don't trip on the raised sill."

The Israeli returned to his room in the house where he was staying.

A little after six-thirty he saw the green Vega parked in front of the house. He heard a light sound of the horn as he went downstairs, pulling on his new, warm coat.

Mary leaned over to open the door. "It's great to see you again. I thought the afternoon would never end."

"I guess my afternoon went quickly because I did so much walking and saw so many different people. But I'm certainly glad to see you again, Mary."

"Look, is it all right with you if we go up to my apartment to eat?" Before he could answer, she added, "There will be other people there, friends of mine."

"I'd like nothing better."

"But we'll probably get talking and won't get to the Christmas Eve service at church. In fact, these friends of mine wouldn't go anyway. They're not the church kind. They're like me—like I was before I met you."

"Supper with you and your friends sounds a lot more interesting—and worthwhile—than sitting through a Christmas Eve service."

"Do you really mean it? I was afraid you'd be like the rest—oh, that wasn't a kind thing to say. I've got so much to learn."

By now they were climbing the stairs to the second-floor apartment. From inside the door came sounds of the Living Dead.

"It'll be noisy," Mary said as she opened the door. "Hi," she called out to the six or seven forms sprawled on chairs and on the floor. "Turn that record player down, someone. I want you all to meet my new friend. I've only known him one day, but in my whole life nobody has ever known me so well. He's from Israel."

"Welcome, Israeli. How are the Arabs?"

"Suffering, as they have for centuries. Like my own people."

"We'll eat soon, gang," Mary called as she went into the tiny kitchen. She turned toward the Israeli, "Come and help me."

Before long, spaghetti was overflowing a large bowl, and long loaves of bread, buttered and flavored with garlic, were placed on the table next to a bowl of green salad. The table had no cloth on it. Paper plates and red paper napkins were set out, with stainless steel utensils.

When the food was on the table, Mary announced, "Before we eat, my Israeli friend will pray."

There was a whisper, "Mary has a new hang-up."

The Israeli stood in the kitchen doorway. "Father," he said, "I thank You for this spaghetti and for Mary's kindness to us all. Make Your name glorious in this room tonight."

No one sat at the table. They ate from their laps, or placed their plates on the floor, where they sat or reclined. At first the music was so loud it was hard to talk, except to one other person. But as they were finishing the meal, Mary turned down the volume. Then the whole group began to discuss war and peace, sex and drugs, life, race (two of them were black), Camus and Christmas.

The Israeli listened most of the time, although he asked a lot of questions. His occasional comments were brief. He also told several stories.

As the evening passed, they began to ask him questions. His answers were direct, without pressure.

At midnight Mary said, "Merry Christmas, Israeli! Merry Christmas, everyone!"

Soon afterward the guests began to leave. The Israeli was the last to go.

"Thanks for a most enjoyable Christmas Eve, Mary. And thank you for introducing me to your friends. They're an interesting group, each one different."

"Thank you for coming. May I go to church with you tomorrow?"

"Of course. I was hoping you would."

"I'll stop at your house about ten-thirty."

"Fine. Good night, Mary."

He walked through the snow—by now almost to his knees—to the house where he was staying. Because most of the sidewalks were not yet shoveled, he walked in the street, where cars had smoothed some narrow tracks.

In his room he undressed, then stood by the window for a moment, shivering in the darkness, looking at the silent snow. He prayed, "Father, I thank You that You hear me. I thank You that things shall not always be as they were that night and as they are this night. Cover earth with righteousness and justice and love as snow covers all things tonight."

He slept.

The blinding sunlight of Christmas morning awoke him, reflecting whiteness all around. From his airline bag he removed an orange, which he peeled and ate.

Just before ten-thirty, Mary came. The green Vega was filled with people who had been at her apartment the previous evening—all except one couple, who rode a motorcycle behind Mary's car. A snowplow had partially cleared the street.

"Merry Christmas, Israeli!" they all shouted as he came out of the house.

He smiled—a pleased, happy smile. "Thank you, friends. And Merry Christmas to all of you. I'm surprised to see you, but I'm glad you're going to the service with Mary and me."

"Mary didn't twist our arms, either," one said. "Yesterday she'd have had to, and we still wouldn't have gone. The fact is, she wouldn't have gone herself, before yesterday. But now we've met you ourselves, and we know you, so we want to go."

At the church, which was already almost full, an usher led them up to a partially empty pew at the very front. They were an odd assortment: miniskirted, leather coated, long haired, one bearded, two black skinned, and the rest white. And the Israeli, who sat between Mary and a young black man.

The service began with the doxology and Apostles' Creed. Carols sung by the congregation, "O Holy Night" by the combined choirs, the Christmas story from Luke's Gospel followed. Next the offering. While the ushers were taking it, and the organ was playing, the pastor looked thoughtfully down at the front pew, at the Israeli and the group of young men and women around him.

After the offering, the children's choir sang "Silent Night."

The sermon followed. It was a carefully prepared, almost exhaustive survey of the Old Testament prophetic passages that predicted Christ's advent.

A prayer, "O Little Town of Bethlehem," and the benediction ended the service.

Mary's little group of friends surrounded the Israeli as they walked behind the slow-moving group out the center aisle. The young black man turned to him. "Sir, could I talk to you before you leave town? Mary says you're heading back down today."

"Of course. We'll find a quiet place."

At the door, the pastor smiled as he shook their hands. "I hope you all felt welcome among us. And you, my friend," taking the Israeli's hand, "I'm sorry there just wasn't time in the service for a word from you. But Christmas morning, you know—people are so anxious for the service to end promptly at twelve so they can get home to their family celebrations. I hope you understand."

"I do," said the Israeli.

Mary spoke to the pastor. "You missed something. We know, because we've been listening to him."

"Well, Merry Christmas," said the pastor, turning from them to greet the last ones to leave.

They went back to Mary's apartment for a bacon-and-eggs lunch. They talked all afternoon.

Around five o'clock Mary drove the Israeli to O'Hare airport. Everybody went. This time the motorcycle, with its two riders, led the way.

He left for Israel on TWA flight 802.

A Christmas meditation on the Incarnation.

Christmas Voices

Joseph

It's cold and drafty. She's cold. Why couldn't the boy have been born while we were still in Nazareth, instead of here, alone, no one to help. Only me, and I've never delivered a baby.

Fear not, Joseph.

I do believe God. I take Him at his word. A baby. But not mine.

Take unto thee Mary.

Mary—how I love her. I love you, Mary. Here.

Hold my hand. I'll see that nothing goes wrong.

No, God will see to that, He'll take care of you.

He's got to—it's His baby. Don't be afraid.

She shall bring forth a son.

He'll work beside me, help me smooth a yoke, build a house. I'll get him a little saw, the boy and I will work together.

Call his name Jesus.

I like that name: Jesus, Joshua—he brought our people to this land. He was a leader, Joshua was. He was God's man.

He shall save his people...

It's beyond me. I'm just a carpenter, not a rabbi. How can he save, even after he comes of age? When Messiah comes...

... from their sins.

Things are so bad. People are so bad, not just the Romans, either. For that matter, I'm bad—I need a Savior. Mary, I'm here. Don't be afraid—cry out, if you feel like it.

Emmanuel.

God with us, Mary. God's with us, and here's the baby. Listen to him cry. Where did you put the bands to wrap him in? I love you, Mary. And I love your son—our son.

Shepherd

It's a night for lambing, a dark one. No moon or stars. It's good we built this fire. —What's that?

Fear not.

Don't be afraid? When you see an angel, big as life? And hear its voice rock the whole countryside? I'm glad this hole is here.

For, behold, I bring good tidings of great joy...

I wish it'd go away. Or lower its voice. "Great joy" sounds good, though. I could sure use some. Do you suppose that's a real, honest-to-goodness angel?

. . . which shall be to all people.

Impossible. How can the same news be good for the Roman swine and for us? The angel must be Jewish, like God. It probably means "to all Jews."

For unto you is born this day in the city of David . . .

In Bethlehem? Little Bethlehem, where I was born? Impossible. Maybe Jerusalem, but not Bethlehem.

. . . a Savior, which is Christ the Lord.

The Messiah, born tonight, born in Bethlehem? We've waited for centuries, and no Messiah. Tonight's a night for a lamb to be born, not a Messiah.

And this shall be a sign unto you; Ye shall find the babe wrapped in swaddling clothes, lying in a manger.

The Messiah born in a stable? A baby all wrapped up? Impossible. A lamb in a stable, a king in a palace. —Hey, look at that, a whole army of angels. More than a Roman legion. And what a bright light.

Glory to God in the highest . . .

They must be able to hear that the whole way to Bethlehem.

. . . on earth peace, good will toward men.

Peace, that's great. Especially if it means the Romans will leave our country. But "good will toward men"? They must mean toward Jews, if they're really speaking for God. —Hey, where did they go? It's dark again. They're gone. Did you see that? Did you hear what they said? Wait till I tell the wife about this. Let's go to Bethlehem and see what they were talking about. Maybe we'll find the Messiah, maybe we'll only find a lamb. In a stable, mind you.

Look at the newborn. A perfect little thing, like a lamb without blemish.

The Father

My Son
Farewell.
A body I've prepared for You
in Mary
Jewish girl
betrothed to Joseph
Jewish carpenter.
You who have been with Me
from everlasting days
who with Me made all things
including earth and man
and Mary
tonight become a creature vulnerable
baby most helpless.
The swirling cloud
takes You to her
through darkest night.
I send an angel army to protect

proclaim Your birth.
You'll grow
and spend a few days' light
then darkest noon
and You'll return.
I'll have the dust of earth
virgin's fruit
at my right hand
forevermore.
Tonight I joy
that You delight to do My will
take God-sized step
to earth and womb
and tree.
My Son, Farewell.

I hear a baby's cry.

Mary

Wretched place to be delivered. Birthplace of oxen, of asses, of vermin. Pain. Travail in a stable.

Fear not, Mary.

Stench of manure. Straw, pungent, acrid. Birth pangs in a stable.

For thou hast found favor with God.

Pain. My first baby. A boy. Born in a stable, born away from home. Nine months. Nine long months.

Thou shalt conceive in thy womb, and bring forth a son.

A son. My son. Strange thought—not his. Pain. My son, my Savior. Our Savior.

Thou shalt call his name Jesus.

Jesus. Jesus. Pain. He shall lead our people into the Promised Land.

Beautiful name. Jesus, my first baby. A boy.

He shall be great, and shall be called the Son of the Highest.

God's Son in a stable? Birthplace of oxen, birthplace of vermin? Pain, what pain. Son of the Highest.

The Lord God shall give unto him the throne of his father, David.

Palaces, not stables, for kings. Pain. Pain. Stables for asses, for sheep. For a little lamb.

Of his kingdom there shall be no end.

David's kingdom ended. Every kingdom ends. Pain. His kingdom . . . Pain. It will never end. Never. Pain. Greater than King David. Pain. Pain. My baby. My Savior. Pain. Pain. Pain. Joseph, *Joseph.*

My baby. Those fingers, so tiny. Round little arms and legs. My baby.

That holy thing that is born of thee . . .

Cover him up. Wind it tight. Drafty old stable. Stars through the roof. Smelly manger, hard and cold.

He shall be called the Son of God.

Those hands, those tiny, perfect little hands. They made the stars, the earth. God's Son, my Savior, my baby. It's cold tonight. Cover the hands, too.

Joe Bayly's last sermon, preached to College Church in Wheaton—his home congregation—on Sunday morning, March 2, 1986. Bayly had been sick in bed much of the previous week and attributed the power of this sermon to the extra time he had been able to spend in prayer. *

Is Holiness Possible Today: With a Warning from Esau

THERE ARE CERTAIN words and terms that are dated. They're anachronisms, relics of the past. *Hippies* is one of them *bobby socks* another. *Railroad journey* is almost one. *Holiness* may be such a word.

For many centuries the word holiness summed up the highest aspirations of the church for its people. As a doctrine, holiness is responsible for the formation of a number of denominations. Today we talk about church growth instead of holiness. We talk about witnessing instead of holiness. We talk about self-esteem instead of holiness. We talk about the health and wealth gospel instead of holiness. We talk about political influence instead of holiness.

Holiness begins with God. In Leviticus 19:2 we read, "Be holy because I, the Lord your God, am holy." And Jesus in Matthew 5:48 in the Sermon on the Mount said, "Be perfect even as your Father in Heaven is perfect." Holiness begins with God. But contemporary theology doesn't begin with God. It begins from beneath, with man. It often ends with man. There is relational theology today: feminist theology, liberation theology, a theology arising out of various human conditions and desires. But holiness arises out of God—the nature and character of God. It is the condition of being set apart for God—totally for God. Which is the only rational situation for any creature to its creator. And even more for the redeemed to their Redeemer.

*If the reader wishes to have an audio copy of this sermon, he may e-mail the Bayly family at <cbmw@earthlink.net> and they will be pleased to provide one.

Holiness is a requirement for every Christian. Man or woman, bond or free, rich or poor, sick or well, married or single. "Be holy because I, the Lord your God, am holy."

Holiness wasn't limited to the biblical ages. It is God's requirement today. The church may have forgotten about holiness, but to the extent that it has, it has forgotten about the God who is supremely holy and demands that of those who belong to Him. Is holiness possible today? Yes, but it's supremely difficult. It's the road less traveled. It cuts across the grain. Not merely of this present evil world, but of much Christian teaching and practice. Hebrews 12 tells us how to achieve holiness today. What we must do, and how God works to bring about our holiness. First we are told that the men and women—heroes of faith—whose lives were described in the previous chapter—Moses and Abraham and the rest—that these men and women should encourage us to run our race in a certain way. We have picked up the baton from them, from Christians in generations past, as they have ended their race, and we ourselves must carry it on to the finish line. It is our great loss today that we have forgotten the more recent heroes of faith, that missionary biography has fallen into discard. People are growing up today without knowing the sacrifices and the trust, the faith in God of men and women in more recent centuries. This cloud of witnesses who surround us, not merely these Old Testament ones, but Hudson Taylor and Maria, Mary Slessor, Charles Simeon. Reading the lives of these men and women would supply some of the power we need to run our own race.

How should we run our race? First, let us throw off everything that hinders, that which is superfluous, that which holds back our commitment to God. These are matters of individual conviction and decision. You know what hinders your growth as a Christian. It isn't sin that I am talking about at this point, but those things that pull you down. Those things that hinder your growth in holiness. Friendships that don't lift you up, but rather have the opposite effect. Lack of discipline in your use of time. Self-centeredness that keeps you from entering into the needs of others, even writing a note to someone who is ill, even calling on the phone and saying "I am praying for you." All these are hindrances that impede our race. But not merely the hindrances, but the sin that so easily besets us. It tangles us in its web so that we may be forced to drop out of the race. This is no matter of individual choice. If the Bible describes something as sin, it is sin. There is no waffling over it—no deciding whether we will obey or disobey if we are the children of God. We must only obey.

Next the writer says, "Let us fix our eyes on Jesus" (verse 2). What are your eyes fixed on? What are you looking at? Jesus or *Miami Vice?* Jesus or murders, rapes, illicit sexual relations? How many murders did you watch last week? How many chapters of the Bible did you read? Did you pray? God says, "Whatever is true, whatever is noble, whatever is right, whatever is pure, whatever is lovely, whatever is admirable—think about such things." You cannot fill your mind with moral sewage and be a moral person. It is as simple as that. And you who have children in your homes, are you raising them with their eyes fixed on Jesus? Or are their eyes fixed on this present, evil world? Someday God will demand an accounting for your stewardship of your children's minds. Now when we look at Jesus, we don't see success in the eyes of the world. We don't see comfort and wealth. We see a man of sorrows who is acquainted with grief. A poor man. A man who stood up to the opposition of sinners—who died on a cross forsaken by His friends as we are told here in Hebrews.

But the writer of Hebrews says, "He endured." He endured; Jesus endured all the suffering and the opposition and the persecution and death on the cross. He stood firm against all the opposition Satan could muster against Him. Jesus' life certainly wouldn't make the Christian best-seller list today. But Jesus is our model of holiness because all this did not deter Him. It didn't hold Him back. He saw beyond it all. All the suffering, all the betrayal, all the pain, all the loss—He saw beyond it all to the joy that followed the cross. That is what carried Him through. He didn't go through on flowery beds of ease. He never had it easy. He taught no wealth and health gospel. He healed people. And of course God still heals people. God shows us in Jesus that suffering is the road to holiness if we endure. Jesus didn't expect to find gratification or fulfillment in this life. An old divine put it this way, "O God, burn eternity into my eyeballs. Burn eternity into my eyeballs. Help me to see all of this life through the perspective of eternity." All that is our part in becoming holy men and women, according to this passage. But God is working to make us holy, too.

What is God's part in our holiness? Very simply, a father's loving discipline of His children. Don't think that Christians are God's spoiled children. We aren't. We are the children that God disciplines, that God will punish in order that someday we may be able to stand in His presence. Because those who are holy are the ones who will see God. It is because we are God's children that He won't let us get away with anything. I remember when our children were growing up, Mary Lou and I imposed standards on them and punished them for behavior that didn't trouble their friends. Those other children weren't ours. They were their own parents' responsibility. I am sure that at times life was easier for those other children than for our own children. But we loved our children enough to discipline them, to train them for life. This is what the writer of Hebrews says about God's part in building holy people. "He is a loving Father who disciplines us because He loves us and therefore, punishes everyone He accepts as His child." That is God's part in developing our holiness. Why? Well, in verse 10 we are told God disciplines us for our good that we may share His holiness.

One time we had a little four-year-old who was seriously ill with leukemia. It was shortly after the Aucas had killed the missionaries. We had a letter from our friend Betty Elliott. Let me read you part of that letter: "My morning reading yesterday fell in Hebrews 12. Verse 10 came with fresh force in the RSV: 'He disciplines us for our good that we may share His holiness.' There are times when we are tempted to say, 'Anything but that, Lord.' Then He must of necessity say, 'Anything but My holiness.' Is any price too great to pay if we may share His holiness? From my heart I say even the loss of Jim is not too great if He will allow me this. But I will have nothing less. So I know you rest too in His will which is forever good and acceptable and perfect."

Let us pray. Our Father God, we have heard Your Holy Word. We pray that Your Holy Spirit will enable us to receive it into our hearts, change our lives, and make us the men and women, boys and girls that You want us to be. Through Jesus Christ our Lord. Amen.

*For twenty-five years, 1961-1986, Joe Bayly wrote the popular column
called "Out of My Mind" for* Eternity *magazine. The best—and still timely—
columns are included here in chronological order.*

Out of My Mind

What Would Happen If . . .
July 1962

If a preacher should arise and say that our biggest problem is not Russian Communism, but the sins of the American people of God, the corruption of our own nation;

. . .and call his own people dishonest, unjust, full of adultery, covetous, liars, oppressors of the helpless;

. . .and say that freeborn Americans have sunk to the level of beasts, behaving like well-fed stallions in our lust;

. . .scorn our high standard of living, condemn our love of luxury, and pronounce God's judgment upon us for exploiting minority groups and the poor;

—And when he spoke of the future

would say that there is no hope of ever returning to the halcyon days of the Coolidge administration,

. . .nor of creating a bright new order by liberal social reform;

. . .that a conservative President—or a liberal Congress—wouldn't make a bit of difference,

. . .nor could economic justice be restored by repealing the income tax, or bringing the labor movement under the antitrust laws,

. . .or by repealing the poll tax, or passing social legislation that would cover everybody from the cradle to the grave;

But the only hope

is a coming King

...not of the USA, but of a better country;

And meanwhile

we had better get ready for some bad times—

...because it won't be long before the Russians overcome

—not just overtake us, but overcome us, take vast numbers of our American people into captivity, to Siberia and Hungary and China;

...and our alliances with England and France and Germany will not help us in that day,

...nor our bases in Spain and Turkey, our nuclear arms and roving submarines,

...because God is going to do this, God is going to help the godless Russian Communists defeat America, citadel of freedom:

What would happen?

Would that preacher

win a Freedoms Foundation award,

...would people flock to hear him,

...would they pay for full-page ads to carry his words in the daily papers,

...time on the radio and TV;

Or would they

cut up his speech in Congress,

...burn it in the governor's mansion,

...threaten his life in Anathothburg, his hometown,

...put him in prison?

I think we know the answers.

...and if we don't, Jeremiah could tell us.

Is Every New Bible Version a Blessing?
October 1962

When the *Revised Standard Version* was completed in 1952, a call to arms resounded throughout Fundamentalism. A new test of orthodoxy was forthwith introduced: continued use of the *King James* Bible.

Copies of the new translation were burned in pulpits. Granted, such instances were few and far between. But even fewer were the critics within Fundamentalism of such blasphemy. Doubtless the objectors had their grounds. Hebrew and Greek scholars are not generally best qualified to communicate in modern written English. (Prime example: the Berkeley Version.) A case could be made for the inclusion of skilled writers, of the same professional caliber as the Greek and Hebrew scholars, on every translation team. Surely writers, as well as translators, are God's gift to the church.

But on the other hand, a skilled writer is not a translator. Many people received enlightenment from the freshness of J.B. Phillips' paraphrases (especially *Letters to Young Churches,* his first and best). But why do author and publisher now call this a "translation"?

For a few years after the *Revised Standard Version* was shot down in flames, no Bible in modern English existed to satisfy any desire these people might have for something fresh. And so demand built up behind the dam erected by Fundamentalism's leaders. Some Christians did not want the *King James* replaced in the pulpit, but personal Bible reading was another matter.

And so, when new translations and paraphrases appeared, demand rushed through the dam's floodgates. *Williams* (republished), *Verkuyl-Berkeley, Phillips, Amplified Bible, New English Bible:* each appeared in turn and was either accepted acritically by Fundamentalism's arbiters, or was subjected to criticism mild by *Revised Standard* criteria.

The *Revised Standard Version* may be superior to the *New English Bible* on doctrinal and literary grounds (the latter especially for American readers), but it would be hopeless to attempt to prove this to a segment of the Bible-reading public. The *Revised Standard Version* may be a model of literal translation beside *Phillips Paraphrase,* but a generation's mind has been molded to

154

exclude the one and admit the other.

Conservative Christian scholars, both biblical and literary, privately bewail the widespread acceptance and influence of a certain version. But outside the classroom, their mouths and pens are silent—probably because this version has grown within the matrix of fundamental authorship and publication. These people are our team—they're Bible-believing Christians—so we automatically accept what they produce. And besides, people are getting a blessing from it.

The most recent addition to the list is *The Teen-Age Version of the Holy Bible.* The preface states that "Teenagers themselves have been the judges of what they want, need, and will use." "Easy-to-understand language" has replaced big words. Reason: "Surely there is little excuse for a translator to force his reader to be constantly translating further as he reads."

Now this version is doctrinally sound. The "translator" is a man who loves the Lord. The Holy Spirit will use this Bible—even as He uses the *Revised Standard Version*—for spiritual enlightenment.

But where are we headed? Will a new version be issued for the gifted child?

And where are we headed when those who stand for verbal inspiration are the very ones who are opening the floodgates to novel, gadgetry ideas in Bible production? Does it matter that a Bible for teenagers says that God created "the heaven and the earth" (Gen. 1:1) instead of "the heavens and the earth"? What would we have said if the *Revised Standard* translators had changed this? Or is "virgin" the only word of Scripture worthy of serious defense? And what about changing our Lord's imperative, "Be ye therefore perfect, even as your Father which is in heaven is perfect" (Matt. 5:48), into a simple future, "therefore, you shall be perfect . . ."

We must be more critical of such translations, not less critical. Those who believe in verbal inspiration and add to or subtract from the Scriptures are worthy of greater censure than those who take a different position on inspiration. Scholarship is as necessary for the conservative as for the liberal. And beauty is a thing to be desired in any attempt to bring forth the Word of God afresh.

Lord, Raise Up a Negro Prophet
November 1962

For a number of years, speaking, writing, and editing, I have espoused the cause of Negroes. I have not merely accepted, but have been thankful for, court decisions in the area of equal civil rights for Negroes. I have repeatedly told my white Christian friends, including those who live in the South, that God will judge us if we are content to enjoy advantages at the expense of others, and the sooner the situation is changed, the better.

Now I have something to say to my Negro Christian friends, something that is seldom said today by thinking white people, especially thinking church people, because we may so easily be accused of speaking without love. Or we may seem to lack understanding of the basic problems confronting Negroes in contemporary culture. Or what is worse, we may seem to be using this as a lever to maintain the status quo, which is so unbalanced in our favor. I run these risks in what I say.

Negro crime and immorality constitute one of the gravest problems in American society today. Whenever I speak at correctional institutions, I am struck by the disproportionate number of Negroes—men, women, boys, girls. I immediately rationalize this situation to myself: If you had been forced to live in the sort of environment these people have always known, if you had always found discrimination based upon color of skin, you yourself would probably have gotten into trouble, your own children might be in this group of young people before you.

A Philadelphia newspaper tells of a public school—located in a Negro neighborhood—in which 70 percent of the children have been of illegitimate parentage. I read in those same newspapers about Negro gangs, about narcotics peddling and numbers gambling among Negroes.

Perhaps the trigger for what I write was the thirteen-year-old child whom a medical friend of mine assisted in a difficult delivery a couple of Sundays ago. Or it may have been the young Negro woman converted in a university, who said, "I just can't face life as a married woman among my people. The standard is too low, at least in the city where I live . . . I'd rather remain single."

Now I am aware of the cultural displacement of the Negro masses who emigrate to our northern cities, week after week. I know something about—nothing of—the poverty, the crowded housing, the discrimination. It is easy for me to sympathize with Negroes and rationalize Negro crime and immorality.

But there is one thing I can't rationalize. That is the almost complete silence of Negro leaders, including church leaders, about the situation. I have listened for a prophet's voice raised against these evils, but heard none. I have only heard the multiplied voices of judges raised against the evils of white discrimination.

It is morally unhealthy to sit in judgment upon another race, another people, another person, demanding and receiving confessions of guilt and sin, meanwhile remaining silent about one's own sin. The sin of discrimination is a heavy weight upon the white Christian conscience, both North and South; the sin of sexual immorality and crime seems to lie light upon the Negro conscience.

Perhaps if I were closer to the heart of Negro affairs, I would hear voices raised. I hope so. Yet I wonder if this is so, since newspapers that report the demands of Negro leaders for Negroes to be appointed to high administrative posts in public education and government would almost certainly report demands of these same leaders for a Christian standard of morality among their own people.

Not that I consider white America moral. I don't, and I can't rationalize the situation. But I hear Christian voices raised, I read articles warning of impending judgment.

I know that social change is accomplished one step at a time. I know, too, that God delivered His people from Egypt before He gave the Divine Law. But today we are not in the darkness of pre-Revelation. We have the Light of our Lord Jesus Christ. And Christian morality has never, to my knowledge, waited for social betterment. Those slaves (white) on the island of Crete, about whom Saint Paul wrote to Titus, were expected to influence their masters by their personal morality (Titus 2:9-10)—not by their demands for equality. And I sense that a significant decrease in the number of Negro births out of wedlock, in the number of unwed Negro mothers on the relief rolls, in the number of Negro youths embroiled in delinquency, a significant improvement in Negro morality would do more to change the climate of white opinion toward Negroes than all the pressure groups can ever achieve.

So, I look for a prophet, a Negro prophet, who will scorn personal advantage, who will warn his people of sin and judgment, and preach Jesus Christ according to the Scriptures. God give us a thousand such men.

Meanwhile I shall continue to speak out to exercise my slight influence on behalf of the Christian and American attitude toward equal rights for Negroes. But as we descend the ladder of white privilege, I hope we meet others ascending up the ladder of Negro morality.

Beauty Out of Cinders
April 1963

Have you ever held a cluster of trailing arbutus in your cupped hands and buried your nose in its delicate pink and white flowers?

If you have, you'll agree with me that this is one of God's best fragrances—a sufficient reason, all by itself, for the creation of noses.

I've only seen this flower three times, yet every spring I think of it. That's because of the first time, when I was six or seven years old. We lived in the mountains of central Pennsylvania; my father traveled a great deal on the railroad.

One night in the spring, just as the moon was coming up over Pleasant Valley, he came home with a bulky but light package, loosely wrapped in newspaper, in his arms.

"Mary, I brought you something," he said. "It was growing in some cinders by the railroad tracks." He probably said where the tracks were, some little town—perhaps Cresson—where he'd been that day.

"Open it up."

We children shoved close. Suddenly the room was filled with the fragrance of those lovely flowers as the newspaper fell apart.

That night I knew that trailing arbutus was the most beautiful flower in the world. And I knew that my father loved my mother.

Every period in life has its special problem, and even a newborn baby has a lesson to learn—to receive and give love. But this problem really began before his birth. It began with you two, his parents. Unless you love each other, you cannot properly love him nor provide a love-warmed home for him.... True, there is no guarantee that your children will grow up healthy and happy just because you two are in love with each other. You must also have the knowledge and the will to raise them right.

One thing is certain, however, the children of parents who do not love each other have a sad time of it. Their home is a spawning ground for mental and moral ills.

No study of what every child needs, therefore, can do better than dwell hard and long on the question of how parents can so replenish each other's affections, can so fulfill each other's need of love, that in its mutual overflow there will be more than enough to envelop the children with warmth and comfort....[1]

Several weeks ago I participated in a student conference sponsored by InterVarsity Christian Fellowship. Students from out of town were placed in Christian homes.

Toward the end of the three days, in a "sharing" session, a young woman said that she had been a Christian for only two years and had never been in a Christian home before. "I've sometimes wondered if there were such a thing as a Christian home, and what it would be like. My own mother and father aren't Christians, or even religious. Well, now I know—and I could just rave about the home where I've been staying here at this conference. It's going to

[1]David Goodman, *A Parents' Guide to the Emotional Needs of Children* (New York: Hawthorn Books, 1959).

make a difference in my entire outlook on marriage and having children.

"This family where I'm staying has eight children. They live in a big old house. Their furniture is old and sort of put together—but lovingly put together. There are separate boys' and girls' bathrooms, like at school. There's a big dining table—the father's at one end, and the mother's at the other.

"The mother's so peaceful; you'd never know she has eight children."

Betty Scott Stam, China Inland Mission missionary killed by Chinese Communists in 1934, wrote to her parents when she was a student at Moody Bible Institute: "Because you loved, I am."

Whether she meant any more than the mere creation of life—which may be accomplished without love—or not, her statement has lengthening implications during the life of a child and teenager.

How many children, even in Christian homes, can say the other truth: "Because you didn't love, I am not . . . secure . . . trusting Jesus Christ . . . walking in His ways."

White is not the mere absence of black; it is the presence of all the colors of the spectrum.

And Christian perfection is not the mere absence of sin; it is the presence of all the beauty of God's holy, loving character.

Arbutus from cinders, beauty from ashes, tender love from a marriage that may be falling to pieces: thus does God work . . . when we turn to Him in faith.

Hush, Hush about Morality

Where Do We Take Our Stand? or Salt Losing Its Savor
June 1963

This year, speaking to college students—especially in dormitory and fraternity discussions—I've been asked one question again and again. It almost always takes this form: "Why is premarital intercourse wrong?"

Often there are explanatory or qualifying clauses: "—with the girl you are going to marry someday"; "—when it seems to work out well in parts of Europe where it's pretty commonly accepted"; "—if neither of you sees anything wrong with it"; "—since he may be shipped overseas any minute"; "—when it seems, like the psych professor says, to be merely a normal response to a human appetite."

Those clauses reveal the more basic question, one that is foundational to the Christian religion: Are there such things as moral absolutes, or is everything relative, subject to the conditions of time and place and opinion? The latter view, probably held (consciously or unconsciously) by a majority on today's academic scene, was expressed by the scientist Sir Julian Huxley in a recent issue of *Nature* magazine: "In adapting our old educational system to our new vision, such cargo will have to be jettisoned—once-noble but now moldering myths, shiny but useless aphorisms, utopian but unfounded speculations, nasty projections of our prejudices and repression. … Children are not born with a load of original sin derived from a 'Fall'… There are no Absolutes of Truth or Virtue."

Now I believe in academic freedom of expression, but I find it hard to understand why a scientific magazine should lend itself to an attack upon the Judeo-Christian religion. Even harder for me to understand is the silence of qualified and respected scientists who are Christians, in the face of such an attack. Why, in scientific publications or in classrooms, is there so seldom a rebuttal of such opinions? The failure of Christians in academe to avail themselves of the prerogatives of academic freedom may go far toward explaining why the historic Christian faith is no longer a live option to the educated person. "The children of this world are in their generation wiser than the children of light" (Luke 16:8).

But the general silence among Christians about moral absolutes today, both in and out of the university community, is disturbing—like the small lump, alarming out of proportion to its size, to one who fears a malignant tumor. This vague disturbance was expressed several years ago by an editorialist in *Christianity and Crisis:*

> For about a generation now there has been a growing tendency among Christian intellectuals to eschew and condemn moralism... One of the things which attracted the ancient Romans to Christianity was the rigorous Christian morality, especially regarding sex, and the self-discipline of the Christian home. Doubtless many of the intellectuals of the Roman world branded these simple Christians as being too simple and too moralistic. I suspect that if Jesus, or Paul, or one of the early church fathers were to preach in America today, many Christian intellectuals would accuse them of the same. I do not know for sure. That is what disturbs me. But at the risk of being a superficial moralist I raise these questions: Have Christians sold too many hostages to the modern vogue of relativism? And where do we take our stand, particularly on the matters of sex and the preservation of the Christian home?

Where do we take our stand?

On the ground of moral absolutes: as a convinced Christian I have no other answer. Jesus Christ and Paul and Moses and Elijah have determined our position. When the Christian church yields relativism, the salt loses its savor, the world loses its light (Matt. 5:13–14).

Our temptation, especially with the unconverted, is to bypass absolute demands of a Holy God, ineffably pure, and "just preach the Gospel." For we know that men cannot achieve moral purity and legal justification before coming to Christ.

But there's a difference between saying, "Come to Jesus just as you are. Don't wait until you're better," and saying, "It doesn't matter what God is like, what His standards are."

God dealt with His people, in the childhood of the race, by revealing absolute moral law. Jesus Christ began His ministry of introducing the kingdom by confirming the law and divining rod's ultimate standards. Saint Paul said that in his personal experience, sin, by the commandment of the law, became exceedingly sinful (Rom. 7:13).

Should we deal with our generation otherwise? Is not the present uncertainty about moral absolutes (including premarital intercourse) one result of introducing boys and girls, men and women, to grace without prior exposure to law? We hedge on the demands of absolute law at the risk of undermining absolute grace; when we lighten law we cheapen grace.

In a fraternity lounge or on the sand at Fort Lauderdale, we must not bypass the moral absolutes that include our hearers under the judgment of God. To do so is not merely to cast our pearls before swine (Matt. 7:6); it is to gain an audience and lose our mission.

The Truth—But Not The Whole Truth
November 1965

The question of authority is basic to any religious system. And so we ask what authority is claimed and recognized by the contemporary evangelical Christian movement in the United States and Canada.

This seems to be one question that can be rather easily answered. Our authority is the Bible, the written Word of God. Anything more than this lacks authority, anything less than the whole Bible is insufficient.

A good, sound, biblical answer. But unfortunately the answer does not accurately describe the existing situation.

Part of the trouble goes back to sixty years ago when *The Fundamentals* was first published. Despite our affection for the first fundamentalists and our respect for what they did, we must admit that fundamentalism was never a biblical word, and perhaps was overloaded from the beginning.

It is at least possible that, with the best of intentions, those Christians who developed and defended the concept of certain "fundamentals" were adopting an extrabiblical (or even a nonbiblical) defense for the biblical position. For when they decided that certain teachings of the Bible were "fundamental," other doctrines were automatically relegated to a position that was less than fundamental (or basic). And so, as a result of their value judgment, *The Fundamentals* tended to become definitive of the Christian position . . . even a half-century later.

In other words, from the very beginning of the movement, the danger was present that a human construct ("the fundamentals") would be accepted in place of the complete Bible from which that construct arose.

These fundamentals are and always have been basic to biblical Christianity. But when they became more or less codified as the "fundamental" doctrines of Christian belief, the assumption was almost unconsciously present that other teachings of the Bible are of secondary importance, and therefore may be neglected or passed over.

Perhaps the deteriorating doctrine of the church during these decades is to be ascribed, partially at least, to the fact that particular doctrine was not included among *The Fundamentals*. And then there's Christian love: if we listen to Jesus Christ in the Gospels, we cannot escape the conclusion that love of the brethren here and now is as fundamental to Christian life as belief in the Second Coming. But Christian love was omitted from *The Fundamentals*, while the Second Coming was included. Is there any relationship between this omission and the generally accepted image of American evangelical Christianity as a bitter, self-centered, fighting movement? We are known for our belief in the Second Coming, but not for our love.

Of course, *The Fundamentals* represented only one factor in this twentieth century doctrinal crystallization, although it was the most far-reaching. (Several million of the volumes were distributed free of charge to 300,000 ministers, missionaries, and other workers throughout America and around the world.) Another significant factor was the increasing use of various "Bases of Faith" as a test of orthodoxy and common ground for interdenominational activity.

Historically, these bases (or doctrinal standards) had their origin at the Niagara Bible Conference early this century, and the Niagara Platform has served as the pattern for numerous other Christian movements that have not been denominationally related. By narrowing the field of Christian doctrines down to a workable five or ten, these Bible conferences, foreign missionary societies, other agencies and institutions have found a test of orthodoxy that is relatively easy to apply and implement. But in the process, disproportionate weight has come to be attached to doctrines explicitly stated in the doctrinal basis, as over against other doctrines not explicitly stated therein.

Some answer this by pointing out that these bases of faith usually begin with an affirmation of belief in biblical inspiration; therefore all other biblical doctrines are implicitly included. This is so, but if the first statement is sufficient to cover all biblical doctrines, why are specific ones singled out for inclusion thereafter?

And so we have come to accept an eclectic type of authority in evangelical Christianity. We select certain doctrines as constitutive and others as secondary. As a concomitant, those books of the Bible that emphasize the fundamental doctrines are given preferred positions in our canon of teaching emphasis and preaching.

Why have the Synoptic Gospels, with their record of the life of Christ, been neglected by many Christian churches, while such books as Romans and Revelation are given prominence? Why is John's Gospel so much more familiar than his Epistles? Why is the Epistle of James less popular than the Epistle to the Hebrews?

In the thinking of believers, what is the effect of sixty years of singling out the deity of Christ as fundamental, while bypassing His humanity and the unity of His nature?

Most of us are seriously concerned about the lowering levels of ethics and morality among evangelical Christians. Is the absence of the doctrine of Law from *The Fundamentals* and doctrinal bases relevant?

I do not intend to make whipping boys out of the writers of *The Fundamentals*—Gray, Orr, Thomas, Torrey, et al.—whose shoes I am not worthy to tie. The fault lies with us, who accepted their masterful answer to heresy in their day as the code of our belief.

The Bible does not lend itself to abridgment or underlining, except at the expense of authority.

The Teaching We Have Neglected
January 1966

Twelve or fifteen years ago, the late Canon T. C. Hammond of the Church of England visited the United States. Toward the end of his trip, in which he visited many parts of the country, I asked Canon Hammond for his predominant impression of evangelical Christianity in America. The author of InterVarsity Fellowship's *Reasoning Faith* and *In Understanding Be Men,* and authority on Roman Catholic theology (*The Hundred Texts,* published by Irish Church Missions) seemed unusually qualified to render an objective judgment on such a matter.

His answer was prompt: He was impressed by our shallow treatment of the doctrines of sin and law. We seemed to introduce children and adults to grace and salvation without laying any adequate foundation in the knowledge of personal rebellion and sin.

The result, he said, was a low view of Christ and grace and righteousness, for our appreciation of salvation is in direct relation to our understanding of the pit of sin from which we were dug.

In answer to a further question, Canon Hammond agreed that a low level of personal righteousness and sensitivity to sin among American Christians might be related to the same cause. Wasn't that what the Apostle Paul was talking about when he said, "I had not known sin, but by the law: for I had not known lust, except the law had said, Thou shalt not covet" (Rom. 7:7).

Who's responsible for the present erosion of American morality and personal ethics? It's easy to blame the days in which we live . . . Hugh Hefner and his *Playboy* philosophy . . . the end times.

When the shoe is on the other foot, whether in England after the Wesleys, or America after the Great Awakening, we know the answer: revival in the church brought about a quickening of the world's standards of morality. The salt had its effect on society.

And today? The church that takes credit for heightened social morality must acknowledge its responsibility for society's moral depression. Perhaps the salt has lost its savor (Matt. 5:13–14).

This brings us back to Canon Hammond's thesis. If the children of the church have not been taught God's standards of righteous living, the children of the world have nothing against which to measure their conduct.

But why has this teaching been neglected? Why have children grown up in the church and in Christian homes without a solid foundation in the biblical doctrines of law and sin?

At the risk of being misunderstood, may I suggest that it has been because of our obsession during the past thirty or forty years with the immediacy of salvation. We have had one continual message for our children: "Ye must be born again" (John 3:7). Every Sunday School lesson has been turned into a salvation lesson; decisions have been the response constantly sought.

We have not taught the Bible with integrity: John's Gospel as John's Gospel; Proverbs as Proverbs; Judges as Judges; Exodus 20 as Exodus 20. Instead we have taught John's Gospel as John's Gospel; Proverbs as John's Gospel; Judges as John's Gospel; Exodus 20 as John's Gospel . . . if we have taught the latter at all. Recently I had a letter from a woman who related her experience teaching Ruth to junior highs the Sunday before. "Suddenly it came to me that what my girls needed wasn't that they should love Christ as Ruth loved Naomi, but that they should be the sort of women when they grow up that Naomi was to stir such a response of love in her daughter-in-law. Ruth was profitable as Scripture itself, not just as a type of Christ—valid though that might be."

What our children (and we ourselves) need is exposure to the whole Bible in its integrity, "for doctrine, for reproof, for correction, for instruction in righteousness: That the man of God may be perfect, thoroughly furnished unto all good works" (2 Tim. 3:16–17).

In the Westminster Shorter Catechism, the Presbyterian Church taught children those doctrines it considered necessary to glorify and enjoy God. The doctrines were arranged according to the pattern of biblical revelation. Thus the sweep and scope of God's revelation in history became the sweep and scope of God's revelation to the child.

A few years ago, Dr. J. C. Macaulay, president of London (Ontario) Bible College, told of an incident when he visited the Scottish islands of the Hebrides, where revival had been endemic for some time. Dr. Macaulay was on his way to a church service and heard a low wailing noise from a cottage.

In response to the visitor's question, a man with whom he was walking replied, "That's William, finding his way to God. He'll come through."

If we trust God's Spirit to bring our children through to salvation . . . in His time . . . we will with patience teach law and depravity and sin and providence and all the other doctrines of Scripture, as the foundation of salvation that means something in moral living, and of an exalted view of Christ.

If, on the other hand, we seek above all else the security of knowing that our children have made a decision, on the basis of which we can reassure them of their salvation from a very early age, we shall probably continue to have spiritual mediocrity and a-nomianism (if not antinomianism) in the Church.

I believe that some children will be saved early in life. But others—even in the same family—will come later. In God's providence, all fruit does not ripen at the same time.

Oh, for the Good Old Days

. . . when one knew that America was far superior to Russia, where marriage was only a physical bond, the Bible was banned from the schools, and the people's lives were government-controlled from birth to death.
August 1966

When I was growing up, I remember, we were impressed by our elders with the evil results of Communist doctrine in Russia.

Marriage was one example. Under Communism, the home was breaking up. Divorce had become a simple civil matter, available to any couple who no longer wished to live together.

Free love was widespread in Russia, we were told. Unmarried men and women could openly have relations without stigma. Moral standards that had formerly controlled attitudes and actions were no longer considered relevant, now that Communism was the dominant ideology.

The training of children was considered the responsibility of the state. Nursery schools had been established for Russian children three or four years old, and their mothers were no longer burdened with responsibility for them. The state also assumed the care of children born out of marriage, the result of casual liaisons.

Freedom from responsibility for their children meant that women could take full-time positions alongside their husbands. I remember news pictures of women repairing streets, then later, of women in scientific laboratories. The new Communist law forbade any job discrimination based on sex.

I recall a series of posters, given me by an elder in the church—perhaps he was my Sunday School teacher—depicting the Communist attitude toward God. One had a crudely drawn coffin in which lay an old, dirty, white-haired man. The Russian characters on the front of the Photostat were translated into English on the reverse side: "God died when Communism freed the people. Nobody needs God any more. God, rest in your coffin."

We were also told that Communism had destroyed personal initiative in Russia. The government was reaching into all areas of life, from the cradle to the grave, and controlling whatever it touched.

And God had been banished from Russian life. I remember a Jewish teacher, a man, in West Philadelphia High School, who would read the prescribed number of Bible verses for the day in homeroom period—always from the Psalms—with deep respect. As he closed the Bible, he often said, "Under Communism, this would be impossible. There they have banned the Holy Books."

All this was evidence, according to our elders, of the demonic nature of Communism. If America ever became Communistic, we were told, these same results would follow. Thank God America was still Christian and still a democracy.

These memories were evoked by an item in the newspaper the other day. An important official in the federal government's Health, Education and Welfare Department said that the education of four year olds would soon be compulsory. We know today, he said, that character (this is the word he used) is formed very early, and so children should be in school at least by the age of four. Otherwise we miss out on the most crucial period of a child's life for training.

Reading the official's words, and a subsequent confirmatory statement by President Lyndon B. Johnson, I considered the United States today, a generation later. Our government has not become Communistic, yet we have entered into a period of social, economic, educational, and moral conditions similar to those we were told were the result of Communism in Russia.

One important difference is that the church in the United States has not been suppressed, as in Russia and China, so that the new order might be established. Instead, the church, through many of its leaders, has gone along with the changes, even providing a theological rationale for some of them.

Well, at least we still have more telephones and color television sets than Communist Russia. And more Bibles.

Is There a Parallel Between Infant Baptism and Early Decisions for Jesus?
December 1966 (partial)

Have you ever considered the possibility of a parallel between infant baptism or confirmation, on the one hand, and early "decisions for Christ" on the other?

Most of us evangelicals fear an act of religious formality early in life that may be trusted in the absence of conversion. "Of course I'm a Christian—I was confirmed at the age of twelve" rings an alarm in our minds.

But "Of course I'm a Christian—I raised my hand in a children's meeting" doesn't set off the same alarm.

Some parents and teachers go even further, trying to convince the doubting teenager that he's really a Christian, because "you asked Jesus to come into your heart in the primary department." Assurance comes from the adult who remembers an act, rather than from the Spirit who may—or may not—indwell the life.

Not all doubts are bad. Doubt may be God's instrument of conviction, and to turn it off by reminding the doubter of a prior act—whether confirmation or hand-raising—may be to perform eternal disservice to his soul.

Even in Christian homes, there are individual differences. Not all children will necessarily trust Christ in childhood. Historically, Polycarp (martyred when he was over eighty) and Jonathan Edwards (spearhead of colonial America's Great Awakening) knew Christ before the age of ten. But Augustine, son of godly Monica, and John Wesley, child of the parsonage and of strong Christian parents, both were around thirty years of age when they converted. For Adoniram Judson, the occasion was a summer between college and seminary.

Somehow most of us feel that if the crop isn't harvested at least by the teen age, there's not much hope. And many Christian parents would settle for the comforting assurance that their child "made his decision when he was thirteen," even if a life of spiritual mediocrity followed, rather than go through the hurt and blind faith in God until their child comes Home from the far country with true spiritual power.

The Missing Ingredient in the New Bibles
February 1967

This year the *Revised Standard Version* of the Bible comes of age. And in these twenty-one years since its publication, a plethora of other translations and paraphrases has been produced.

Each represents a particular viewpoint and satisfies a part of the market.

None satisfies every group. The monopoly of King James and Douay in Protestantism and Roman Catholicism has ended during this generation.

In their place we now have, in addition to the RSV (which, in America at least, is the dominant new version), a considerable list of options: *The New English Bible New Testament*; Kenneth Taylor's paraphrases; *Today's English Version* of the New Testament; *The New American Standard Version* (New Testament only thus far); Berkeley; Williams; Beck; the Knox and Confraternity (Roman Catholic); and some fragments, such as *God Is for Real Man* (inner city).

Just published is *The Jerusalem Bible* (Roman Catholic). In the planning stages are two evangelical committee efforts: *The New American Standard Old Testament*; and a second, yet to be named.

I suppose that I should rejoice at this proliferation, and I do. "Every man" in America, 1967, should be able to read God's Word in the idiom he understands, rather than in that of his ancestors almost 400 years ago.

But proliferation may lead to confusion. And choice may lead to privatism. And a glut of Bread in America may dull our sensitivity to the hundreds of millions elsewhere who lack even a crumb.

I can't help thinking of what the same amount of time, money, and scholarly resources would have accomplished if they had been expended on missionary translation and Bible distribution.

Why should I own ten different Bibles when my brother doesn't even have a verse?

But bypassing that uncomforting aspect, here are some of the problems that I see in the present embarrassment of biblical riches. You may want to add to the list, or suggest compensating values that I may be assuming.

1. Confusion has resulted. The Bible's use in public worship has been complicated by the variety of versions and paraphrases in the congregation. Bible memorization has become a knotty problem, especially with children.

2. A subjective element is present in all translations, but especially in one-man translations and paraphrases. The evangelical Christian public is quite aware of this problem when it comes to the RSV: "young woman" in Isaiah 7:14, which

was the *cause célèbre* for rejecting this version, even burning it, in the late 1940s.

But while the front door was being zealously guarded against the RSV, the back door was left open to all comers. Evangelical attitudes toward every other Bible production have been almost a-critical, by contrast.

So we accept—in place of the inspired Scripture—a fictitious, allegorized hash of Song of Solomon in the *Amplified*. We seem to have no objections to changing the all-embracing term "salvation" to the limited "bring you to heaven" (Rom. 1:16) in *Living Letters*. And the latter in a day when Christian morals and ethics are declining, and God's present saving work in this evil world desperately needs emphasis.

Examples could be multiplied; I have merely chosen from two that are totally within the evangelical community. (Incidentally, some months ago I mentioned these two illustrations to the publishers.)

Every translation is an interpretation. A paraphrase, by nature, is even more interpretive. And the fact that God's Word is changed to correspond to evangelical thought patterns is hardly less blameworthy—perhaps more so, since we hold to the doctrine of inspiration—than that it is changed to reflect liberal bias.

3. Committee translations, on the other hand, tend to be pedantic. W. H. Auden, the poet, found fault with the *New English Bible* on this score.

Who is least likely to be able to write in the current idiom, especially if you add the necessary dimensions of grace and beauty? I think there is little doubt, with few exceptions, that the answer is scholars. The man who translates from Hebrew and Greek, whether he is English or German or American, is not the man who has the gift to talk the language of Everyman.

Yet this is the necessary reason for any new translation. I doubt that many scholars would say that new manuscript discoveries, or changed linguistic concepts are of sufficient scope to necessitate another translation. It is rather the communication of God's Word in the 1967 American idiom.

Then why start with the scholars? Why not start with writers, who would use common sources—such as the *King James* and the *American Standard* of 1901, both of which are in the public domain—to render the Word of God in modern English? Then have the scholars check what the writers have produced against the original, returning the corrected manuscript to the writers for rewriting.

It seems to me that this is technically feasible, but that the other way around is not. Once scholars set the Word in concrete, capable writers would find it hard to breathe freshness—and to change the scholars' minds about the wording.

Before this new evangelical translation project gets too far down the track, I hope someone with influence (in the evangelical lowerarchy, this means money) says, "Look here, Committee on a New Translation of the Bible. Let's turn this thing over to some people like Frank Gaebelein and Elisabeth Elliott, maybe even W. H. Auden and John Updike, to see what they'd come up with. You'll have your innings on the rewrite. But give them a go at it first."

Who knows, maybe the new Bible would come out beautiful as well as faithful to the original languages.

Recently we've been using *The Jerusalem Bible* (translated from the original languages, via the French) in family prayers. From youngest to oldest, we like it. Simplicity, beauty, clarity, power, felicity of expression are in the parts we've read.

J. R. R. Tolkien, British novelist and poet, is listed as one of the collaborators in its production.

Are We Undermining Authority?
May 1968

If there's been one doctrine strongly taught and defended by evangelicals during the past several decades, it's the inspiration of the Scriptures. Among many, perhaps most, who taught the doctrine, verbal inerrancy of the original manuscripts has been upheld.

Now with all this emphasis on inspiration and inerrancy, you'd think that young people who have grown up in an evangelical milieu would be firmly grounded in the Bible's authority.

They're not. In my experience, at least, I don't usually find the reflex,

"The Bible says it and so it must be true," among young men and women.

The reaction of a student in a Christian college, on being reminded that the Bible forbids premarital intercourse, is rather typical of the attitude I've found. "Maybe the Bible says it, but if it does, that isn't what it means."

The element of doubt about what the Bible teaches in areas of less emotional involvement is also significantly high among our evangelical teens and students. Does God have purpose in human suffering? Is God powerful enough to act today? Will Christ return to this earth? For a large number of evangelical young men and women, such questions are not settled by what the Bible says.

If my impressions are correct, we are in danger, period, since it is questionable whether morality and ethics—even faith (Rom. 10:17)—can stand, apart from the support of accepted biblical authority.

How do we explain this weak attitude toward the Bible's authority? Have we unwittingly undermined confidence in the Bible?

I think we have got things out of the right order, at least as far as ordinary Christians—especially the young—are concerned. We have stressed the Bible's inspiration and assumed that authority would take care of itself. But it hasn't.

Theologians may conclude that inspiration is the ground of authority, and therefore must come first. And they are probably right in a theological context.

J. Gresham Machen once said that theology begins with the doctrine of inspiration, while apologetics ends with it. I suspect, if this is so, that we have made the mistake of treating our young as theologians rather than as potential converts or young Christians.

I believe the debate about biblical inerrancy during recent decades has had the unfortunate result of weakening the Bible's authority in the minds of the young. The possibility or impossibility of infinitesimal error has tended to obscure the great, overarching areas about which there is no question.

By arguing about whether there is dust on the piano, or whether the kitchen floor is completely clean, a husband will lower his children's overall impression of their mother's faithful loving service and diminish her authority in their eyes. When they are older, the children may see things in true perspective; then they are likely to blame the picayune, judgmental father. But meanwhile the harm has been done.

So it may be with the authority of the Scriptures in the eyes of the young. We argue about whether 3,000 or 30,000 soldiers fought in a battle and we lose a greater battle.

Children, teens, and students need to be brought into Christ's kingdom by faith, by their own personally exercised choice. From a human stand-point, they need examples, adults who say and live the principle, "I believe the Bible." And I think this is the really important thing to communicate to the young—complete submission to the Bible's authority—rather than, "I believe in the inspiration of the Bible."

I know that full conviction of the Bible's authority over all of life comes through the Holy Spirit's work. But it is often, perhaps usually, communicated through the Christian community.

Perhaps this low view of Scripture's authority is related to a low view of Christ's authority. We may be reaping the results of recent decades when we appealed to the young to "receive Christ as Savior," bypassing His demand of absolute Lordship and doing violence to His Person.

A fresh breath of submission to the authority of Christ and the Scriptures in the church, and in the lives of Christians—especially the young—could be the catalyst needed to change the world's drift toward anarchy and nihilism.

And I am not usually a prophet of doom.

Does Christian Coffee Save Men?
September 1968

"Pre-evangelism" has become a familiar concept in these years.

We cannot assume that we have the respect or attention or interest of the person to whom we want to bring the life-giving Christ; we must earn these by entering his life, by becoming concerned about his whole person. The process by which we do this is pre-evangelism, breaking up the ground for seed we intend to plant.

This is a pendulum swing away from the former concept of "a tract, a testimony, a decision for or against." And in the opinion of most of us who were raised in an atmosphere of success stories about soul-winning conversations with total strangers on streetcars and trains, the swing is healthy.

We may not have formulated it, but the question at the back of our minds when we listened to those soul-winners was, "What about your children, your neighbors, your business and professional associates? Are you reaching them? Does the Gospel stand exposure to more than a twenty-minute conversation on a streetcar, does it speak to 'life that is so daily?'"

We weren't hearing about conversions in the ongoing peer group of the soul-winners. It was the transient and casual situation that was presented as a pattern.

Street meetings, prison and rescue mission ministries were another part of the picture, a part that did not remove the question about Christianity's effectiveness with one's peers.

Now we have settled in to evangelize our neighbors and close associates and the first step is to gain a hearing.

So we pre-evangelize.

Great.

But when is the prefix removed? When does pre-evangelism turn into evangelism?

If it doesn't, the term is a misnomer. We may be displaying the fruits of righteousness, but we aren't evangelizing. We may be doing the good works God has commanded, but we are not evangelizing.

This is so in personal relationships and in group activities. A Christian coffee shop without evangelism is merely a coffee shop run by Christians, regardless of the high-sounding pre-evangelism theory that led to its establishment. Christian coffee doesn't save lost men.

Are we really concerned that men shall be saved? Are we convinced that they're lost? Are we certain that only Christ can save them?

When the pendulum was at the opposite extreme, the answer to those questions was in no doubt. It was the strong conviction that prompted train conversions and promoted street meetings.

Maybe the part of the spectrum covered by that former evangelism was limited, but it was covered. Maybe the presentation of the Gospel was too either-or, too take-it-or-leave-it, but the effect was to communicate urgency.

Urgency. Strange, isn't it, that the word today is more applicable to the community of atomic scientists (who have just advanced their eschatological clock to seven minutes to twelve) than to the Christian community.

What is the goal of evangelism?

In the former day, it was simply stated: to save men from hell's eternal separation from God and take them to heaven.

On the way, things happened. But evangelism wasn't primarily to mend marriages or heal loneliness or solve life's problems. It was to get men right with God and settle an eternal destiny.

Do you sense that we have lost this dimension in much of our evangelism today, that our lingering at the way station of pre-evangelism is because we're not sure of the real destination?

It takes faith to believe that nice people are under God's judgment for sin, and that only Jesus Christ can save them. This faith is somehow different from faith that divorce can be avoided or problem drinking controlled. After all, marriage counselors and programs for alcoholics are achieving results without reference to any narrow Christian claims.

And we hate to be narrow in a day of widening highways.

Tolerance is the spirit of pre-evangelism. Evangelism says that there's only one road to God, and Jesus Christ is it; only one hope of heaven, the reconciling cross and empty tomb; only one saving response, believing what God has said in His Word about our sin and His Son. Even for nice peer-group people.

When everyone else is involved in an agonizing search, it's not easy to say, "I have found. Taste and see that the Lord is good." But that's evangelism.

High Price of TV
February 1970

As we enter the '70s, psychologists have become our conscience in areas of human behavior. Warnings about the effects of TV-watching are coming from psychiatrists and educators—not from pastors.

The church has apparently defaulted on its responsibility in favor of the psychologists. Whatever threat pastors see in television is not related to its effect on the human mind and behavior, but the effect on Sunday evening church attendance and pastoral home visitation.

Dr. S. I. Hayakawa, the embattled president of San Francisco State University, points out that by the time a typical American boy or girl has reached the age of eighteen, he or she has had 12,000 to 15,000 hours of TV-viewing. These are not hours stolen from school, but from relating to other people: parents, siblings, neighbors, the elderly, strangers. He concludes that it's small wonder so many students drop out; they did not learn how to get along with other human beings during their formative years.

Dr. Graham Blaine, chief psychiatrist in the student health service of Harvard University, has said that the most serious problem of TV is not poor programming, but that it has destroyed the average family's exchange of views and information at the evening meal. People are anxious to get to a favorite program, he says, and so they hurry to finish eating. What happened during the day, the little things, and bigger matters are never discussed.

When was the last time you heard a preacher or Sunday School teacher warn about the family-fragmenting effects of television?

Is the church even remotely concerned about what this electronic communications medium is doing, may eventually do, to the human behavior of Christians? I think not. What I hear—when I hear anything—is the soul-destroying effect of the theater in the theater, not the theater in the living room. Movies seem to have a baptism of purification when they are shown on TV.

The daughter of a friend's pastor put it this way: "I can hardly wait till that movie is shown on television, so I can see it."

What will be the long-range effects of TV on the American mind and morals, on the Christian mind and morals?

For perspective on the question, one psychologist says that the average child today, who follows the typical American viewing pattern, will by age sixty-five have spent nine years of twenty-four-hour days sitting in front of a TV set. (If he went to Sunday School every Sunday during those years, he will have spent about four months studying God's Word.)

Even if TV were morally neutral, it would have serious effects on Christian life and thought. You don't spend nine years of life watching anything without being affected by it. Or even six or seven years.

"It's so cute the way our little boy can sing all the commercials." I've heard that statement several times; so have you. But even if it's cute, is it worthwhile? Is such mental conditioning, perhaps, in the long view dangerous?

What view of life do people get from TV? Secular, materialistic, man-shall-not-live-by-bread-alone. What view of family life? Fragmented, strong mother, feeble father. What view of human life? Cheap, meaningless, here-and-now, hedonistic. What view of reading? What's a book? What view of God? Who's He, apart from a Billy Graham special?

Do Christian people even think of what Dean Martin, Tiny and Vicki Tim, Johnny Carson do to them and their children? Is this the sort of guest we want to invite into our living rooms every week?

What about family Bible reading? Prayer? If these are missing and Dean Martin, or Rowan and Martin are welcomed, aren't we shouting something to our children and ourselves, something about the real values of life now and hereafter? No Sunday School, or later a Christian college, can replace that value system.

But TV is not morally neutral. It was a secular writer in the *Detroit News* (Kathy Sudomier, a thirty-six-year-old newspaper woman), not a preacher, who screamed loudly enough about TV advertising—"You dirty old ad men make me sick"—to awaken *Advertising Age* to a potential threat.

Has the church yielded its role of moral guidance, along with other roles, to secular society in our time?

After giving examples of sexually arousing pictures and dialogue in TV advertising, Mrs. Sudomier concludes: "If you think this generation represents the New Morality, then look out for the next one, Granddad. You'll have our kids turned into the most over-sexed, over-sated monsters since the fall of the Roman Empire."

A medical doctor in West Germany warned several years ago that the country that once knew the tyranny of Hitler now faces the tyranny of evil. And the United States, which has never—except in localized situations—known totalitarianism, seems to be embracing a tyranny of evil.

In my opinion, this represents an interesting switch on George Orwell's *1984:* It is not Big Brother observing human life in every room by TV cameras who thereby controls life; Big Brother performs on TV in every room and thereby determines life.

If our Lord Christ returns during the '70s, will He find faith in the United States (Luke 18:8)?

Raison d'Être

What's worth the investment of a woman's lifetime?

In a recent column I questioned the contemporary attitudes of some women toward child-bearing and abortion, and pressures for governmental controls in the areas of birth and eugenics.

Some women wrote to me.

One wanted to know whether I was talking about single women when I asked, "Is a typewriter or sales counter sufficient [reason] to justify the devotion of her life?"

No, that was a question aimed at Catherine Drinker Bowen, whom I quoted in the previous paragraph: "No woman can devote a life to the rearing of two [children], she cannot even make a pretense of it."

God uses many single women, as well as childless women—whether without children, or having children who are no longer dependent on their mother—in a variety of careers. They represent some of the greatest assets in business, medicine, teaching, and in many Christian organizations and missions.

I'm glad for the increased recognition and opportunity women are receiving today: equal pay for equal work, increasing opportunity to compete with men for executive-level positions and professional status.

The American Bible Society recently appointed Ruth Culley to direct its Philadelphia office. Miss Culley also directs the Pennsylvania Bible Society, the first woman to hold these positions. It's hard to say that I commend the Bible Society for this step without appearing to be a condescending male, but I do.

But a woman with children, especially young ones, should not scorn child training as a career of sufficient magnitude to provide her *raison d'être*. This is my opinion, and I believe it has a biblical basis.

The Christian welcomes some cultural changes, accepts some, rejects some. Our criterion in each decision must be the Bible, if the Bible speaks on the matter. If it does not speak, we are dependent on a Bible-programmed, Spirit-enlightened conscience. And the Spirit may use Christian teachers and the Christian community as one means to that enlightenment.

Another letter came from a woman who wrote about "the main point that is glaringly missing [from my prior column]—the right of a woman to say what will happen to her own body. I have a wonderful Christian husband, several kids of high school age, and a six-month-old baby. I cherish him—now. But I pray earnestly that my daughter will live in a time when she will have the ability to decide how many children she will have, and when. No man will ever understand the emotions and physical stress that come to a woman who unwillingly bears a child."

I suppose not. But "emotions and physical stress" are known to the God who made us, to the Christ who redeemed us. And it is He to whom we must answer, whether male or female, for our attitudes and actions.

Do women really have to wait for their daughters' time to "decide how many children to have and when"? Not if we're talking about the control of conception, and that husband is really a "wonderful Christian."

But the decision to abort existing life is not the same as the decision not to conceive life, in my opinion. As a Christian, I consider the new morality of abortion by choice evidence of the post-Christian, pagan nature of our society. (I have no question about aborting in the event of rape, a slight question about aborting when the girl is single, although I am inclined to accept this as well. Perhaps I am inconsistent in my views,[1] but Old Testament law usually was also fitted to a variety of occasions.)

How often the womb is mentioned in the Bible: "Thou didst knit me together in my mother's womb" (Ps. 139:13); "the Lord who made you, who formed you from the womb" (Isa. 44:2; Job 31:15). Perhaps we Christians need a fresh sense of awe at God's involvement in the creation of a new life through two of His children whom He has brought together, rather than so much light talk of curettage and vasectomy.

Another woman wrote to rebuke me for the fact that I have fathered my own children, instead of raising other people's "unwanted" children. This is her solution to overpop: "voluntary vasectomies—by the millions."

But at the risk of losing those who see things differently, I do not believe adoption is, or should be—in most instances—a substitute for a Christian couple's bringing their own children to birth, and then raising them.

As I understand the Bible, a "goodly heritage" (Ps. 16:6) involves familial lines of descent, not just environment. It seems to me that great stress is laid on ancestors in the Bible, not just on who raises the child.

Therefore I believe the world and the church need more children of Christians, not just more children raised by Christians.

I hasten to add that God delights in taking roots out of a dry ground (Isa. 53:2), and turning them into great giants of trees. From the standpoint of His contemporaries, Jesus was such a root. And God brings the mighty low. So what I have said previously is not to downgrade adopted children. But I hope adopted children who love God will—when they are married—have their own children, rather than limiting themselves to adoption.

But let's not put all our problems into the overpop basket. Writing in the *New Republic*, Ben Wattenberg suggests that overpopulation is the current scapegoat for various national ills: pollution, depletion of natural resources, poverty. Among the examples he gives is the panic button apocalyptic demographers have punched in connection with our wilderness, that

---

[1] *Editor's note:* Compare Bayly's position here with his later understanding of the abortion issue in the December 1981, June 1984, and January 1986 articles. When asked once why a major evangelical leader of his acquaintance had taken the position reflected above (abortion acceptable in certain extraordinary cases), he answered, "Ignorance."

has been vanishing "because of too many people." But in less than twenty years, visits to national parks have gone up by more than 400 percent, while population has increased only 30 percent. So there must be other factors. These factors (in all areas, including poverty) are more difficult to control and program for change than over-population. So this takes the front of the stage.

Wrong Fences
How false landmarks can lead to disaster
January 1971

In a lecture at Haverford College several weeks ago, Dr. Kenneth Boulding, noted economist, gave a mind-stimulating view of the world.

The world, Dr. Boulding said, makes him think of a mesa, one of those high plateaus with precipitous sides that are found in the Southwest.

Fences are necessary at the mesa's edge to keep people from stepping off to destruction. We all recognize the need for such fences.

But some people build fences in other parts of the mesa, places where there's no danger. These fences are not merely unnecessary; they are dangerous.

The unnecessary fence is dangerous because people who manage to breach it without injury and who then only find more of the mesa beyond the fence are likely to conclude that all fences are extraneous—including those vital ones that guard against the precipice.

But we have not been satisfied with the fences God erects in the Bible: fences of morality and ethics, justice and righteousness. We had to get in the fence-building business ourselves.

We've spent fifty years cluttering up the mesa with fences. And we've given these man-made fences the same coat of authoritative paint as biblical ones, the "thus saith the Lord" ones.

There's a fence against a white person marrying a black person, a fence against movie-going, against fellowship with true Christians who belong to the wrong church council, a fence against cosmetics and hair and music, a fence against various political, social, and economic systems.

We've been a generation of fence-builders, of mesa-dividers.

Now our children come along and breach the fences we've built so carefully, located so logically. They breach them and find that nothing happens.

So they come to scorn fences. They lump all fences together, God's and ours, and will have none of them.

"The mesa has no danger; see, we've gone through the fences with impunity"—until they face the precipice.

Has your heart ached for a Christian girl who had a baby out of marriage, a Christian boy who shacked up with a girl without marriage, a young person on drugs, a teen who became involved in shoplifting, a Christian man who marries a non-Christian woman, a Christian couple who slide into divorce and remarriage?

The list is heartbreakingly long. And I guess I've concentrated too heavily on the sex-oriented ones; it's easy in our American culture. But the point is our fences divert attention from God's fences. Sometimes, I am tempted to think we locate them where we do with this in mind. We build a fence against the intermarriage of white and black so that the warning of God's Word against sub-Christian attitudes toward the stranger and the poor are obscured. Our fence of patriotism hides the fence Jesus Christ erected against yielding to Caesar the Christian conscience that forever belongs to God.

We see these fences of God so clearly in another culture, another age.

We recognize that Shinto-shrine worship was patriotic but wrong for Christians in pre-World War II Japan, and that persecution of the Jews was patriotic but wrong for Christians in Hitler's Germany.

But for Christians in the United States, are there no parallels? Has God given us the privilege of living in the first "Christian" state in history? If we think this is so, we may be in danger of totally yielding our conscience to the judgments of our rulers.

God's fence is still there. Our man-made fences may hide it, but it remains. And it judges us if we allow the American flag to become our Shinto shrine, the black our Jew.

Let's tear down our fences so that we may get a fresh view of God's fences. Then maybe our young will begin to run from the edge of the precipice.

Women's Lib and the Bible
November 1972

My recent column on the proposed Equal Rights (for women) Amendment to the United States Constitution evoked letters in favor of pacifism. Every woman who responded to the column singled out my objection to women in military combat duty, rather than the other effects of the amendment I had noted.

The argument goes like this: "If it's wrong for women to drive tanks and get killed in war, why is it right for men? Women's Lib forces us to reexamine the war." "The fact is that God did not intend that anyone should be a soldier to destroy anything."

Quite obviously, I don't believe God originally created man to destroy. Satan is the destroyer, and by his temptation our first parents fell. Sin entered the race, and with sin the necessity for policemen and soldiers. Sin and policemen and soldiers will cease with the millennium, or with the new heavens and new earth, but not before. Women's Lib cannot hasten or delay the millennium.

The Old Testament is embarrassing to pacifists who claim to believe in its inspiration, because it does not merely say that God permitted war; it says that He commanded it and used it to right wrong, correct injustice, and destroy His enemies. And He commanded His people to fight.

I know that many of my fellow Christians are pacifists because of Jesus' teachings, and I respect their position. Yet there is no record of Jesus or the apostles commanding a soldier to forsake his military career. And a key Pauline illustration of the Christian life is based on soldiers at war (Eph. 6:10-17). (Can you imagine one based on stealing or prostitution?)

I do not believe God has given *carte blanche* approval to war, including

American wars. One big problem with contemporary Christians is our inclination to sing "The Star-Spangled Banner" to the tune of the "Doxology." In my opinion, this "laboratory of death" (a phrase I heard in Mexico recently) we are perpetuating is quite different from World War II. Sometimes I am sobered by the possibility that I may be standing with German Christians who were silent in the face of Hitler's attempt to exterminate the Jews.

But my point here isn't whether war is right or wrong, whether the Vietnam War is right or wrong, whether Christian participation in war or the Vietnam War is right or wrong. I am rather speaking about the necessity of our having biblical authority for what we believe about war or Women's Lib or anything else.

I was recently at a conference where a distinguished liberal theologian rejected certain teachings of Saint Paul on the grounds that he was an arrogant old bachelor and what he said wasn't the Word of God.

I disagreed, but I disagree just as deeply with those who claim to believe in the Holy Spirit's inspiration of the Bible, including the Epistles of Paul, but who then proceed to say or imply that we can disregard what he said about the relationship between men and women.

Women's Lib, the ordination of women to the Gospel ministry, women's participation in war, the whole concept of unisex, and every other part of the present rethinking of women's role in society and the church: All are subject and subordinate to the Bible's teaching. Christians start with the Bible, not with Gloria Steinem or Hugh Hefner.

Writing about women's place in the church, Paul roots it in Creation principles (before the Fall). "I suffer not a woman to teach, nor to usurp authority over the man, but to be in silence. For Adam was first formed, then Eve. And Adam was not deceived, but the woman being deceived was in the transgression" (1 Tim. 2:12-14).

You can rationalize that statement and other statements about the relationship between man and woman that are made in the Bible. You can scorn the Bible's description of male and female roles, husband and wife roles, mother and father roles.

If you do, admit that you've been liberated from the Bible's authority.

On the other hand, if you think the Bible is still true and relevant in this area, why don't you say something, or write something, that reflects your belief? Just make sure that what you say takes into account everything the Bible says, including those statements that Women's Lib ignores or rejects.

If We Could Rewrite the Bible
December 1973

When you stop to think about it, there are a lot of improvements we could introduce to make a better case for our cherished ideas.

I was listening to Eugene Chamberlain, coordinator of the children's section of Southern Baptist Sunday School Board, as he explained some difficulties in writing curriculum materials, especially telling the Bible story—for children.

"It's hard to maintain suspense," he said, "because you can't whomp a different ending on it."

Suppose we could write Bible stories differently, I thought. What changes, what surprise endings, would we be likely to introduce?

In today's charismatic climate, we'd hardly have Saint Paul take a medical doctor with him on his journeys. Luke would be left behind, to carry on his practice among the pagans.

Neither would Paul leave Trophimus behind, sick, at Miletus. A word from Paul, faith on Trophimus' part, would have healed him and restored him to the ministry.

And we'd probably remove Paul's thorn in the flesh.

We'd save lots of people from premature death: John the Baptist, Stephen, maybe even Jonathan. Samson would work his way out of the shambles of Dagon's temple, his sight restored by the shock of falling pillars, and serve God to a ripe old age instead of meeting a tragic end.

Some people would die sooner. Ahab and Jezebel, for instance, and Saul. Why should he have been permitted to hound David all those years and delay David's wonderful kingdom?

We could probably use some people's time and talents to greater advantage. How can you explain the one godly man of his day, Noah, spending years in the shipbuilding business? Wouldn't it have been more appropriate for him to travel around preaching the love of God, or the Quadruple Torah? Maybe, if he had done that, the Flood wouldn't have been necessary.

I guess we'd let the life of Jesus stand as it is, except we might have Him start His public ministry at the age of twenty instead of thirty. Of all men to spend most of His life as a carpenter, He's the last one you'd expect.

We might change a few of His teachings, if it were possible. After all, He was pretty tough on rich people—the camel and the needle's eye, and the rich man who died and was told that he had had his good things on earth. And we'd probably bring Jesus' account of future separation between sheep and goats more into line with Paul's teaching. Jesus' knowing people, and admitting them to heaven, on the basis of their visiting prisoners, clothing the naked, feeding the poor? That sounds a little like salvation by works.

I've always felt sort of sorry for Eli. He seems to have done a good job of raising Samuel, but his own sons were such a mess. Why not make his sons excel him in spiritual vigor and devotion? That would be much more encouraging to us parents today.

At the same time, Eli wouldn't have been overweight.

There's all that wine in the Bible that could be changed to water, or grape juice. And Paul could have advised Timothy to take Maalox, or pray over his upset stomach.

We would surely do something to clean up the violence in the Old Testament, including spikes through foreheads, cutting off big toes, and daggers embedded in fat flesh. And all those battles God's people fought at His command—surely we could find an easier way, and a more moral one, for them to obtain the Promised Land.

One incident, at least, could be changed so that world affairs 4,000 years later would be vastly improved. That's the brief affair Abraham had with Hagar, which need never have happened.

Or if it did, she could have aborted.

How about Jacob and Esau? Jacob was such a worm, and Esau was such a man's man. He must have had charisma beyond Jacob's, so let's make him a leader.

Another turn-around could be Joseph and Potiphar's wife. Why should he go to prison, when he was innocent, while she was free to seduce the next houseboy who came along?

Women: the word conjures up scores of changes we could make in the Bible. The most obvious is to introduce some women among the twelve disciples. Then there's Paul, who could keep his ideas to himself.

A bit more organization of ideas would help in the Bible. It would be great if at least one book were organized as a systematic theology.

And Revelation could be less vague, more specific, like eschatological books today.

When you get right down to it, there are only two incidents you'd really have to change to affect the whole thing: the rebellion of Satan and the fall of man. Those are the ones I'd really like to whomp a different ending on.

Revise Our "Sexist" Scriptures?
Target of Christian revisionists
September 1974

A recent news release indicates that the *Revised Standard Version* is to be revised yet once more, this time to eliminate sexist language.

What is sexist language? "Sons of God," which will become "children of God." "If any man thirst," which will be changed to "If any person thirst." "He who endures to the end will be saved" will be either "He or she," or "They."

I happen to think the whole idea is stupid, the sort of tampering with the Scriptures that Bible-burners accused the RSV translators of twenty-five years ago.

Before persons begin to write letters accusing me of being a M.C.P., please listen to me say that I think women have a valid and serious cause for complaint in our present American society. I'm for gymnasiums at Christian colleges for women as well as men, equal sports facilities and equipment at Christian camps, women on boards of directors of Christian organizations, equal pay for women for the same work—in Christian as well as secular situations, opportunity for women to advance along with men to executive positions.

And a lot of other things, more basic.

If a woman works all day at employment outside the home, elemental justice would indicate that her husband should share the work of the home.

No husband should be content to flower while his wife vegetates. Every Christian married man is responsible to see that his wife realizes the potential God has built into her life.

But it's not just husbands who must free women to be themselves, to achieve the goals they'd like to achieve. Women's libbers (including many of the Christian ones) need to learn the same lesson. Their scornful put-down of interest in motherhood, in providing a warm and beautiful home, in being a "traditional" wife and mother—forcing a contented wife and mother into a "meaningful career" outside the home, or imposing guilt—is as destructive to many women's freedom as a husband who thinks his wife only exists to further his goals.

Now back to the Bible.

Up to the present time, men have pretty well known who they were, and women have known who they were. There were clear distinctions, both in the Bible and in the general culture.

Nobody felt the need of unisex or bisexuality. In fact, the Bible clearly warned against blurring the lines between the sexes.

Now Germaine Greer and Gloria Steinem come along, and part of the Christian community begins to feel guilty that we are not keeping up with the world. So revisionists take over the Bible and set to work to change it. (I have intentionally chosen a pejorative word; Christian revisionists are comparable to Communist revisionists, in my opinion. Both represent an attempt to rewrite history for their own purposes, and tamper with source material.)

Some of the changes—such as the ones I suggested in the second paragraph—aren't too important, although I think it's stupid to change a grammatical usage, such as the generic "man." We need a term such as "mankind"; "chairperson" may be all right, but "personkind" is flawed, in my opinion.

But where will the revisionists stop? Will Adam come from Eve's rib, the Serpent tempt Adam, Sarah lead the pilgrimage out of Ur and have a daughter by Abraham's servant, Mrs. Hosea track down a male prostitute husband, Jesus have six women along with six men disciples, Paul travel with a woman doctor? Will the Prodigal Son become the Prodigal Daughter (or person)?

Granted that we have stressed God's maleness too much (He is compared to a mother in Scripture, as well as a father), but does the Incarnate Son become a Daughter? Do we erase the Creation-based, not Fall-based, distinction Saint Paul makes in 1 Corinthians 11?

When you start to rewrite history, you're in trouble, whether it's Communist history or biblical history. It would be more honest to say, "They were wrong; we've discovered new truth in the twentieth century," or "Times have changed, and we must reflect those changes," than to tamper with source material.

In defending the Bible as it stands, I'm not implying that it wouldn't be different in many places if God were revealing Himself today instead of millennia ago. With girl runaways outnumbering boys, the prodigal might well be a daughter, if Jesus were telling His story today. With women's education equal to men's, today's Bible might have books written by holy women. Surely the exploits of women missionaries would be headlined. And Herod might be a woman.

But these changes, reflecting the times with which God was burdened in His self-revelation, would not obscure the original Creation, nor the peculiar identities of men and women. Biblical principles about sex are unchanging.

Thank God for making women different from men.

I think an awful lot of men would agree with me. Men like Abraham and Moses and Aquila and Gloria Steinem's husband, if she's married.

Why Don't Sinners Cry Anymore?

Not just for cartoons
October 1974

About fifteen years ago I wrote some chapters for a book I never finished. One of those chapters was about the lost grace of repentance.

It was occasioned, I think, by British thinker-preacher Martyn Lloyd-Jones' comment that people no longer weep at evangelistic meetings. They laugh, he said, they come happily to the front, but they don't mourn over their sins. Nor does the evangelist indicate that weeping, or repentance, is part of a transaction with God.

It seemed to me then that a lot of Christians felt that repentance was not for this dispensation, that the call of the prophets to repent culminated, and ended, with John the Baptist.

Nothing that has happened in these intervening years has changed my mind. Godly sorrow for sin that leads to repentance (2 Cor. 7:10) is almost totally absent from our preaching and from our lives. The one who enters the kingdom without repentance hardly finds need for it as a resident.

We have lost the ability to say, "I'm sorry," to God and to one another. We have lost it as persons and we have lost it in our churches and we have lost it as a nation. For if Christians do not feel the need to repent, shall we expect non-Christians to do so?

A national leader tells of being invited into former President Nixon's office almost a year before the resignation. The President asked him and others gathered there what they thought he should do about Watergate.

This man, who is a Christian, says that he told the President that the American people are very forgiving. "Even at this date, if you went to them and said, 'I did wrong, I'm sorry. Please forgive me,' they would."

The President listened, then turned to the next person for his suggestion.

I'm inclined to agree with the advice this leader gave the President. I think that up until the very end, almost, an admission of culpability and a plea for forgiveness would have been honored.

According to *New York* magazine, a reporter asked one of the key

Watergate participants, "Aren't you and the others sorry for what happened?" His answer: "Contrition is b.s."

I am very aware that tears and sorrow for sin is only part of the truth, that true repentance involves a radical change of conduct. Thus Judas Iscariot "repented" after he betrayed Jesus—the Greek word means he had an "after care," he was sorrowful (Matt. 27:3). But if his mind was not changed, he would not have embarked on a new and different life if his suicide attempt had failed.

The New Testament word for repentance of the kind that pleases God means being sorry enough to change conduct and involves an about-face.

But do we need to repent today? Or is this one of those "works of righteousness" from which God's grace frees us? Jesus taught repentance: "Do you suppose that these Galileans (who died at the hands of Pilate) were sinners above all the Galileans, because they suffered such things? I tell you, No; but unless you repent, you shall all likewise perish" (Luke 13:2, 3).

Peter taught repentance. In his first sermon, on the Day of Pentecost, he said, "Repent and be baptized, every one of you" (Acts 2:38).

Paul taught repentance: "The goodness of God leads you to repentance" (Rom. 2:4). "I have taught you . . . repentance toward God and faith toward our Lord Jesus Christ" (Acts 20:21).

And the last book of the Bible teaches repentance: "Repent, or else I will come to you quickly, and will fight against you with the sword of my mouth" (Rev. 2:16).

Our attitude toward God affects our attitude toward others. Maybe one reason marriage and family relations are in such desperate straits today, including those of Christians, is that we've lost the grace of repentance.

Joseph C. Macaulay, interim pastor of New York's Calvary Baptist Church, told of a visit to the Hebrides Islands some years ago, when revival was going on. On his way to church, where he was to preach, Dr. Macaulay heard a man sobbing in a cottage as he passed.

"What's that?" he asked his companion.

"That's John. He's on his way to God. He'll come through," was the reply.

For many years, the *New Yorker* magazine has had two subjects of cartoons repeated again and again. One is Noah's Ark. The other is of a man with a sandwich sign that reads, "Repent. The end of the world is at hand."

I think we need that message—not just a cartoon, but in our pulpits and in our lives.

Power of Providential Praying
Concerns beyond the family circle
December 1975

"I'll pray for you."

How often I've said that, only to forget, or to remember for a brief period of time and then forget.

Of course, some people and needs are always present in the mind; there is no need to be reminded to pray for them. Family—immediate and more distant, work and associates, neighbors, pastor and church staff, familiar missionaries and Christian workers, government, the persecuted of earth: these come to mind almost automatically.

A prayer list is a help, perhaps a necessity, for responsible praying. But periodic editing, including both additions and removals, is necessary if it is not to become unwieldy. And often, when time is suddenly available for praying, I find the list is not at hand. (I'll admit that it should probably be always available, but it isn't.) Or I realize I've removed a name for whom I should still be praying.

The result for me, and I suspect for a lot of other people, is recurring guilt over my prayer life—especially intercessory prayer. "When we work, we work; when we pray, God works," is never far from my mind.

In the past couple of years, several things have helped me pray more, and, I trust, pray more effectively.

First is a fresh awareness of God's amazing closeness to me. I am never removed from His presence, except by sin. "Pray without ceasing" (1 Thess. 5:17) means that as I write this on an airplane six miles above western

Pennsylvania, I can pause to speak to my Father. Driving a car, sitting at my desk, shaving in the morning are other situations when I can turn to God and find Him there. When I am awakened at night and cannot immediately return to sleep, I can pray to God.

Praying with other people has also been a great encouragement to me: with my wife, when we are alone in the car; with my sons, when I'm driving them to school.

But my greatest help in remembering has come from realizing that God can bring to my mind those people and situations for which I ought to pray. He can stir my memory through associations—something I see, something I hear, something I read. If I forget to pray for someone, He can remind me.

A stewardess on this flight reminds me of a woman whose husband recently died. I pray for that woman and her children. The pilot makes me remember to pray for friends who are also airline pilots, and for JAARS and MAF.[1]

Driving the car, I see a street name, a billboard advertisement, a real estate sign, a church: each leads to an association that results in prayer.

A friend mentioned something that E. Stanley Jones wrote in connection with prayer; this has been a help to me: If your mind wanders to something else when you're praying, Dr. Jones suggested, pray for that something else.

God can stir our minds to pray: God can bring an image from the past, or from a far distant place, before our mind's eye, and lead us to pray.

Another part of faithfulness in praying for others is not to wait until a convenient, quiet time—rather, to pray in the midst of life's pressures. I think I'm learning this, as well as the rightness of saying, "Let's pray about that now," when someone talks to me about a problem.

We do not pray enough together, as Christian brothers and sisters. We talk, and we forget that our Father is there listening—and that it should be the most natural thing to include Him in our conversation.

Recently I said good-bye to Abe Vander Puy at the Quito, Ecuador airport. As we stood there with people moving past us, Abe said, "Let's

[1] *Editor's note:* JAARS stands for Jungle Aviation and Radio Service, an arm of Wycliffe Bible Translators, and MAF is Missionary Aviation Fellowship.

pray." His arm went around me, and he committed me, for the trip and for my life, to the Lord. It's the most satisfying departure from an airport I've ever had.

"Pray without ceasing" has implications for life that are so daily, too. While driving a car, you see an accident; do you think to pray for the injured one, the worried, upset ones? When you see the poverty-stricken, the old and feeble, the alcoholic on the city streets, do you think to pray for them? God answers prayer; His answer does not depend on the possibility of our personal intervention in the situation about which we pray.

Prayer may be our children's greatest enlightenment that we have concerns for people and situations beyond our own family circle.

Reading *Time* or *Newsweek* or the daily paper are other occasions to pray. Can God intervene in the Patty Hearst case to bring about justice, to bring about truth? Can God solve the problems of Northern Ireland and Lebanon? Do we ask Him for these things?

I remember one day early in the Watergate affair when I was driving my two sons, one teen-age, the other on the threshold of teen-age, to school. (A year or so earlier, when the federal judge and former Illinois governor Otto Kerner was on trial, one of them said to me, "But doesn't everybody in public office accept bribes? Do any of them live on their salary?" I was suddenly struck with the image he had—and other children probably had—of public servants.) This morning as we prayed together in the car, I asked God to bring truth to light, to make corruption surface, to judge the guilty and protect the innocent.

Later, looking back, I was glad that I had a part—an infinitesimal part, but a part—in the resolution of Watergate, by turning to a judge greater than the Senate or the federal court.

Bloodthirsty or Biblical?

Hang the man or hang the logic
May 1977

One element has been missing from discussions of Gary Gilmore's recent execution, and of the larger question of capital punishment.

We've heard a lot, mostly con but some pro, about the deterrent effect of capital punishment, and about the thwarted possibility of reformation. And more has been said about "murder" by the state, about the effect on the condemned man of waiting for time and appeals to run out, about society's voyeurism, even about the suffering of the condemned man compared to that of his victim and the victim's family.

But I have not seen a serious presentation of the one element in capital punishment that has found general historical agreement among Jews and Christians: retribution, the punitive effect.

Perhaps it's not surprising that this is absent from our consideration of the ultimate punishment, since it is also the missing element from our consideration of punishments for lesser crimes.

I am not especially concerned about the rejection of retribution by the secular mind, which in our day to a large degree is humanistic. Reformation of the criminal is the only reason for incarceration or other punishment, according to this way of thinking. But I am deeply concerned about its rejection by the Christian mind. As in so many other recent instances, it seems to me that we have in this turned from the Word of God and accommodated our theology, attitudes, and values to this present evil world and its ruler.

Behind all the Bible's teaching about sin and crime is one central proposition: The reformation of the offender is not the primary object of punishment; nor is the deterrent effect upon others. Rather, punishment is inflicted to satisfy justice. That justice may be God's or (by derivation from God) the state's. Why did God inflict destruction on men at the time of the Flood, in Sodom and Gomorrah and Jerusalem? Not for the good of the offenders or for their reformation, but to satisfy His justice. And God's future punishment of fallen angels and of men who ultimately refuse His offer of salvation likewise will not be for the purpose of reformation; this the Bible rules out by declaring that the punishment is eternal.

The prevention of crime is desired by all who desire justice and righteousness. And this is sometimes a side effect of punishment. But whether capital punishment or lesser punishments are deterrent or not is, for the Bible-believing Christian, irrelevant to the central reason for punishment of the criminal.

Theologian Charles Hodge distinguishes between punishment and chastisement. "A father chastises a child in love, and for the child's good. And God, our heavenly Father, brings suffering upon His children for their edification. But evil inflicted for the benefit of the sufferer is chastisement, and not punishment. Punishment, properly speaking, is evil inflicted in satisfaction of justice."

Punishment of the wicked is always related to the anger of God in the Scriptures. Chastisement of His children is related to love.

Even for God's children, there is punishment as well as discipline. Saint Paul relates the sickness and death of many in the Corinthian church to their sin and lack of self-judgment. And we are told that "if we confess our sins, he is faithful and just to forgive us our sins" (1 John 1:9).

Isn't the penalty removed by confession, by saying we're sorry, please forgive us?

No, and here, it seems to me, is the heart of the matter.

The penalty is removed by our Lord Christ's action in taking it upon Himself on the cross. His death was as our substitute. A penalty always results from the violation of law, and that penalty is always borne. It may be borne by the sinner or it may be borne by Christ. It may be borne by the criminal or it may be borne by the victim and by society. But in a moral universe, the penalty is borne; it must be borne.

Retribution is at the heart of our Lord Christ's redemptive work. The sentence imposed by God upon me was death; Christ fulfilled the sentence, bore the punishment, and therefore I am pardoned.

Not all theologians agree with this view. I remember hearing Dr. Clarence T. Craig tell a class in Pauline theology at Union Seminary in New

York (commenting on Romans 3, and the concept of propitiation), that any attempt to show that there is something in the essential nature of God that requires the satisfaction of His justice against sinners "ends only in blackening the character of God."

According to an alternative view, it was not necessary for sin to be punished, with judgment falling either on the sinner or on the Son of God. Rather, the death of Christ, along with His life, teaching, and other acts, produces a moral effect on the hearts of men. The results of this moral influence (which is what the theory is called) is that the sinner turns from his sin. He is reformed.

I am aware that some Christian theologians hold and have held the moral influence theory of the work of Christ, rather than the substitutionary atonement theory, the punitive theory that I have just mentioned. And it is true that Christ's life and teachings and death exert a powerful influence on the Christian. By His example our Lord does affect our conduct. But this follows the satisfaction of God's just judgment; it does not replace it.

Most theologians have found this theory inadequate. So have most of our Christian organizations and institutions, which incorporate a statement about the substitutionary atonement in their bases of faith.

Now we are back at our initial question: What is the state's purpose in punishing the criminal? Is it simply reformation, or is it the exacting of a penalty, retribution?

According to the Old Testament, homicide is to be punished by the death of the murderer (Ex. 21:12, 14; Lev. 24:17; Num. 35:16; Deut. 19:11, 13). These passages distinguish between murder and manslaughter, providing for escape from the penalty for those guilty only of the latter.

The rationale for capital punishment is found in Genesis 9:6: "Whoever sheds man's blood, by man shall his blood be shed; for in the image of God made he man."

This command was given to Noah, the second head of the human race. Therefore it does not seem to be limited to one particular age or race. Rather, the reason is ageless: Man bears God's image; therefore the destruction of man is an outrage against God, to be punished by execution.

The New Testament confirms the state's authority to carry out executions in Romans 13:4. And neither Jesus Christ nor Saint Paul challenged this authority in their own confrontations with the state. In fact, Saint Paul affirmed it: "If I be an offender, or have committed anything worthy of death, I refuse not to die" (Acts 25:11).

As Christian people, we believe that there are unavoidable results of disobeying God, whether the disobedience is personal or national. If this is so, whether capital punishment is a deterrent to murder or not, we are suffering those results as a nation and will suffer them in the future.

Again quoting Hodge: "Experience teaches that where human life is undervalued, it is insecure; that where the murderer escapes with impunity or is inadequately punished, homicides are fearfully multiplied. The practical question, therefore, is 'Who is to die? The innocent man or the murderer?'"

The Old Testament prophets ("All Scripture is given by inspiration of God and is profitable" [2 Tim. 3:16]) pronounced God's judgment on nations, including Israel, and cities that were characterized by violence and the shedding of innocent blood. The judgments they mentioned are frightening, as were their later fulfillment.

And is God not already visiting judgment on our callous disregard of human life, as children murder parents; parents murder children, including infants; teens and young adults kill old people; arsonists kill ghetto-dwellers; lust-ridden men rape and kill innocent women; bombers and sharpshooters kill numbers of innocent people?

I am aware that some who read what I have written will ascribe bloodthirstiness to me, desire for vengeance, lack of Christian concern for a brother human being who happened to commit murder.

I am also aware that when it was still practiced by the state, capital punishment fell most heavily on the poor and members of minority races. The rich, who could afford prestigious lawyers, often went free. God punishes nations for unequal treatment of the guilty. God's people must crusade for justice in all areas, including capital crimes.

I am thankful for decisions of the Supreme Court in recent years that have reinforced equal treatment under the law, for instance requiring legal counsel for the poor and indigent.

And if the viewpoint I espoused is considered bloodthirsty, what shall we say of a nation that gets its "kicks" out of watching murders and other acts of violence as a chief form of entertainment—in television, movies, theater? A nation that is made up of increasing numbers of onlookers who watch other human beings beaten, raped, and murdered in real life, without intervening? A nation that seriously discusses televising (with sponsor) the execution of murderers?

We're sick.

God, heal us. Soon.

Empty Calories
February 1980

George Kraft is a retired member of Overseas Missionary Fellowship (OMF), a veteran worker with China Inland Mission. Detained by the Communists in 1950, Mr. Kraft continued his ministry (with Mrs. Kraft) in Taiwan and Singapore.

Mr. Kraft interrupted a silence of many years by writing to me several months ago in response to one of these columns. His letter is disturbing to me; it is also beautiful in its expression of the deepening of a husband/wife relationship through suffering. With his permission, I share the following excerpts:

> More than forty years of marriage plus [his wife's] terminal cancer bring new joy and meaning to our marriage vow, "till death do us part." But almost weekly we are pained with news of the marriage breakup of evangelical leaders so that one almost wants to cry out, "Stop! For God's sake stop!" What's happening, Joe?
>
> . . . Many years ago I read an article by a German Lutheran theologian with which I strongly disagreed at the time. But now I won-

der if he did not have some legitimate insights. As I recall in his thesis he maintained that the pietistic emphasis was dangerous and in some cases bordered on heresy and that its fruits would be bitter. As I considered the Moravian missionary movement, some of the rich devotional hymns coming from the pietistic sources and the obvious devotion to the person of Christ I dismissed his work as more of the dead orthodoxy against which I had rebelled in my youth. But there was more to his thesis than mere protest. He maintained that the solid theology of the church fathers with its emphasis on Christ and objective truth rather than on subjective experience was much more productive of true scriptural holiness than pietism.

For some decades now American evangelicals have been feeding upon pietistic literature. . . . I have enjoyed reading them myself but along with my wife have often had a gnawing feeling that something was amiss in the emphasis. What has been the fruitage from this type of thinking? Has it produced vigorous, loyal, covenant-keeping, vow-respecting believers? Or has it induced a sloppy sort of sentimentality which passes for the real thing in undiscerning circles? Has this type of mindset contributed to or at least failed to prevent the marital problems which have produced so much heartache in evangelical circles? This needs to be explored by someone who can put things in perspective. No names and books need be mentioned but the deeper issues do need to be brought forth. For as a man or a generation thinks in their hearts so are they (Prov. 23:7). And sloppy, sentimental thinking will not produce strong homes for God and his church.

Pearl Kraft, George's wife, recently died, after what was described as "an incredible illness" of almost seven years, that involved much suffering and constant care. A memorial fund has been established by OMF, and will be used for scholarships at Singapore Bible College, and an OMF-sponsored Gospel broadcast to China.

I'm inclined to comment on the beauty of a long marriage in the Lord, which inevitably involves some suffering, and to say that Christian growth and the development of a personality are rooted in such a relationship—not in the "I need space in which to grow, I'll divorce you for my own good" type of thinking that is so prevalent in the world, and even in the church, today.

But the essential point of George Kraft's letter goes far beyond the crisis in marriage. It extends to Christian morality and ethics in every area of life, in every business and profession, to priorities established by the church, to our parachurch organizations and institutions.

We need a rebirth of Christian doctrine, of biblical theology. We need iron in place of straw, emphasis on God's work through suffering in place of this overweening emphasis on success and growth.

Maybe a good goal for the decade just beginning would be one doctrinal sermon every month. We've had enough milk; bring on the meat (Heb. 5:12).

New Fig-Leaf Dictionary
May 1980

Language changes. Today's understandable words will be tomorrow's quaint archaisms. And yesterday's clear expressions seem old-fashioned and outmoded today.

As an example, it is probable that a majority of people in the United States, for that matter the world, would consider the statement "as American as McDonald's" clear, and the statement "as American as apple pie" obsolete—an archaism.

The church is no exception. Yesterday's words and the ideas they represent pass out of vogue, become archaic; they are replaced with new and different concepts.

Here are some archaisms of biblical and theological derivation, familiar to past generations of Christians, words that seem to have been discarded or replaced by new words and the ideas they represent.

Adultery: "Voluntary sexual intercourse between a married man and someone other than his wife, or between a married woman and someone other than her husband" (*Webster's New Collegiate Dictionary,* 1975 ed.).

Biblical usage: "Thou shalt not commit adultery" (Ex. 20:14).

"Affair" is the less judgmental word used today. The concept itself is not generally mentioned in preaching, even when divorce is discussed.

Awe: "Emotion in which dread, veneration, and wonder are variously mingled, as: (a) a profound and humbly fearful reverence inspired by deity or by something sacred or mysterious; (b) submissive and admiring fear inspired by authority or power; (c) wondering reverence tinged with fear inspired by the sublime" (*Webster's*). Biblical usage: "Let all the earth fear the Lord: let all the inhabitants of the world stand in awe of him" (Ps. 33:8).

Awe was damaged in the churches, destroyed by the electronic church. Awe has been replaced by good feelings toward oneself and God, by a happy-face image of God.

Cleave: "To adhere firmly and closely and loyally and unwaveringly, syn. stick" (*Webster's*). Biblical usage: "For this cause shall a man leave father and mother, and shall cleave to his wife. And they two shall be one flesh" (Matt. 19:5).

"Loyally," "unwaveringly," "stick," "one flesh" are related archaic terms. "Cleave" is only used in its other sense: "Divide, split, separate into distinct parts."

Guilt: "The fact of having committed a breach of conduct, especially violating law and involving a penalty" (Webster's). Biblical usage: "When one has sinned and become guilty, he shall restore what he took by robbery, or what he got by oppression, or the deposit which was committed to him, or the lost thing which he found, or anything about which he has sworn falsely; he shall restore it in full, and shall add a fifth to it, and give it to him to whom it belongs, on the day of his guilt offering" (Lev. 6:4–5 RSV).

"Feeling guilty" in current usage has replaced guilt, which is archaic. Feeling guilty is bad; it may lead to deeper emotional problems.

Hate: "To feel extreme enmity toward" (Webster's). Biblical usage: "Hate evil and love good, and establish justice in the gate . . . I hate, I despise your feasts, and I take no delight in your solemn assemblies. . . . Take away from me the noise of your songs; to the melody of your harps I will not listen. But let justice roll down like waters, and righteousness like an everflowing stream" (Amos 5:15, 21, 23-24 RSV).

Today hatred is perceived to be a harmful, destructive emotion for human beings (including Christians), and is antithetical to an image of the God of love.

Humble: "Not proud or haughty; not arrogant or assertive" (*Webster's*). Biblical usage: "If my people, which are called by my name, shall humble themselves, and pray, and seek my face, and turn from their wicked ways; then will I hear from heaven, and will forgive their sin, and will heal their land" (2 Chron. 7:14). During World War II this verse was frequently quoted in Christian assemblies. Numerous days of prayer and prayer meetings were held on the basis of this divine promise.

Today the word is archaic; no national crisis has caused Christians generally to act upon it. This may be related to a rightful feeling of strength among Christians, based upon George Gallup, Jr.'s, research. "Growing," "successful," "respectable" are now used instead of humble.

Pollute: "To make . . . morally impure; defile" (*Webster's*). Biblical usage: "For if after they have escaped the pollution of the world through the knowledge of the Lord and Savior Jesus Christ, they are again entangled therein, and overcome, the latter end is worse with them than the beginning" (2 Peter 2:20). In the 1930s movies were considered a polluting influence by many boycotting Christians.

Today this idea is considered quaint, narrow, archaic. There is a great resistance to the concept of TV as a moral and spiritual pollutant in the living room. Any use of the term is limited to Webster's secondary definition: "To contaminate (an environment) especially with man-made waste." Theological status is given the idea of polluting air, land, oceans, etc. today.

Repent: "To be sorry. To turn from sin and dedicate oneself to the amendment of one's life" (*Webster's*). Biblical usage: "The men of Nineveh shall rise in judgment with this generation, and shall condemn it: because they repented at the preaching of Jonah; and, behold, a greater than Jonah is here" (Matt. 12:41).

Individual repentance is a lost emphasis in most preaching and evangelism today, as evidenced by the lack of sorrow (tears). When repentance is used, it is applied to social injustice, the rape of the environment, United States intervention in Vietnam, etc.

Sunday: "The first day of the week: the Christian analogue of the Jewish Sabbath" (*Webster's*). Biblical usage: "If you turn your foot from the Sabbath, from doing your pleasure on my holy day, and call the Sabbath a delight and the holy day of the Lord honorable; if you honor it, not going your own ways, or seeking your own pleasure, or talking idly; then you shall take delight in the Lord, and I will make you ride upon the heights of the earth; I will feed you with the heritage of Jacob your father, for the mouth of the Lord has spoken" (Isa. 58:13-14 RSV). Earlier in this century, when American Christians worked six days a week, eight to ten hours each day, they set apart one day—Sunday—for God.

Today the Christian Sabbath (or Lord's Day) is an archaic concept, probably because there are too many things to do to set one day apart for God and deeds of mercy.

Vow: "A solemn promise or assertion; specifically by which a person binds himself to an act, service, or condition" (*Webster's*). Biblical usage: "When you make a vow to the Lord your God, you shall not be slack to pay it; for the Lord your God will surely require it of you, and it would be sin in you. But if you refrain from vowing, it shall be no sin in you. You shall be careful to perform what has passed your lips, for you have voluntarily vowed to the Lord your God what you have promised with your mouth" (Deut. 23:21-23 RSV). The word has been used in a church context of the promises made in the wedding ceremony, before God and to the other person, to cleave to the spouse "for better or for worse, for richer or for poorer, in sickness and in health, until death us do part."

This is only a beginning. To be really impressed with Christian archaisms, read a theology text written before 1940. Better still, read the Bible.

One Sage's Testament
July/August 1980

It was the summer of 1940. The Netherlands had fallen. A surgeon, talking to an elderly Friesian farmer, asked, "And what are we to do now?" The old Christian replied, "Before men we must be as eagles; before God, as worms."

Last week, on my sixtieth birthday, I had a warning of my mortality, that a day is coming when my voice in this world will be stilled and I shall awaken in my Lord's awesome, joyous presence.

The warning was a tap on the shoulder, not hands around my neck or a shove to the ground. But it caused me to think deep thoughts, consider separations, ponder my life and work.

I found peace, "the peace of God that surpasses understanding" (Phil. 4:7). Not anxiety, not fear, but peace: the peace of those who know that no force, not even death itself, can come between us and the love of Christ (Rom. 8:35-39).

"The just [those who have been justified before God through faith in his Son] shall live by faith" (Rom. 1:17; Gal. 3:11). Yes, but the just shall die by faith also.

One heavy thought that came to me was what final testament I would leave for my children, our own and other Christians of their generation. This was not a new thought; in recent weeks—perhaps in anticipation of my birthday—it had been recurrent. But now there was an edge of urgency to it: I could not avoid the evidence that my generation is in the process of turning the game over to a fresh team.

Here are some parts of that testament.

1. Read the Bible. Read it all and read it carefully. Read it first and last with your own eyes, but in between read it with the eyes of the poor, the persecuted, the dispossessed, the uneducated, the prisoner, the stranger, the minority person. By that I mean consciously acknowledge that this isn't just a private pillow of precious promises (a sign of my age: I've avoided alliteration previously), but the voice of the Judge of the universe.

There are two dangers in reading the Bible. The first is private interpretation, which means coming up with ideas and dogmas that are "original" with you. Check your interpretations with those of other Christians, both writers and speakers who have the gift of understanding God's Word and teaching it.

The second danger is not so obvious, but is at least as serious:

Watch out that you don't accept the private interpretations of anyone else. As I see it, this is a grave danger today. Test the ideas and interpretations of Christian leaders, preachers, seminar leaders, and gurus by the Bible. That includes any ideas you've learned from me.

I know this isn't new to you, but I'm amazed at how many Christians follow teachers who start with a statement and then find proof texts to support it. More often than not the texts must be warped ever so slightly or isolated from the context to "prove" the idea.

Don't let anyone trade on your respect for God's Word by winning you to his/her private interpretation of it. And remember that heresies have seldom arisen full-blown; they were first of all the seeds of warped ideas from seemingly godly leaders.

2. There is one "simple" idea in the Christian faith. That is salvation by faith alone in Jesus Christ. Never complicate that wondrous provision of God. When I was a teenager, my confidence in God's power was immeasurably strengthened life-long by seeing hopeless alcoholics in New York missions saved from their derelict ways, reunited with their families, and living for God; all this by merely responding with faith to that simple message and the Spirit's invitation.

Now this may be a slight overstatement, but after we enter God's family by faith, I believe there are only a few uncomplicated ideas or courses of Christian action. Choices must be made, sometimes, in a murky mist, and paradoxes resolved—or lived with. Things don't always turn out right on this tent-ground. So watch out for Christian leaders who would seek to entice you with their simplistic, foolproof, guaranteed answers. It's appealing to a sincere Christian when an obviously authoritative person says, "This is the way and here are the verses to prove it" (note *verses,* not usually *chapters* or *sections*). Be discerning as you listen to that person; don't entrust him/her with your inner soul. And be careful with other people who quote him/her as final authority.

(I have yet to hear a poor or persecuted Christian give a seminar on success as the result of learning biblical principles. And I have yet to hear a hurting Christian parent lecture on the foolproof biblical way to raise teenagers.)

3. Look for humility in the leaders you choose to follow, the voices you choose to hear. Pride, I increasingly believe, is the most damnable sin: the creature's refusal to acknowledge that he/she is a creature responsible to the Creator. No person can foster the impression that he/she is great and then exalt a great God.

A true leader for God speaks and acts with authority. This may (and should) be coupled with humility and meekness. But their aim is to build disciples for Jesus Christ, not their own personal disciples. He/she is horrified to hear people quote them as the authority for their beliefs or actions.

Look for God's little heroes. Let others adulate the Christian superstars. And when you find them encourage them, appreciate them, love them.

4. If God should lead you into a ministry of counseling others, be careful lest you take the place of God in their lives. Never back people—including your children—into a corner where freedom of decision is destroyed. Never manipulate people. And if a person responds to the Holy Spirit's urgings through you, cut the umbilical cord as quickly as possible. Don't get your kicks out of a person's continuing spiritual dependency on you.

I hear a lot of talk about "discipling" today. I'm disturbed by much of it (and much "shepherding"). We must want to make people disciples of Jesus Christ, not of ourselves. One of God's most beautiful gifts is freedom; don't let anyone prevent you from exercising it by coming between you and God. And don't let any group, either.

5. You won't be able to stem the national tide that is running against the family. But determine that your marriage, if God gives you a partner, will be inviolable, that it will continue until death separates for a time. Make your home an oasis of morality and love in a pagan world.

6. Train your children for persecution. I hope it won't come, but prepare them for it. Work toward building a tough character that will stand

in the evil day. Read the Bible to your children and pray with them daily. And do other activities with them: take walks, play games, read books aloud. Where will the time come from? Don't have TV. Refuse to rent your living room and your time—your own, your spouse's, your children's—to pagan hucksters. Ask whether you'd want these people as guests and friends in your home, if you'd want your children to grow up under their influence. And ask similar questions about Christian hucksters. Is their image of God, the Christian life, the church, the biblical one you want "sold" to your children?

Perhaps persecution won't come in your children's lifetime, but the same principles will prepare them for an increasingly popularized evangelical Christianity or a period of civil religion.

7. I'm glad you like to read. Guard your literacy and that of your children: thinking Christians, able to reason on the basis of God's Word, may become scarce in the future. Note how often Saint Paul speaks of the mind, of wisdom, knowledge, understanding in his epistles. We understand true doctrine with our minds, not with our feelings.

Your generation has reminded mine of the importance of feelings. I love to see radiant Christians, to be part of a group that "feels" the Gospel. But I sometimes get uneasy about endless repetitions of simple phrases. Sing with your understanding as well as your feelings.

Remember that truth without feelings is still truth, but feelings without truth are at best mawkish, at worst heresy.

8. This one may surprise you, but I believe my generation's greatest loss—next to the inviolateness of marriage and the family—has been the sanctity of the Lord's Day. My wife and I started out our home with a rather serious attempt to "keep it holy": no work, no group sports for our children, quiet activities, occasional visits with Christian friends and their children. But somewhere along the way we changed, and our attitude became much more secular (or pagan) than Christian—in the sense that I now believe the Bible teaches and our own parents and earlier generations practiced.

For yourself and for any children God may give you, try to recapture the Lord's Day as a day of rest and deeds of mercy, of retreat from the world;

try to turn it into the happiest day of the week.

9. Be tolerant of different styles among Christians, different emphases. Remember that Jesus said, "He who is not against Me is for Me." Be intolerant of heresy—not of the right to speak; defend that with all your strength—but of accepting it as a viable option. Seek pure doctrine and life in the church, always remembering that "the wisdom that comes from above is first pure, then peaceable" (James 3:17).

10. If you see another person fall, help him up. And withhold judgment, at least that final kind reserved to the Judge of All that I think Jesus was referring to when He said, "Do not judge, and you will not be judged" (Luke 6:37).

And when you see somebody fall, let your first thought be, "That could have been me. It's only God's grace that enables me to stand."

11. Never forget that human beings are the most important creation in the world to God, and they should therefore be to you. Not just yourself, nor your family, nor other American Christians, but every other human being in the whole world. I think I can understand the concern of some people over endangered species: seals, whales, snail darters. But there are endangered humans, too: Amazon Indian tribes that may soon be extinct, Chicago inner-city kids, Cuban refugees, all created in the image of God. Give your life for men and women, teenagers, children—not for dollars or status.

Life is short, and every treasure on this earth will ultimately fail to satisfy the possessor: even a corner on the silver market or a Nobel or Pulitzer prize. So, in living your life, make your choices for God's glory and the good of others. The old divine's prayer is still a good one, "Oh God, burn eternity into my eyeballs."

When I was young, a couplet was often quoted:
Only one life, 'twill soon be past,
Only what's done for Christ will last.
It's still true.

Unlikely American Hero
His lackluster resumé would never get beyond the church secretary's wastebasket, but ...
July/August 1981

It isn't likely he could serve on the board of most churches because he was a single young adult.

It isn't likely he'd be asked to speak at a liberated Christian women's conference because all his disciples were men.

It isn't likely he'd be asked to speak at a men's retreat because he cried publicly.

It isn't likely he'd pass most evangelism training courses because he adhered to no soul-winning formula and approached each person differently.

It isn't likely he could be the pastor of most churches because he said that people who remarry after divorce (except for marital unfaithfulness) are guilty of adultery.

It isn't likely he'd be asked to supply many pulpits because he often just told stories. And they were short.

It isn't likely he'd prepare Christian education materials because a lot of his stories were open-ended.

It isn't likely he could serve on a Christian college faculty because he drank wine.

It isn't likely he'd be asked to teach at a seminary because he had no earned doctorate and spent most of his time in practical work with his students.

It isn't likely he could serve on the board of a Christian institution or organization because he was poor.

It isn't likely he could preserve a reputation for leadership because he regularly took time out for rest and washed the feet of his followers.

It isn't likely he could be a counselor because he reinforced people's sense of sin, was directive, and turned from those who didn't respond.

It isn't likely he could run an electronic church because he told a rich man to give away his money to the poor, not to support his own ministry.

It isn't likely he could fill in at a youth conflicts seminar because he stood up to his parents when he was twelve (Luke 2:39-50), appealing to a higher responsibility, and refused to obey his mother when he was in his early thirties (John 2:1-4; Matt. 12:46-50).

It isn't likely he could fill in at most other seminars because he defined success in nonmaterial terms.

It isn't likely he'd be used as an example of dying, because in his last hours he felt alienated from God the Father.

It isn't likely his opinion would be sought or heeded because he spoke of his followers in terms of a "little flock" and "two or three," warned against times when all men speak well of believers, and said that they should expect to be persecuted.

It isn't likely he'd expect people to come into church buildings; he'd probably be preaching in Central Park or the Boston Common.

If Jesus were here today. Poor church, poor world.

The Birth of an Ethic
December 1981

Behind Christmas 1981 exists a controversy that swirls around us like a winter storm

Christmas 1981.

When did the fetus Jesus become a human being in Mary? When "He was conceived by the Holy Ghost," as the Apostles' Creed puts it, or at some later time during fetal development? The controversy over pro-life, pro-freedom of choice, proabortion, antilife, antiabortion swirls around us like a winter storm.

I have some thoughts on the subject that probably will reflect my lay status in both medicine and theology. (Lay is frequently a synonym for ignorance.)

In all the discussion by pro- and antiabortion activists, I have seen no reference to the fact that a criminal felony was changed into a permissible action overnight by a simple majority of the Supreme Court.

Prior to that decision, abortion (except for an abortion performed to save the life of the mother) was abhorred by almost everybody, including all Christians and most physicians.

It's hard for those of us who lived many years before that simple act of decriminalization to accept abortion's changed status. Imagine if infanticide or child abuse were suddenly declared legal. And we're puzzled by the medical community's immediate unquestioning acceptance, including that of many Christian physicians.

Those physicians are more likely to be obstetricians than pediatricians or orthopedists. I suppose the cynic in me comes to the surface when I ask why they were so ready to begin to abort pregnant women when the Court ruled it legal, although physicians resent any judicial impingement on other medical decisions? Was it the vast new source of income that suddenly opened up?

And the strident objections to cutting off government payment for abortions of poor women: was this caused by pity for the poor or by the loss of income? If the former, physicians are still free to abort poor women as a charitable act. I suspect few are thus aborted.

"The love of money is a root of all kinds of evil" (1 Tim. 6:10 NIV).

I understand that Christian theologians fall into two opinions about the origin of the soul in the fetus. First are those who believe the act of conception results in a living soul—a true, albeit embryonic, human being. Second are those who believe that sometime during the development of the fetus in the womb, God implants the soul. Nobody is sure when, but from that time on the fetus is not a "thing," but a human person.

Back to my first question: when did the fetal Jesus become a human being in Mary? From the Holy Spirit's conception, or later in its development?

And how about the fetal John's leap for joy when the sound of Mary's greeting reached his mother's ears (Luke 1:41-44)? Was that fetus a human being?

Canadian psychiatrist Thomas Verny has collected evidence, recently published in *The Secret Life of the Unborn Child* (Summit Books), that a fetus can feel emotion and respond intellectually months before birth. Item: a test shows that as early as twenty-five weeks a fetus will jump in time to the beat of an orchestra drum. It will grimace when sour liquids are injected into the amniotic sac, and double the rate of sucking when the liquid is sweet. Item: a mother in Oklahoma City discovers her one-year-old daughter reciting breathing instructions for Lamaze childbirth. But the terminology and technique are observably Canadian, not American. The mother had taken Lamaze while living in Toronto more than a year earlier.

This proves nothing; it does warn us to be careful about killing fetuses because they don't feel pain and aren't human.

One other question: could a not-yet-human inherit a sinful human nature? Yet David says, "Surely I have been a sinner from birth, sinful from the time my mother conceived me" (Ps. 51:5).

So it seems to me that I fall into the company of Christians who believe a fetus is human, a living soul, from the moment of conception.

One theologian suggested recently that for the second group (those who believe that at some point in time in utero the fetus becomes a living soul), abortion is defensible.

My son Tim, who has helped my thinking in this whole area of abortion, has a good answer for that.

"If a hunter is out looking for deer and sees something moving through the trees, he won't think it's either a deer or a human being and shoot. It's up to him to be sure it's a deer before he shoots, or he'll be in court for manslaughter.

"Isn't it logical that if we don't know exactly when a fetus becomes a living soul, a human being, we have no right to terminate its life on the chance that it may not be human yet?"

I am convinced that the legalization of abortion on demand has opened a Pandora's box of evil upon the United States, and that the silence of many Christians, especially Christian physicians, and churches is sinful—a condoning of evil.

Not speaking too strongly, Dr. R. G. Hammerton-Kelly, dean of chapel at Stanford University, put it this way: "In the time of Adolf Hitler—you must understand me, I know that arguments by historical analogy are very difficult—we do not ask of a church of that time, how was your singles' program? We do not ask of the church of that time, what was the quality, what was the intellectual quality of your preaching, how many books did your clergy produce? We ask only one thing: where did you stand when they led away your brothers and sisters? Where did you stand? Well, it is in those terms I'm afraid that I have come rather reluctantly to see this [abortion] issue."

—And I.

Who Are We to Judge?

Is the Gate widening, or are we just not taking God's Word seriously anymore?
November 1982

A man who is separated from his wife writes a book that presents a new view of divorce—a view that permits it today for the same reason God permitted it in the Old Testament: the hardness of His people's hearts. The man is respected; the book is accepted. In fact it is welcomed by one of our most conservative evangelical periodicals, which headlines the review, "Remarriage as God's Gift." Calling the book "monumental," the reviewer summarizes the new doctrine as "God's gracious action in permitting us to sin, then forgiving us and giving us another chance to succeed." And how many chances? Two, three, five?

Another man writes a book on how Christians should have a caring attitude toward others. He's divorced. Others continue in positions of leadership, including youth work, after divorce and remarriage.

The reviewer of the book I alluded to earlier says that "evangelical thinking about divorce has been cast in concrete since the early 50s, with the works of John Murray, Guy Duty, and Charles Ryrie forming the basic framework for that thinking." I wonder why he only went back thirty years instead of to Jesus' teaching in the New Testament. Surely Christian thinking about divorce was cast in concrete then and continued until ten or fifteen years ago when evangelical Christians discovered that divorce with remarriage was acceptable. Subsequently new and exciting (or comforting) discoveries were made by so-called theologians to rationalize the disdain of Christians for the teachings of the Bible.

A similar pattern is displayed in liberation theology, women's theology, black theology, homosexual theology. Maybe I shouldn't lump these together; I am not implying that some of them don't have valid, biblical goals. But they are alike in starting with a problem, a need, a desire, rather than with God; then building a construct that is unbalanced, to support their teaching about that need. If Bible passages have to be explained away or even rejected to support their thesis, so be it.

I remember studying under C. T. Craig, New Testament scholar and *Revised Standard Version* translator at Union Seminary the summer of 1942. The course was "The Pauline Interpretation of the Gospel." For the first few weeks Dr. Craig could not have been more clear in his understanding of the Pauline teaching if he had been teaching at Dallas or Wheaton.

Then, at a critical point in the course, he said, "Up to this time we've been studying what Paul actually said. Now we shall proceed to reinterpret his writings in the light of the twentieth century." From then on he cut down what he had previously built. Saint Paul was "a child of his times"; cultural change necessitated drastic revision of his ideas.

I could not have been persuaded in 1942 that forty years later a respected professor at an evangelical seminary would reject Saint Paul's teaching about gender differences with almost the same words.

How far we've strayed from believing and obeying the Word of God.

The evangelical church is sick—so sick that people are crowding in to join us. We're a big flock, big enough to permit remarriage of divorced people (beyond the exception Jesus allowed), big enough to permit practicing homosexuals to pursue their lifestyle, big enough to tolerate almost anything pagans do. We're no longer narrow; it's the wide road of popular acceptance for us.

"When the Son of man cometh, shall he find faith on the earth?" (Luke 18:8).

That question asked by our Lord haunts me. To me its implications are far more serious than the timetable of His return, over which we spend so much time arguing.

What do I suggest?

First, that we begin to take the Bible seriously again, as God's Word—

God's Word. Not something to hold conferences about, to give lip service to; something to reckon with and to obey.

If we take the Bible seriously, we won't rationalize the parts that convict us of sin—whether the sin of divorce and remarriage, the sin of homosexual relations, the sin of scorning the poor, or the sin of genocide by nuclear weapons.

Somehow we must restore the sacredness of the marriage vows. Maybe there could be two different ceremonies: one for those who have forsworn divorce and remarriage, another for those who consider divorce and remarriage an option "if this doesn't work out." I'd like to see all latter such ceremonies relegated to the county clerk's office.

By revealing my thoughts, by writing these words and submitting them to the editor for publication, I have stepped away seemingly from the tolerant, caring, loving, "who am I to judge?" attitude of many evangelicals, including many of my friends. I'm considered judgmental; I ought to cast the beam out of my own eye (Matt. 7:3-5); I've forgotten to show love; I'm getting old.

To those who consider the latter a valid objection, especially since I've been married to the same person for thirty-nine years, I'd like to say that pressures on marriage are nothing new. Don't think my generation and previous generations were free from the relational, emotional, financial, health, and spiritual problems—including the temptation to commit adultery—that confront you today. We were confronted; some of us had good marriages, some poor ones.

But divorce wasn't an "out" for previous generations of Christians. Maybe that was the reason we honored our promise to stick to our mate for life, "until death us do part."

I like to think that a lot of us were persuaded that we'd made the best choice in the whole world and that nobody else (including young flesh) could be better. And I like to think that we had a bit more concern for our children.

Our Reich of Indifference
June 1984

We castigate the apathy of Christians in Nazi Germany—and ignore our own silence on today's holocaust of abortion.

There is a sin of indifference. It is the sin that binds evangelicals as the Lilliputians bound Gulliver, preventing us from exercising the influence that God has given us in these years—years that are destined to come to an end and may never be repeated.

To me, the outstanding example of indifference is in our reaction to the great sin of abortion that is the shame of our nation. Each year, one-and-a-half million humans who bear the image of God are murdered, many, perhaps most of them, with accompanying great pain to which a group of non-Christian physicians recently attested. The pain is that of poisoning by a saline solution or dismemberment, being torn apart and removed in pieces from the uterus. (In the latter part of the second and in third trimester, this is now the procedure of choice, since it removes the possibility of delivering a viable infant.)

Many Americans who protest Canada's annual seal hunt, in which baby seals are clubbed to death, are the most vociferous in defending a mother's right to have her not-yet-born child killed, with greater pain than the baby seals suffer.

We Christians are indifferent. After all, the Supreme Court of the United States by an eight-member majority condemned these millions to death (by some estimates, seventeen million since *Roe v. Wade* in 1973). As good Christian citizens we accept this as the law of the land.

Our Christian physicians will be judged for their indifference. With notable exceptions the United States medical establishment, including Christians, has been silent about our great national sin.

Why this silence?

According to Father John Powell, Roman Catholic spokesman for the antiabortion movement, the answer is money. "I have heard many doctors say that even if the Supreme Court reverses *Roe v. Wade* and declares abortions illegal, they will continue to perform them. I have never heard a doctor say that he will continue to perform abortions if he is not paid for them."

We blame Christians in Germany during the Third Reich for their indifference to the murder of Jews. "Why were you silent?" we ask.

Someday we will be asked the same question. And a righteous God will not judge the German nation without also judging our nation.

Ironically, in 1975 (two years after our own Supreme Court's decision that a fetus is not a person) West Germany's Federal Constitutional (Supreme) Court firmly stated the unborn child's right to life. Thus the heirs of the Third Reich alone among Western nations that ruled on abortion statutes during a two-year period (United States, Austria, France, Italy, West Germany, and Canada) affirmed the historic, Judeo-Christian position.

Why are we silent, indifferent to the antiabortion movement? (I prefer this to pro-life, just as I'd have preferred an anti-gas oven movement in Germany to a pro-Jewish life movement. We like to turn horrible matters into more pleasant positive statements.)

One reason for our indifference, I believe, is the silence of our preachers. Few are crying out against this great evil, pronouncing judgment on a nation of killers. "After all, we don't want to make a young woman in the congregation who has had an abortion feel guilty."

Maybe a woman should face up to the fact that her action has destroyed a human life—a life totally independent of her own—that was growing within her.

I think another reason is that our priorities are skewed. We emphasize growth in the congregation's size, new buildings, exciting programs; these are the test of our effectiveness. Yet how we'd scorn a German Christian who said, "Let me tell you about the new building we put up and paid for during 1938–40," or "We had such a great singles' program."

Still another reason is the identification many make of the American government, including the Supreme Court, with the kingdom of God, or at least an Old Testament theocracy. The lines have been blurred between God and Caesar. We have a knee-jerk reaction that Caesar's decree is morally and ethically right; this determines our evangelical ideas of morality and spirituality. We're really convinced that God is only concerned about personal morality, and that only as it is related to narrow areas of life. Let the state handle the big issues.

In 1948 I was in Europe for a Christian student camp. One night we were discussing the recently ended war. The group of ten included French, British, and German students, all of whom, except for me, had seen active duty. A German student told about the crucial experience that stood out for him. He had taken a stand against dancing. (Afterward another German student, from the same small evangelical denomination, said he had taken the same stand.)

"I ruined my chances for officers training," the German student said, "because I refused to participate in social dances, which was required of officers. But I had been brought up, in home and church, to believe that dancing is wrong."

Dancing is wrong—but what did they teach you about the murder of Jews? I remember how the thought raced through my mind. Perhaps to my shame, but out of concern for Christian unity and peace in the cabin, I didn't say it aloud.

Are we giving moral training to the teens and young adults—and older adults—in our evangelical churches? Or are we silent as government and television train them—while we're satisfied to guard them from dancing and other similar perils to the soul?

God, forgive our indifference. Make us burn with white heat against injustice, especially the destruction of the weak and totally vulnerable, who bear your divine image.

The End of an Era
October 1985 [1]

Remember that the greatest strides in Christianity's history—the first-century church—were taken when the church had no money or property.

[1] *Editor's Note:* This month Joseph Bayly began his twenty-fifth year of writing "Out of My Mind."

My generation of evangelical Christians is in the process of passing the torch to the next generation. Thus it has always been in the church; thus it will always be until our Lord returns.

The end of World War II brought a fresh impetus to Christian activity and leadership in this country. Our torch-passing forty years later therefore represents a more distinct period of time than many other less clearly defined transitions in the past. It is the end of an era.

This is a good time to consider the inheritance we received from those who passed the torch to us, and the inheritance we are bequeathing to those who will stand for evangelical principles and serve our Lord during the next forty years.

If I were to suggest a broad generalization, it would be that we were pioneers and our successors are the settlers.

I write as an observer of the evangelical scene, a participant in some of the movements. Many of my contemporaries will see things differently; they may be right and I may be wrong. But here are my impressions, my interim report on the stewardship exercised by my generation.

I present this report in terms of what we received from our predecessors, including our children.

Storefronts and Liberals

We inherited a religious scene dominated by liberals; we bequeath liberalism in shambles.

We inherited a Berlin Wall between evangelical Christians and Roman Catholics; we bequeath a spirit of love and rapprochement on the basis of the Bible rather than fear and hatred.

We inherited 11,000 overseas missionaries; we bequeath 40,000.

We inherited a church torn by strife and schism. We bequeath a church in which healing and reunion have taken place.

We inherited a reputation for anti-intellectualism; we bequeath a generation of scholars and scholarly work.

We inherited aging church buildings, plus some storefronts and roofed-over basements—construction started but interrupted by the Great Depression. As a result of the biggest church-building boom in history, we bequeath a treasure of up-to-date properties and facilities.

We inherited a handful of poor, struggling Christian colleges. We bequeath a score of accredited institutions of higher education.

We inherited three or four small independent seminaries; we bequeath nine or ten healthy institutions that are the major source of trained evangelical leadership for America's churches and parachurch movements.

We inherited one national youth movement—Christian Endeavor, working through the local church—and a Sunday evening young people's meeting, often attended by adults. We bequeath a sophisticated understanding of teens and young adults applied within the local church and outside the church by thousands of professionals. Parachurch youth organizations we founded include Youth for Christ, Young Life, InterVarsity Christian Fellowship, and Campus Crusade for Christ.

In other areas of the churches' concern, we inherited denominational, church-centered programs for children, youth, and adults. We bequeath Child Evangelism Fellowship, Christian Service Brigade, Pioneer Ministries, Christian Business Men's Committee, Bible Study Fellowship, Neighborhood Bible Studies, Christian Medical Society, Christian Legal Society, Nurses' Christian Fellowship, and many other parachurch programs.

We inherited *Christian Herald* and the *Sunday School Times*, rather quaint magazines with limited circulation, that looked shabby next to *Time* or the *Saturday Evening Post.* We bequeath more than a hundred periodicals with a circulation of many millions that don't look strange next to the secular magazines on the coffee table.

We inherited scattered local radio programs, while the rest of religious radio—except for Charles E. Fuller's "Old Fashioned Revival Hour"—was monopolized by the National Council of Churches. We bequeath an end to the monopoly (and the National Council's power), innumerable local radio and television programs, several networks, many independent stations, and an electronic church that takes in $500 million a year.

We inherited camp and conference facilities that were as primitive as the motels of those earlier days. We bequeath many more camps and conferences, as modern as today's resorts, with professional leadership.

We inherited a few publishers and several hundred bookstores. We bequeath a hundred publishers and five thousand bookstores.

Looking at that list, I wonder at all that God has done through His weak, failing people during the past forty years. "This is the Lord's doing; it is marvelous in our eyes" (Ps. 118:23).

But the bequests are not all good.

Success Here and Now

We inherited the integrity of marriage and the family; we bequeath a new permissiveness toward divorce and a new pattern of single-parent families.

We inherited a clearly defined, biblical value system; we bequeath shattered values.

We inherited belief in the humanness of unborn babies and the criminality of murdering them in the uterus. We bequeath an unending American Holocaust of 19 million corpses, increasing at the rate of 1.5 million a year. We also bequeath a general unconcern among evangelical Christians.

We inherited doctrinal, expository preaching with a heavy emphasis on prophecy. We bequeath relational preaching with a heavy emphasis on success here and now.

We inherited leaders who spoke out against evil in society and the church; we bequeath leaders who are specialists in public relations and fundraising.

We inherited a four-week Daily Vacation Bible School; we bequeath one-week schools or the end of DVBS.

We inherited deep distrust of commercial entertainment, typified by sanctions against movie-going. We bequeath acceptance of every kind of entertainment in the living room, available to children. (But we also bequeath a Christian entertainment industry.)

We inherited Christians who were loyal to the church, consistent in their living, and restrained in talking about their faith. We bequeath Christians who are loyal to many religious organizations in addition to—sometimes in preference to—their church, who are less concerned about consistent living, and who have been taught to talk constantly about their faith.

We inherited homes and churches that were patriarchal, overseas missions that were to a large extent matriarchal. We bequeath an unsolved problem of reconciling the Bible with cultural change in the role of women.

We inherited the Lord's Day as a day of rest. We bequeath a completely secularized Sunday.

We inherited family togetherness and activities; we bequeath age-level activities and small groups in the church.

We inherited government friendly toward the church and a church uninvolved in government. We bequeath government hostile toward the church and the church enmeshed in politics and civil religion.

We Cannot Program God

What do I think the agenda for the new generation of leaders should be?

It may surprise you, but I don't think an agenda is advisable, even possible, for the evangelical Christian movement.

Looking at my list of positive bequests above, I'm impressed with the lack of long-range planning shown by the various developments.

Certainly there was little interrelatedness among them, except that one person's step of faith encouraged another to exercise similar faith. Or it may be more accurate to say that the Holy Spirit's blessing in certain areas led to expectations of like blessing in others.

For instance, Jim Rayburn and Stacey Woods were at small Dallas Seminary at the same time. Rayburn's success with high school kids may have led Woods to undertake a university movement. And the recent risk taken by the founders of that seminary may have affected both of them.

In a similar manner, a rash of overseas missionary societies arose after World War II. (Servicemen had been exposed to foreign cultures and observed at firsthand the needs.) Each new society encouraged others to take the plunge.

We cannot program the Holy Spirit. Where He wills, He works.

We also cannot program such factors as the economy, government, taxes, and public—or Christian—response.

The public may turn on evangelical Christianity, especially if government policies supported by evangelicalism's self-appointed spokesmen fail.

The government may become increasingly hostile toward the church, private Christian colleges, and other institutions.

Taxation may force us to sell many of our properties. There is no guarantee against persecution by the time the new generation stands with the forty-year perspective from which I write—in the year 2025.

Rather than an agenda, I suggest several attitudes to our heirs based on our experience.

Fresh Risks; Old Faith

Don't avoid risks. You are settlers rather than pioneers; therefore the risks may be different—and greater. The ramifications of making a wrong decision increase as the organization grows. More is at stake. But risk is a concomitant of faith.

Watch out for a temptation to consider the universe as within the province of your organization. I see this tendency already in organizations which started out with a specific objective: Navigators, InterVarsity Christian Fellowship, Campus Crusade for Christ, and electronic churches, for instance.

Attempts at monopoly are even more dangerous in Christian work than in secular business. An effective money machine may be Satan's provision rather than the Holy Spirit's direction.

Constantly aim at increasing the degree of lay involvement, even if it means cutting down the number of professional workers. Laypersons, if trained, have an "in" that professionals usually lack. Further, if the time comes when professionals are excluded because of government decree or lack of financing, laypersons can carry on the work.

Guard the doctrinal and spiritual integrity that has been bequeathed to you. Keep the faith with previous generations in this area above all others.

Institutions, like individuals, grow middle- and old-aged. Avoid this not only by taking fresh risks, but by trusting younger leadership.

Rather than increasing organizational/institutional lands and goods, ask what you can do without, what alternatives exist to the expenditure of funds for capital growth. Good stewards do not dream up ways to spend money just because the money machine can produce it. Remember that the greatest strides in Christianity's history—the first-century church—were taken when the church was unencumbered by money and property. Maybe, just maybe, there's an organization somewhere that will say to its constituency, "We're satisfied with our headquarters building, the size of our staff. Yes, we're a bit crowded and could use more space; yes, we could figure out where to place more staff. But give your money to digging wells and sending agriculturists to Africa."

In this passing of the torch, this changing of the guard, I commend you to the God of all grace, the never-changing One. May He give you grace, wisdom, humility, and courage.

When the Nazis invaded the Netherlands, some villagers asked the local medical doctor what they should do.

"Before the invading army we must be as lions," he replied, "before God as worms."

Great advice.

Rome Fell While Moralists Slept
January 1986

Like environmentalists fighting for laws for clean air, we have the right to fight for laws against moral pollution.

"You can't legislate morality" has become the battle cry of libertarians in recent years whenever Christians have forsaken their trenches and spoken up for moral principles as a basis for civil laws.

Abortion, homosexuality, pornography—even prostitution—have been defended against any attack with those words.

Sadly, many Christians have accepted the argument and become silent about these evils. So the trenches are full of sleeping moralists, and victory has been won by fighting libertarians.

You may not be able to legislate morality, but our country has certainly legislated its approval of immorality. (This seems to me to be a close parallel to the total exclusion of Christian religion from public schools and the total freedom of expression given to advocates of agnostic religion—some call it secular humanism.)

And so we have seen homosexuality and abortion decriminalized during the past twenty years. Prostitution is legal in much of Nevada. Only child sexual abuse and pornography—though on public display, even in neighborhood convenience stores—are illegal. Even here libertarians are fighting for the right of adults to introduce children to sexual experience. Attacks on laws against incest are frequent. After all, we're told, with new birth control methods the danger of genetic anomalies is practically eliminated, so what's the harm. "You can't legislate morality in the home, of all places."

Besides, why should Christians force their moral ideas on the whole population through laws? Here's why.

1. We believe that there is such a thing as moral pollution, a climate of decadence that characterized Rome and other civilizations in their declining years. As good citizens we have the right—even the responsibility—to fight for laws that will prohibit prostitution, pornography, abortion, homosexuality, and other evils. We have the responsibility to provide a safe moral climate for our children and grandchildren to grow up in. This right is as clear as that of environmentalists to fight for laws that will insure clean air, water, and soil for present and future generations.

2. There are public consequences of the private acts of "consenting adults." A prime example of this is AIDS. Open sewers lead to typhoid epidemics; homosexual practices have led to the AIDS epidemic.

I'm troubled when I read statistics that are aimed at exonerating homosexuals for the AIDS epidemic. Users of contaminated needles, hemophiliacs, and heterosexuals—not just homosexuals—are spreading the fatal disease, we're told. But where does the virus come from that infects those innocent parties—even babies? Homosexuals. That there should be any question about closing public bathhouses in New York or San Francisco, places where homosexuals engage in promiscuous sex, angers me. This is as much a matter of public health as prohibiting drainage of sewage into our cities' gutters.

Further, we Christians are paying for the epidemic homosexuals have introduced with our tax and health-insurance dollars. No one has come forward with statistics related to the escalating cost of this disease. This would seem harsh and unsympathetic toward sufferers, as do my words. Sympathy and understanding have become prime virtues in our society. Do any citizens, including Christians, have the right to object to the decriminalization of a lifestyle that carries such heavy costs in human tragedy and economic loss?

3. From a Christian standpoint (but remember that Christians are also citizens of a democracy), we cannot escape the words of Jesus Christ about nations being judged. The United States is our nation as surely as Germany during the Third Reich was German Christians' nation. Silence before the slaughter of Jews, silence before the slaughter of the unborn; either one, we believe, lays us open to the judgment of God. Therefore we have a duty to influence legislation and the courts by our murmurings, or thunderings, and voting.

4. The prohibition of alcohol in the twenties is usually the example used to prove the dictum, "You can't legislate morality." I'm not sure Prohibition was really a "noble experiment" that failed. It failed with the sophisticated and wealthy; I'm not sure it failed equally with the poor and middle class.

Regardless, I'd prefer the abolition of slavery rather than Prohibition as an example of moral change brought about by Christians. Nobody calls the war that brought freedom to slaves a holy war. Yet that freedom was a direct result of Christian intransigence in the face of a great social evil, a moral blot on our nation.

The writings of Jonathan Blanchard, first president of Wheaton College, reveal this intransigence, this unwillingness to accept half a loaf. In fact, he scorned any sort of compromise with slaveholders.

We have become a compromising Christian community to such an extent that we are now compromised. We invite proponents of "evangelical" practicing homosexuality to speak at our training institutions and sacred assemblies. We seriously propose compromise on the abortion issue rather than excise the evil.

You can't legislate morality? Tell that to William Wilberforce, or to William Lloyd Garrison. It will have to be in heaven, unfortunately, when we're rationalizing our own inaction toward the evils of our times. "Had we lived then," we'll say, "we'd have stood with you."

Jesus said it: We dedicate memorials to dead prophets and kill living ones on our way home from the cemetery (Matt. 23:29-34).

Comforting the Afflicted

Originally published in 1966 and entitled Three Sons.

When a Child Dies

OUR FIRST CHILD was a boy, born on Valentine's Day, 1945. When he was four years old, a mild hemophilia of the Christmas type was diagnosed.

Just before his sixth birthday, Joe nearly died after surgery. At the time there was widespread praying for him among our Christian friends, and God gave him back to us in full health. (The means: a young pediatrician, not on the case, who came to me after two weeks and said, "Professional ethics be hanged. If you leave your boy in this hospital, he'll die. They've given up on him. I suggest you transfer him immediately to Children's Hospital.")

When he was in high school, Joe wrote about something that happened less than a year after that hospital experience: "When I reached the age of seven, I began to examine my actions. It seemed that I was living in a way which was displeasing to God. I was doing things in school and hiding them from my parents, and was pretty miserable.

"At this point, portions of the Bible which I had been taught from a very young age came into play. I thought of Christ's claims of lordship upon a redeemed life, and wondered if I had ever faced up to this decision to accept Christ as Savior and Lord. I finally decided that if I hadn't, I was going to. So I made the decision then.

"I cannot say that there was any immediate, radical change in my life. I did not have a rosy glow inside, and my teacher at school didn't immediately notice a difference. However, things did change. Gradually, I found I wanted to do the right thing more often. Gradually, I found that the feelings of others meant more to me. But most important of all, I began to see God at work."

Three years later, when Joe was ten, we found that his younger brother, Danny, who was four at the time, had leukemia. If ever there was a child who brought joy to a family, it was Danny, who had been described by a German student visiting in our home as a "little he-angel." Joe and eight-year-old Debbie were crushed at the thought that Danny might not come home from the hospital.

"It's like something is pinned to the front of your mind all the time," Debbie said.

But Danny did come home, and then the children joined us in a prayer that we believed was of faith, that God would heal him. Again, Christian friends across the country prayed: some for Danny's healing, all for our stability and strength as a family.

One night early that fall Danny was anointed for healing (James 5:14-15) in a simple service in our living room in suburban Philadelphia. Joe and Debbie, although they were in bed, knew of the anointing and of our firm belief that God would heal Danny. Timmy, who was three, was too young to know.

And our children weren't the only ones who knew of our confidence. I remember talking late one night with a young resident physician at Children's Hospital. I had been trying to share Jesus Christ with him, for he was not a Christian.

"If your boy didn't die of leukemia, do you know what we'd do?'" he asked, leaning on the crib as we looked down at the small figure. "We'd work and study until we found out why he didn't die like all the rest. We'd never believe it was God." He didn't say it unkindly.

After Danny returned home from the hospital he had eight months of almost normal health. Then, one morning in March—while Joe and Debbie were still asleep, he began to bleed. It was a hopeless, slow hemorrhage. The children left for school; the doctor came and left, and Mary Lou and I talked about Jesus and heaven with our almost-five-year-old, who even before his illness had wanted to be a missionary.

Joe's diary entry for that day explains what happened after that: "At about 2 p.m., something told me to pray for Danny. When I got home from school, I discovered that he had died just then! Debbie and I went up to the bedroom and saw him. The undertaker took him. We went and looked at a burial ground for four of the family. After we all ate (Daddy arranged for the funeral), a lot of people came over and we read the Bible, sang and prayed."

And two days later his diary entry was this: "Today we had Danny's funeral. There were a lot of flowers. The coffin was white. The service was a blessing. Then we went to see the grave. It was very unhappy, but Danny is with God. After we got home, Jerry Sterrett and I played ball in the yard."

About nine months later, John was born. A congenital condition required surgery before twenty-four hours. Eighteen days later, just after Christmas, he died. The autopsy revealed no cause of the condition. When Joe was just starting to high school, David was born. In Joe's junior year, our new baby Nathan had the same condition with which John had been born. In his case, however, the surgery was successful. But the diagnosis was cystic fibrosis.

Joe's reaction to all that had happened in his life and our home is in the same high school paper in which be told of trusting Jesus Christ at the age of seven. "The main reason I am a Christian today is that I have seen God at work. I have seen Him work in my life, in the lives of my family, and in the lives of my friends. I have seen Him work in extremely practical ways, such as the provision of money; I have seen Him work in quiet ways changing lives. I've seen Him work in ways which were unpleasant to me, but through which I could tell He was trying to teach me lessons. I've seen and heard of His working in direct answer to prayer. And I have the greatest peace within me which comes from seeing God work, and knowing that He's working on my behalf and is taking complete care of me."

In his senior year Joe qualified as a National Merit Scholarship finalist. He had to write a brief paragraph about himself, this would be one factor in the decision about a scholarship. His paragraph began, "My chief aim in life is to glorify the Lord Jesus Christ by whatever I do." I almost suggested that he rewrite that sentence—I wanted him to get a scholarship. Thank God I was silent.

He received the scholarship and went to Swarthmore College. There he was known as a Christian, a rather good philosophy student, and a rather slow cross-country runner. Like most college students, Joe was coming to certain conclusions. In a letter to the girl he loved, and with whom he planned to serve Jesus Christ overseas, he wrote: "I simply fail to see what there is to look forward to in a job and a car, or anything of the sort for that matter, as long-range goals. It seems to me that (for me, at least) the only thing worth doing with one's life is some sort of Christian service. Other things (such as the cycle I rebuilt last summer) come in as secondary reinforcements, and even sometimes interfere, I guess, but I would really be lost if I didn't have some such thing to look forward to. I just cannot see anything worth wanting in the prospect of a job with salary, however big, a suburban house, etc., etc. I know that such people can be used of the Lord, but I feel quite sure that I couldn't be, with my temperament. Somehow, all I can see in that is a primary allegiance to the job, and giving God part of my spare time. I know this isn't so, but it seems to me to be a losing struggle to do two things at once, and a life that leads to increasing comfort, narrowness of viewpoint, complacency, as one goes on in it. As you can see, I think it is probably harder to be a Christian businessman than a Christian missionary."

On another occasion, Joe wrote: "One must get out of one's head that service to God is the pleasantest thing on earth. One must also rid himself of any idea that service to God can be put on and taken off at will. I think we need more emphasis today upon the sternness of God's commands, the all-embracing character of the Christian life—in short, the cost of discipleship."

On Christmas Day 1963 Joe had a sledding accident. When I saw him he said, "Dad, I'm ready to die." But we didn't expect him to die. (His maternal grandfather, with a prolonged bleeding time of the same intensity, was then in his middle seventies.) We prayed that he would live, and many, many Christian friends joined us in that prayer.

Two weeks later I stood at his side and said the Twenty-third Psalm, as I had in the moment when we thought death was overtaking him thirteen years before—only this time death really came—violent, awful death.

As Joe wrote when Danny died, for those who loved him it couldn't have been more unhappy. Yet for him it was entrance into life with the God he loved and served.

Moses once prayed, "Show me now thy ways, that I may know thee."

God answered, for the psalmist says, "He made known his ways to Moses, his acts to the people of Israel."

During these thirteen uncertain years, which continue into the future for our youngest, we have been concerned lest we see only God's acts and miss His ways—the revealing of His divine character and purpose toward His children.

What ways of God have we seen?

1. God is sovereign. Our peace is not in understanding everything that happens to us and our children, but in knowing that He is in control of sickness and health and even death itself. We accept life's mysteries and sufferings unexplained because they are known to God, and we know Him. Of course we seek answers from the Bible and from experience, our own and that of others. But when no answer is forthcoming, we don't attempt to rationalize ("It could have been worse," "Look at how many people heard the Gospel through the funeral service," or "Things are getting so bad on earth; think of what he's been spared not growing up"). Reason, we believe, is a deceptively weak crutch for faith. Reason gropes in the dark for answers, while faith waits for God.

2. God is love. We have never been more convinced of His love for us and our children than when we have turned from a fresh grave.

3. We have seen God's love reflected in His people at times of crisis and loss. Christian doctors have been unusual sources of strength. Some have seemed to understand suffering to a depth foreign to most other Christians, even including some ministers. We have come to love several doctors who are not yet Christians who have also been examples of selfless devotion to our children's welfare.

4. We believe that God's primary work, for our children and for us, is not to shield us from suffering but to conform us to the image of Christ. And like Him (mystery beyond comprehension), we also learn obedience through the things we suffer.

5. We believe that God is pleased when His children are identified with the world in suffering, and that the Christian response to suffering is a powerful testimony to the reality of the Christian Gospel.

6. We believe that our response is more the work of God's Spirit than our own.

7. We believe that God's primary work in the world today is not world evangelization but the conforming of His children to the image of Christ. Some of the most godly young men and women we have known, the most concerned for soul-winning and foreign missions—including Joe—have been called Home at an early age rather than given long lives here to serve God. We believe that His work in them was finished, sooner than for most of us.

8. We consider it strange that Christians claim to believe that heaven—being present with God—is so wonderful, and yet act as if going there were the greatest tragedy.

9. We believe that death will someday be destroyed, but it is still a painful experience which all of us must face. We believe that some Christians may have idealistic views of deathbed rapture and be unprepared for this enemy's grim violence. God has not promised His children an easy death or deathbed visions of glory. He has promised an open door beyond.

Joe and Mary Lou Bayly were intimate with death, losing three of their children in their first two decades of marriage. Out of those losses came a book, first published under the title, The View from a Hearse, *but later titled* The Last Thing We Talk About. *First published in 1969, here are excerpts of that work.*

The Last Thing We Talk About

The Predictable Event

THE HEARSE BEGAN its grievous journey many thousand years ago, as a litter made of saplings.

Litter, sled, wagon, Cadillac: the conveyance has changed, but the corpse it carries is the same.

Birth and death enclose man in a sort of parenthesis of the present. And the brackets at the beginning and end of life are still impenetrable.

This frustrates us, especially in a time of scientific breakthrough and exploding knowledge, that we should be able to break out of earth's environment and yet be stopped cold by death's unyielding mystery. Electroencephalogram may replace mirror held before the mouth, autopsies may become more sophisticated, cosmetic embalming may take the place of pennies on the eyelids and canvas shrouds, but death continues to confront us with its blank wall. Everything changes; death is changeless.

We may postpone it, we may tame its violence, but death is still there waiting for us.

Death always waits. The door of the hearse is never closed.

Dairy farmer and sales executive live in death's shadow, with Nobel prize winner and prostitute, mother, infant, teen, old man. The hearse stands waiting for the surgeon who transplants a heart as well as the hopeful recipient, for the funeral director as well as the corpse he manipulates.

Death spares none.

The certainty of death, and of participation with all mankind in this terminal event, might be a source of individual security. But it is not. It is rather the focus of man's insecurity and fear, his inability to be completely sure of anything on earth because he cannot be sure of drawing his next breath, or the one after.

What is death?

In the spring of 1957, I sat in the waiting room of Dr. Irving Wolman, hematologist at Philadelphia Children's Hospital. The day before, we had buried our almost-five year old, who had died of leukemia. Now I was waiting to thank the man who had been so kind to our little boy and to us during the nine months between diagnosis and death.

Dr. Wolman's secretary beckoned to me. When I approached her desk, she did not tell me, as I expected, that the doctor would now see me. Instead, she looked toward a little boy playing on the floor. In my preoccupation I had failed to notice any others in the waiting room.

"He has the same problem your little boy had." The secretary spoke quietly.

I sat down next to the little boy's mother. We were far enough away from him, and we talked softly enough, that he could not hear us.

"It's hard bringing him in here every two weeks for these tests, isn't it." I didn't ask a question: I stated a fact. The uncertainty whether a child is still in remission or the fearful cells will reappear under the microscope makes the mind run wild.

"Hard?" She was silent for a moment. "I die every time. And now he's beginning to sense that something's wrong. . . ." Her voice trailed off.

"It's good to know, isn't it," I spoke slowly, choosing my words with unusual care, "that even though the medical outlook is hopeless, we can have hope for our children in such a situation. We can be sure that after our child dies, he'll be completely removed from sickness and suffering and everything like that, and be completely well and happy."

"If I could only believe that," the woman replied. "But I don't. When he dies, I'll just have to cover him up with dirt and forget I ever had him." She turned back to watching her little boy push a toy auto on the floor.

"I'm glad I don't feel that way." I didn't want to say it, I wanted to leave her alone with her apprehension. I wanted to be alone with my grief. But I was compelled to speak—perhaps with the same compulsion that made me write this book.

"Why?" This time she didn't turn toward me, but kept watching her child.

"Because we covered our little boy up with dirt yesterday afternoon. I'm in here to thank Dr. Wolman for his kindness today."

"You look like a rational person." (I was glad she didn't say, "I'm sorry.") She was looking straight at me now. "How can you possibly believe that the death of a man, or a little boy, is any different from the death of an animal?"

Death's True Colors

Each spring the road that goes north from our home in Illinois has a succession of animals that have been struck by automobiles. You pass dog, cat, muskrat, and mole, as well as masses of unrecognizable fur, flesh, and gore, all cold and motionless.

One day a bird struck the windshield of my car as I was driving at high speed. The flash of blue hit with a sound I hear now and then was tossed aside.

I felt pity for the bird, as I have felt pity for dead animals on the road: one moment graceful, beautiful, flying, singing, scurrying, burrowing; the next moment dead.

There is something unnatural and grotesque, even wrong, about death.

I think that if we were confronted only with the death of animals, if human beings never died, we would still have a problem. Perhaps it would not be moral (although a ton of metal, under my control, against an ounce or two of bird would seem to involve morality), but it would certainly be an aesthetic problem.

Death destroys beauty.

Violent death creates obscenity—tasteless, horrid, raw.

We cannot beautify death. We may live with it and accept it, but we cannot change its foul nature.

The Apostle Paul spoke of death as an enemy, "the last enemy to be destroyed." Death is the enemy of God, of man made in God's image, or animal with which man shares flesh, blood, nerve endings.

When the automobile's victim is human, when a child not a bird, a man not a mole lies dead on the road, we see the true nature of death, the dimension of the problem.

We see death's colors when an ounce of metal explodes in Robert F. Kennedy's brain, in Martin Luther King, Jr.'s, neck. Images of the dying leaders etch our memory core beyond smashed bird or crushed animal, infinitely beyond, as human potential is terminated so suddenly, so terribly, so early.

Beauty destroyed by ten pills, achievement terminated by a seven-story fall, youth's glory ended by a grenade, women and children charred by napalm; there are the faces of death.

Coronary, cancer, stroke, infection. Death comes even normally, in a multitude of ways to every human condition, every age.

Shall we deny death and try to make it beautiful?

A corpse is never beautiful, animal corpse or corpse of man.

Death is an offense to beauty; no embalmer's art can possibly restore it.

We may soften the horror of death by honoring the corpse. We may patch it up, preserve it, dress it in going-away clothes, place it on a restful couch, surround it with flowers, arrange the pink, pale lights, burn it or bury it.

But disposing of the body does not provide a satisfying answer to the mystery of death, at least for most people.

Nor for humanity's thinkers, who have pondered the subject since the beginning. Socrates held that the essence of philosophy is preparation for death. Before Socrates, the Old Testament Book of Job described death as "the king of terrors." King David put it bluntly: "The terrors of death have fallen upon me. Fear and trembling come upon me, and horror overwhelms me."

Death's horror is universal.

Surprisingly, one of the two events common to every human being's existence has been considered unnatural by every generation of man, including our own.

What is it about death that creates this unnatural horror in us?

For one thing, death is the supreme enigma. We cannot explain its mystery and the unknown makes us fear. This mystery is greatest in a generation whose stance toward death is denial.

Another element of death that is unnatural, and makes us dread, is the pain that frequently accompanies dying. Pain may be extended over a long period of time, or it may be sudden and overwhelming. But it's a part of death.

Then there's the termination of every human relationship. This termination may be quite abrupt, providing no opportunity to set affairs in order. Death is the great interrupter.

Decomposition of the body is another element of death that contributes to our sense of dread. We spend a lifetime caring for our bodies; it is hardly pleasant to contemplate a time when they will return to dust.

In spite of death's endless repetition, it is still not natural. Nor will it ever be.

"Why Would a Kind God . . . ?"

A letter posed the question for me. But the problem was already there, in my own experience, years before the letter came.

The woman wrote from a small town in the East: "On January 25th, 1973, in Memorial Hospital, John Riso, red-haired, laughing, tall, eighteen, tractor-driving, cow-scratching, flirtatious, shy, died after two and a half years of leukemia. After six weeks of a raging temperature, experimental drugs, bleeding, and an abscess in his rectum that became gangrenous, he died soft and gentle, finally, after six hours of violent death throes. His face so thin, his hair only a memory, a soft red fuzz, arms blue and green from shots and intravenous feeding, he looked like an old picture of a saint after his tortures were over . . .

"Why would a kind God do what was done to John, or do such a thing to me? I am poor, have only secondhand furniture and clothing. The things of value were my husband and sons. All our lives we have struggled to make ends meet. How can I live with the memory of the agony he suffered? Part of the time he was in a coma, and he kept saying, 'Mama, help me. Mama, help me.' I couldn't and it's killing me. I whispered in his ear, 'John, I love you so much.' All of a sudden his arm came up stiffly and fell across my back, and very quietly he said, from some vast depth, 'Me too.'"

There's the question: "Why would a kind God do what was done to John, or do such a thing to me?" Who has not asked it in the hours and days of suffering, of watching one close to his heart suffer?

I find no easy answer. Nor, probably, do you.

But finding none, we are in good company. Old Testament Job was in the dark too, when all his children died a violent death. And a great theologian, Charles Hodge, said that if anyone thinks he has a simple solution to the problem of suffering, he should hold an infant screaming with pain in his arms, and any simple solution will fly out the window.

But somehow we start with the fact, admitted by the woman who wrote to me, that God is kind. Strangely, we continue to believe in His kindness, in spite of evidence that would seem to lead to a contrary conclusion.

Moses once prayed, "Show me now thy ways, that I may know thee" (Exodus 33:13). And God answered, for the psalmist says, "He made known his ways to Moses, his acts to the people of Israel" (Psalm 103:7).

Many people, like the Israelites at the time of the Exodus, are only interested in the acts of God. But the ones who want an answer to the problem of suffering must get behind and beyond the acts of God, as Moses did, and discern His way.

God is sovereign. This is where we begin to answer our questions. Our peace is not in understanding everything that happens to us and our children, but in knowing that He is in control of sickness and health, and even death itself. We accept life's mysteries and sufferings unexplained because they are known to God, and we know Him. Of course we seek answers from the Bible and from experience, our own and that of others. But when no answer is forthcoming, we don't attempt to rationalize. ("It could have been worse," "Look at how many people heard the Gospel through the funeral service," or "Things are getting so bad on earth; think of what he's been spared by not growing up.") Reason, we believe, is a deceptively weak crutch for faith. Reason gropes in the dark for answers, while faith waits for God.

But we also believe that God is love. He is kind; "He does not lightly afflict the children of men" (Lam. 3:33). I cannot explain it, but my wife and I have never been more convinced of His love for us and our children than when we have turned from a fresh grave.

Jesus wept with the suffering sisters of Lazarus, who had died. He suffered anguish of the soul the night before His execution; He cried, "My God, My God, why have You forsaken Me?" on the cross. He shared our humanity, our grief, our pain. But He also taught that God is sovereign, and He was the personification of His love on earth.

Here is the mystery: the kind and sovereign God permits suffering and agony.

One thing we must remember is that His is not "the best of all possible worlds." It is a world in rebellion against the kind God, a world of evil and sin and pain. It is a world, as Jesus explained, where God's Enemy is at work.

In such a world, it is easy to forget God, to live only to enjoy the banquet hall without thinking about the painful exit door. But God will not permit this. He interrupts the banquet with suffering. "God whispers to us in our pleasures," C.S. Lewis wrote in *The Problem of Pain*, "speaks in our conscience, but shouts in our pain. Pain is God's megaphone to rouse a deaf world."

We believe that in this world of evil, God's primary work, for our children and for us, is not to shield us from suffering, but to conform us to the image of Jesus Christ. And like Him (mystery beyond comprehension), we also learn obedience through the things we suffer.

God intends life to be character building, and to this end He brings His people, the people He loves, into suffering situations. This was true of Job, although he was in the dark the whole time of his agony. A Christian response to suffering is a powerful testimony to the reality of Christian faith.

Death will someday be destroyed, but it is still a most painful experience which all of us must face. Many religious people have idealistic views of deathbed rapture and are unprepared for this enemy's grim violence. God has not promised His children an easy death, or deathbed visions of glory (although sometimes He may give them). He has promised an open door beyond.

Helmut Thielicke, contemporary German theologian, gives the final word, the answer to those who see in such a death as that of the "tractor-driving, cow-scratching" young man absurdity or meaningless suffering. *In Death and Life,* he writes a "letter to a soldier about death."

I do not want to close this long letter, dear comrade and brother, without opening to you yet one last perspective. Luther says in similar situations that only He who inflicts the wounds and permits them is able also to heal them. No one else. Illusions about death cannot do this; neither can hushed silence on the subject. Even the atheistic method of easy dying effects no healing; it only teaches how to bleed to death without looking. It proclaims the demise of an impersonal collective entity, not the end of a human being who is wrenched from just such anonymity when he is called by his name to be God's possession. No, God alone can heal the wound because He is the one who has inflicted it. Only He can heal it whose love reveals to us— so painfully and yet with such joy and promise—"the infinite value of the human soul." . . . I am one whose history with God cannot stop, since I am called by my name and I am the friend of Jesus. The Resurrected One is victorious and I stand within His sphere of power. Once more it is His "alien" life with which I am in fellowship and which brings me through everything and receives me on the other side of the gloomy grave. It is not the intrinsic quality of my soul nor something supposedly immortal within me that brings me through. No, it is this Wanderer who marches at my side as Lord and Brother and who can no more abandon me on the other side than He could let me out of His hand here on this side of the grave.

Two Kinds of Death

The Bible describes death in various ways. It is "being gathered to one's people," "taking down the tent," "sleeping with the fathers," "departure," "dissolution of one's earthly house," and "rest."

These descriptions are for the event of dying and what follows.

The Bible uses the same word, death, to describe man's spiritual condition. We are "dead in trespasses and sins" according to the Apostle Paul. Death is a state of sin and darkness in which all men are alienated from God, the Fountain of life and light.

Used in this sense, death represents God's judgment for our rebellion against Him—our refusal to admit that we are creatures responsible to the Creator—and for our sin. (But physical death is part of the judgment. God condemned the first man for his disobedience with these words: "You are dust, and to dust you shall return.")

At the time Jesus Christ was born, according to Saint Luke, the world was sitting "in darkness and in the shadow of death" (Luke 1:79). Jesus described His mission in this way: "I came that they may have life, and have it abundantly" (John 10:10). And He made a great claim for Himself, related to death: "I am the resurrection and the life; he who believes in me, though he die, yet shall he live" (John 11:25).

By His own death on the cross for our sins, and by His resurrection, Jesus Christ has brought life to men who were dead in rebellious sin. This life is available to all who turn to Him and put their trust in Him.

Therefore when we begin the life of faith in Christ, Saint Paul says that we "arise from the dead" and become "alive to God."

We will someday die, like everyone else, but the enemy has been conquered; we have no fear of God's judgment in the afterlife. For that judgment was already suffered by Jesus Christ in His own death "for our sins."

Death then becomes for us, in the words of King David, "the valley of the shadow." Beyond the valley is unending and unshadowed life with God.

One blustery Sunday afternoon in February, I spoke at a service in a convalescent home near Chester, Pennsylvania. Men and women were in wheelchairs, some listened from their beds in adjoining rooms.

Several of the patients were in their nineties; one lady was almost a hundred. She was weeping before the service began; as I leaned over to speak to her, she whispered, "I'm afraid to die."

When I spoke, I asked a question: "If I could promise to take you where you would be forever free from all your aches and pains, where you could walk and even run, hear and see, and never had any more loneliness or sorrow ever again; but if I had to take you first through a dark tunnel to get you there: how many of you would want to go?"

My question was rhetorical, but almost all of those dear old people raised their hands.

"Death is that tunnel," I explained. "It is not to be feared if we trust Jesus, for He will take us through it to heaven."

Our experience of heaven, according to the Bible, will be in two stages: first, immediately after death, a purely spiritual existence; later, a reunion of body with spirit.

During the first stage, our bodies will return to dust in the grave, while our spirits—the nonmaterial part of us that constitutes the essential person—will go to heaven to be with God. One reason for this conscious spiritual existence without a body may be to convince us once for all that we are more than a body, that—like God Himself—we can find completeness and fulfillment in a purely spiritual state.

(Some Christians believe that this first stage does not involve continued conscious existence of spirit without body, but rather a period of rest without consciousness. This state of soul sleep, according to these Christians, continues until the resurrection. Although no large part of the Christian church has held this view of what happens immediately after death, it creates no great problem. If you have ever gone to bed exhausted after a full, busy day of work, you know that sleep is a wonderful prospect, and that there is no consciousness of the passage of time before morning's awakening.)

The second stage will occur at a future date, when our spirits will be united again with our bodies. Christianity is not dualistic—it does not teach that spirit is good, the body evil. Instead it says that the body itself has dignity and worth, and will be raised from its place of rest in the last day, to be reunited with the spirit, as Jesus' body was raised. As Job put it in the Old Testament, even though "worms destroy this body, yet in my flesh shall I see God" (Job 19:26, KJV).

After His resurrection, Jesus Christ had a body that was somehow different from the one that had been lovingly taken from the cross and placed in a tomb by His friends. It was His body, recognizable, including nailprints in the hands; yet it possessed a glory beyond.

This reunion of the individual's spirit with the body he shed at death, reconstituted and glorified, will take place at the time of Jesus Christ's second coming to the world.

Many questions about death are shrouded in mystery in the Bible.

The Bible has nothing to say about the current search for reliable guidelines to determine when death has occurred. It knows nothing about organ transplants or other death-delaying medical procedures. It doesn't describe the kind of funeral customs we should follow.

What it does tell us, and tell us clearly, is that by the death of Jesus Christ on a cross, death itself has been conquered, its bitter sting has been removed, and in a day yet to be, it will be destroyed.

It is enough.

"Death Be Not Proud"

The hearse has come and gone. The brief graveside service is ended, a handful of symbolic dirt has been scattered, the mourners have left, the casket has been lowered, damp ground now covers it.

A slight mound of earth stands above the surrounding turf. Flowers in disarray are its small badge of beauty.

The workmen go off down the gravel road, dragging their shovels.

Soon it will be dark. The rain will come, and in a few months the snow, the bitter cold.

When he dies, I'll just have to cover him up with dirt and forget I ever had him.

Perhaps someone will visit the grave. Jesus' mother and a few friends visited His grave.

Some people find comfort through such visits. They sit and think, perhaps pray. Others find no comfort, only greater grief, and so they stay away.

But God is there. He does not despise the decomposing body. It belongs to one whose spirit lives with Him in heaven. Perhaps He sends His angels to guard it until the day of resurrection, as they guarded Jesus' body.

Someday He'll raise it up. He'll raise that body from the dust and unite it once again, part and parcel, indissolubly, with the spirit that made it live, that gave it consciousness and personhood from the womb.

You look like a rational person. How can you possibly believe that the death of a man, or a little boy, is any different from the death of an animal?

I once saw some workmen move a little cemetery full of graves to make way for a building. One man, standing in a deep hole, held up a small zinc plate: "Jennie Steward, Died 1908." And then some moldy wood, a little dirt, a blackened skull.

"That's all there is of Jennie," he said, and laughed a short laugh. Then he put her in a box and began to dig a foot or two away.

You look like a rational person. How can you possibly believe . . .

Believe that God will raise up Jennie at the last day, the day of resurrection? Raise her up from two different graves?

Raise up your little boy, my three sons? Raise up you and me?

Because God is God. Because He's promised to. But most of all, because He raised up Jesus Christ, His Son who died, from the grave.

Death be not proud
though some have called thee
mighty and dreadful
for thou art not so.
For those whom thou thinkest
thou dost overthrow
die not, poor death.
Nor yet canst thou kill me . . .
One short sleep past
we wake eternally

and death shall be no more.
Death, thou shalt die.
—John Donne

One Saturday morning in January, I saw the mail truck stop at our mailbox up on the road.

Without thinking, except that I wanted to get the mail, I ran out of the house and up to the road in my shirtsleeves. It was bitterly cold—the temperature was below zero, there was a brisk wind from the north, and the ground was covered with more than a foot of snow.

I opened the mailbox, pulled out the mail, and was about to make a dash for the house when I saw what was on the bottom, under the letters: a Burpee seed catalog.

On the front were bright zinnias. I turned it over. On the back were huge tomatoes.

For a few moments I was oblivious to the cold, delivered from it. I leafed through the catalog, tasting corn and cucumbers, smelling roses. I saw the freshly plowed earth, smelled it, let it run through my fingers.

For those brief moments, I was living in the springtime and summer, winter past.

Then the cold penetrated to my bones and I ran back to the house.

When the door was closed behind me and I was getting warm again, I thought how my moments at the mailbox were like our experience as Christians.

We feel the cold, along with those who do not share our hope. The biting wind penetrates us as them.

F. Scott Fitzgerald, writer of the '20s, who coined the phrase "the Jazz Age," spoke of the end that was "desolate and unkind, to turn the calendar at June and find December on the next leaf." We have had this same desolate feeling, many of us.

But in our cold times, we have a seed catalog. We open it and smell the promised spring, eternal spring. And the firstfruit that settles our hope is Jesus Christ, who was raised from death and cold earth to glory eternal.

A Psalm on the Death of an Eighteen-Year-Old Son

What waste Lord
this ointment precious
here outpoured
is treasure great
beyond my mind to think.
For years
until this midnight
it was safe
contained
awaiting careful use
now broken
wasted
lost.
The world is poor
so poor it needs each drop
of such a store.
This treasure spent
might feed a multitude
for all their days
and then yield more.
This world is poor?
It's poorer now
the treasure's lost.
I breathe its lingering fragrance
soon even that

will cease.
What purpose served?
The act is void of reason
sense
Lord
madmen do such deeds
not sane.
The sane man hoards his treasure
spends with care
if good
to feed the poor
or else to feed himself.
Let me alone Lord
You've taken from me
what I'd give Your world.
I cannot see such waste
that You should take
what poor men need.
You have a heaven
full of treasure
could You not wait
to exercise Your claim
on this?
O spare me Lord forgive
that I may see
beyond this world
beyond myself
Your sovereign plan
or seeing not
may trust You
Spoiler of my treasure.
Have mercy Lord
here is my quitclaim.

What will heaven be like? Facing major surgery just a couple years prior to his death, Joe Bayly wrote this meditation on heaven which echoes the desire of God's children through the ages: "I may not long for death, but I surely long for heaven."

Heaven

IT'S SIX-THIRTY on a Tuesday morning. Here I am waiting. Waiting to be wheeled into an operating room at Mayo Clinic's Methodist Hospital.

For some reason I am at the beginning of the long line of carts, soon to number thirty, each holding another human being who also waits. Next to me is a man in his eighties, beyond him a man younger than I. The older man is asleep, the younger is himself a medical doctor. I learn this when another stops to talk briefly with him.

"Does being a doctor help at a time like this?" I ask.

"Not really," he answers with a wry smile. "It's a mixed bag."

A nurse stops at the head of my cart, reads the piece of adhesive tape on my forehead, then asks, "What's your name?"

"Bayly," I answer. "Joseph Bayly."

She moves to the sleeping older man next to me, reads his name, but doesn't disturb him. Then on to the doctor, and so down the line.

As people are wheeled past me to take their places farther down, I nod or smile at the ones who are still awake. Otherwise I wait.

For what?

I wait for the merciful anesthesia, then the surgeon, and then . . . to come back to consciousness in the room where dear Mary Lou, my wife of thirty-two winters—and summers—also waits.

Or to come back to consciousness in the presence of my Lord Christ.

The surgery will not be very serious, there is little risk, but I am equally at peace, as far as I can plumb the depths of my heart, with either prospect.

I wonder how many others in the long white line have this hope. How would I feel, approaching the radical surgical procedures some of them face, without it? Would I have their courage?

My courage is Christ. My hope is Christ and the door to heaven He flung open by His own death for my sins, my hope His resurrection.

What will heaven be like, whether I go there as a result of this operation (a remote possibility), or go there later (a certainty)?

Heaven will be my eternal home with Christ. I'll just move into the part of His Father's house He prepared for me. No fixing up that home, no parts unfinished, no disappointments on moving day.

No, He's prepared it, He's made it completely ready, completely perfect, completely mine.

What's a home like, one that He prepares?

A place of peace and beauty, of joy and glory, of celestial music, of fresh, unchanging, purest love.

I'll say: "Hello, Lord. I'm tired." And He'll say, "Rest, because I have work for you to do."

"Rest?"

"Yes, remember that I Myself rested on the seventh day of Creation. So, rest is not incompatible with heaven's perfection."

"And work?"

"Of course. Did you think heaven would be an eternal Sunday afternoon nap? My people serve Me in heaven. I have work for you to do."

"Keeping all the gold polished?"

"Ruling angels. Managing the universe for Me. Someday, being responsible for whole cities."

"Whole cities? Like New York and Toronto?"

"Like them if everyone were living for my glory, every person safe, Harlem with trees growing in it and a river of pure water running through it, and people laughing."

I remember how He wept over Jerusalem.

"And Las Vegas without people desperately trying to be happy?"

"Happy without trying."

"Those golden streets . . ."

"What about them?"

"Why gold? Not for show, maybe for beauty?"

"Everything in heaven is turned upside down from earth. Values are reversed. What's most important on earth? What have men lived and died for, for millennia?"

"Gold."

"You'll walk on it in heaven. Like concrete or asphalt."

"Can I see my sons who died a few years ago? And my parents, Mary Lou's parents? My brother?"

"Of course you'll see them. All of them trusted Me on earth."

"Except John, the infant. He couldn't understand. So he couldn't believe."

"But he's in heaven because of my atoning work."

"Will I recognize them?"

"Didn't My servant Paul tell you that the assurance of reunion with your loved ones should bring you comfort? Where would the comfort be if you couldn't recognize them?

"And didn't My servant David find comfort, when his infant died, that he would go to be with that son?"

"I wonder if my infant son will still be an infant, my son who was eighteen when he died still eighteen?"

"You'll soon see."

"You know, just a few weeks ago, I saw a man I hadn't seen for thirty-five years. And I immediately recognized him, even though he was more than a third of a century older than when I saw him last. The surprising thing was that within ten minutes the image of thirty-five years ago had faded, and I knew him as he is now."

"You'll know the ones you love."

"How about people like Moses or Abraham or Stephen?"

"You'll know them, too. Didn't my disciples, Peter, James, and John know Moses and Elijah on the Mount of Transfiguration?"

"Wow! I can hardly wait. But will I recognize them when their bodies . . ."

"Are still on earth? Still in the grave? Yes, you will. Again, remember how My disciples recognized Moses. You'll be as much My son Joe Bayly as you were on earth. But without your earthly body. That awaits My return to earth, and your return with Me, when that dead and disintegrated body will come alive, when you'll reinhabit it and find the glory of your new body."

"I sort of like that body. It served me well for all these years."

"That's not surprising. And your angel will guard it in its resting place, just as angels guarded My body in the period between My death and resurrection. I love the whole you—the body that is My Spirit's temple during your life on earth, as well as your spirit that will be in heaven until your own body's resurrection."

"Heaven seems more of a city than anything else."

"Yes, it is a city—not people living in isolation, like on a vast Texas ranch, but living together. Not independent, everyone living his own life, but living together in perfect love, perfect harmony, perfect cooperation. Some of My children may have lived lonely lives on earth, but never here in heaven. Isolation, the ultimate aloneness, is not for My people, but for those who would not respond to My Spirit, who would not trust Me for life eternal."

"Will I really be able to sit down with the Old Testament patriarchs—and the matriarchs—and talk with them?"

"Yes, you will. Don't you remember that I said people like you, who weren't physical descendants of Abraham and Isaac and Jacob, but who trusted Me, would have fellowship with them in the kingdom of heaven, while their own descendants who refused to receive Me would be denied entrance into heaven?"

"I have a question. Maybe it's sort of presumptuous, Sir, but You can tell me if it is. Will I bring anything with me, is there anything in heaven that belongs to me?—Except my children, that is. Or will I come as I was born the first time, naked, taking nothing with me?"

"Of course you'll bring something with you, or rather, part of it will be waiting for you, while the rest is still to come. Birth into heaven isn't the same as birth into the world. Here you had preexistence on earth, there you didn't—except during your growing period in the womb.

"And by the way, you don't need to be afraid to say anything in heaven, that it may seem presumptuous. You'll be known as you also know others. No need to conceal yourself any longer. No masks. If you want to know anything, you'll just ask. But to answer your question, yes, you will have treasures in heaven. You have Tony as a treasure."

"Tony? I don't remember any Tony who would be treasure."

"Tony, the older man you witnessed to on your first job, while you were still a teenager in New York City. Tony's in heaven. He's a treasure."

"The very best."

"Not necessarily the best treasure. There's also the treasure of another man who tenderly cared for his wife in old age, during the ten years she was totally paralyzed. There's her treasure of an uncomplaining, grateful spirit. There's the treasure of purity—a teenager who kept himself from the world's stain, who did not obey the lusts of his flesh. There's the treasure of an important man who remained meek in all his relationships. And the treasure of parents who were faithful in raising their children, sacrificing their own independence and gratification for them. There are almost limitless treasures for people in heaven."

"How about money?"

"Nobody brings his money with him, but many have sent it on ahead. There are some South American Indians here who look forward to meeting you. You helped support the missionary who took the Gospel to them, who introduced them to Me."

"Are all those things the 'gold, silver, and precious stones' the Bible talks about?"

"Yes, but *don't* look for precisely what My servants said in the Bible about heaven."

"What do You mean?"

"I was limited in what I could reveal to them, limited to what their eyes had seen and their language could express. Can you imagine the difficulty of describing a pineapple to an Eskimo on the Arctic tundra? 'Sweet and juicy blubber' is about as close as you could come. Or how could you describe ice to a desert tribe? How could I tell earth people about heaven?"

"What about the Bible writers who had visions?"

"They had the same problem of communicating what they saw to others who had not shared their vision. How would the Eskimo describe a pineapple to others in his village, even if he were transported to Hawaii and then returned? 'Sweet and juicy blubber' is still about as close as he could come. I remember how frustrated My beloved disciple John was as he tried to describe his vision of the future and of heaven."

"So, it's far beyond what the Bible says."

"Far, far beyond. How could a twin born into earthworld describe what he saw, just in the delivery room even, to his twin not yet born? And beyond the delivery room would be the Rocky Mountains, the sky on a starry night, animals on an African game farm."

"Maybe that's why Isaiah's vision and Daniel's descriptions of the great beasts always seemed so strange to me, and a lot of things in Revelation. I could never get a clear sight on what angels looked like."

"You'll soon see them. And they won't seem strange any longer, just beautiful and full of power, like all that I create."

"I'll have a lot to see."

"It will take you ages to see it."

"And to learn?"

"You'll be learning and growing forever. The structure of the atom is child's play compared to what you'll learn here. And did you think you understood the mystery of My incarnation? The problem of pain? You haven't begun."

"I can hardly wait to study all of human history on earth from Your standpoint, Sir, with all the facts available.

"This work You mentioned earlier. Will it just be managing Your universe?"

"Of course not. You can also plant a garden—without sweat or drought or weeds. Like Eden, you'll find grass on the other side of the fence that really is greener. Or you can create a poem or an oratorio. You can carve wood or paint a landscape."

"To praise You."

"Everything in heaven is to My praise. My people intend it, so I accept it. But that doesn't mean that they only sing My praise—their work is praise to me."

"Will I be able to sing? I've wanted to, since I was a child."

"Handel's choir always has room for one more. But for that matter, you may want to have your own choir, or learn to conduct it—or an orchestra."

"There'll hardly be enough hours in the day to do what I'll want to do."

"There's no night in heaven. You won't need to sleep. You needed sleep on earth for restoration of your strength, of your dissolving powers. But in heaven there will be no wasting away, no dissipation of energy."

"Is there any group, any people, whose entrance into heaven brings You special joy?"

"The persecuted of earth, men and women who are imprisoned, tortured, killed for My sake. When My servant Stephen was stoned, I stood to welcome him into glory. So I welcome all who are faithful unto death."

"What a great thing—to be freed from all persecution at last. To be totally victorious."

"But not just My persecuted ones. Everyone in heaven will be freed from all kinds of evil. There are no guns in heaven, no bombs, no drunkenness or violence or war. And the doors don't have locks on them. All these things that make earth life fearful for so many people are forever gone."

"How about people who weren't able to do things on earth—the severely handicapped, Mongoloid, and retarded people?"

"They are My greatest joy in heaven, next to those who were martyred for My sake. To see them whole, able to do everything they couldn't do on earth . . . to those who had not, it has been given."

"'And from those who had, it shall be taken'—does that mean that the geniuses on earth, the ones who had great power and great gifts, but never turned to You in simple faith—does that mean their gifts are now taken away?"

"Yes, hell is a place of total loss. The world-famous violinist who turned from Me is tone-deaf, the physicist can't manage an abacus, the world leader has no one to control. For them that is unending sorrow. And it is unending sorrow to Me. How often I would have gathered them into My family on earth, but they would not consent to be gathered."

"They must have an awful lot of regret, of 'if only' feelings. How about in heaven: will I think 'if only'?"

"If you do, I shall wipe away your tears. Sorrow is forever gone. You will not face the past, but the future."

"Are there many people in heaven?"

"A multitude beyond numbering. From every tribe and nation on earth."

"Can they understand each other?"

"They speak one language, as it was before Babel."

"It seems to me that a lot of things are the way You originally intended earth to be."

"Yes, but different, better, even as I excel the first Adam."

"If there's such a great crowd in heaven, doesn't one individual person get lost, or absorbed?"

"There's a great crowd on earth too, and yet you're different from every other person who ever lived. Even your fingerprints are different. You'll be the same unique you in heaven. And you'll be uniquely Mine—I call everyone by name. Moses is Moses, Priscilla is Priscilla, and you'll be Joseph Bayly throughout eternity."

"I'm ashamed to admit it, but I'm a little scared. I really like this world: the Rocky Mountains, the beach at Cape May, the fields behind our house, the barn through mist on a gray wintry morning. How can I adjust to heaven when it's so different?"

"That world you like, it is but a womb."

"A womb?"

"Yes, you may not perceive it in that way, but you are bound within earthworld as surely as a baby yet unborn is bound within the womb. Maybe the baby would be scared to be born, too, to leave the womb."

"Then death is . . ."

"Deliverance to life beyond your imagining. The death incident is merely a passage from earth life, from the womb that has contained you until now, into the marvelous newness of heaven life. You'll go through a dark tunnel, you may experience pain—just as you did when you were born a baby—but beyond the tunnel is heaven. I promise you, you'll enjoy heaven."

"And I'll enjoy You. Somehow in our conversation I've gotten so excited about what a wonderful place heaven is that I've almost forgotten You, forgotten that eternal life is to know You, Lord Jesus, that Your presence makes heaven heaven."

"That's all right—a child sees all of life with a child's eyes. But in heaven you will be full-grown, you will be perfectly mature. Then you will learn to worship and praise and be thankful.

"Now you stand on a mountain, like My servant Moses, from which you can see the wilderness of your earth life and the approaching happiness of the promised land, both at the same time. Do you find your perspective changing?"

"I do, I surely do. Some things I enjoyed seem to be fading away as I see heaven in the distance. Others are vastly more important. My values seem to be changing. I may not long for death, but I surely long for heaven."

"Happy are you who weep now; you will laugh! . . . Dance for joy, because a great reward is kept for you in heaven."

I heard a loud voice speaking from the throne: "Now God's home is with mankind! . . . He will wipe away all tears from their eyes. There will be no more death, no more grief or crying or pain. The old things have disappeared."

Luke 6:21,23; Rev. 21:3-4 (GNB)

The editor of Eternity magazine, Russell T. Hitt, inserted this note at the beginning of this, Bayly's last column, in the September 1986 issue: Joe Bayly was chosen in 1961 as columnist a few months after the death of Dr. Donald Grey Barnhouse, Eternity's founder. Although he had heavy responsibilities at David C. Cook Publishing Company, most recently as president, Joe enlivened the pages of Eternity for a quarter of a century.

Recently he decided to retire the column in favor of other writing commitments. This is his final column.

Then on July 16, 1986, after open-heart surgery, Joe went to he with the Lord. With love, we bid him farewell. —Russell T. Hitt, editor emeritus

The Severity and Goodness of God

September 1986

Since I've shared the severity of God with my readers, I want to share the goodness of God in this final column.

With the present issue, I complete twenty-five years of writing this column for *Eternity*. Since all things temporal come to an end, this is also the last column I shall write.

From my standpoint, the best result of this sort of writing, apart from the documentation of my opinions over a period of time, is the audience to whom I have had the privilege to speak. Often they talk back, sometimes through letters, other times when I meet them.

I was speaking on the West Coast about ten years ago when a brief incident occurred, which I prize. An elderly man came up to me afterward and said, as he shot out his hand, "I told the missus I had to come tonight because I already know you, but I wanted you to meet me."

On another occasion, a little farther south on the West Coast, a woman told me that she had read my column for a number of years, then stated quite firmly, "I don't really think you are."

"You don't think I'm what?" I asked.

"Out of your mind." Of course I thanked her for this affirmation, which others might not be willing to give.

Some readers know of the losses Mary Lou and I experienced around the time I began writing this column. (Over a six-year period three of our sons died, aged four years, three weeks, and eighteen years. Cause of death was different for each.) Our grief was reflected in certain columns.

The severity of God was evident in those crises. I couldn't hide it, although I felt then—and continue to feel—that this was more of a problem to some of our friends than to Mary Lou and me. We have found great comfort and peace in the sovereignty of God. And in the darkest hour we have not doubted His love.

Last week at Moody Bible Institute's pastors' conference, a man who had previously only known me through my writing asked, "I know you had three children die. What about the others who are still living?"

Since I've shared the severity of God with my readers, I want to share the goodness of God in this final column, as I did with that pastor.

We have four children in addition to the three who died. I suppose we have had a heightened concept of our stewardship in raising them, being keenly aware that God could terminate our responsibility and call one of them home at any time.

Now they have all finished their training years, and, by God's grace, all are active in Christian ministry.

Deborah felt a strong call to work with inner-city kids.[1] After five years teaching in a public school on Chicago's West Side (an area that was burned out after Martin Luther King, Jr.'s, assassination), she has taught twelve years, and is now principal of Lake View Academy, a small alternative high school for a multiethnic group of students, many of whom have dropped out of public

[1] Deborah Bayly continues to serve as principal of Lake View Academy, which celebrated its twenty-fifth anniversary in October 1997.

schools. The school is located in Lake View Presbyterian Church, a poor church that stayed put when many others moved to the suburbs or closed their doors.

I wish you could meet most of the kids who attend Lake View, as well as the graduates. The commitment of Deborah, Anita Smith (who founded the school), and the teaching staff—commitment to God and to their students—has had life-changing results.

Tim, our next oldest living child, is married to Mary Lee Taylor.[2] They have three children: Heather (nine), Joseph (four), and Michal (six months). Tim is beginning his fourth year of ministry at two Presbyterian churches in Wisconsin: Pardeeville (small town) and Rosedale (country). He is also active in the pro-life movement, serving on the board of Presbyterians Pro-Life. Tim and Mary Lee's door is always open to men and women in need.

Mary Lou and I recently gave Tim and Mary Lee a tenth anniversary present: a weekend at a Chicago hotel while we took care of their children and I preached for him. When I approached the pulpit in Pardeeville, I saw a small yellow "Post-it" on the preacher's side of the pulpit. Printed on it was "Dad, I love you."

David is our next child.[3] He graduated from seminary this spring. This past year he has had an invaluable experience as an intern at First Evangelical Free Church (where Chuck Swindoll is senior pastor) in Fullerton, California.

Two years ago David was a summer missionary with SEND in Glennallen, Alaska. In its different way, this was as valuable an experience as his more recent internship. Nurses at the small hospital and the couple who were responsible for the summer program made an indelible impres-

---

[2] Tim and his wife, Mary Lee, now have five children: Mrs. Douglas (Heather) Ummel of Nashville, Tennessee; Joseph (seventeen), Michal (fourteen), Hannah (eleven), and Taylor (seven). In 1996 Tim accepted the call to serve Church of the Good Shepherd in Bloomington, Indiana. He is also Executive Director of the Council on Biblical Manhood and Womanhood.

[3] David Bayly and his wife, Cheryl (McHenny) Bayly, now have five children: Nathan (ten), Elizabeth (nine), Benjamin (six), Tessa (three), and Isaiah (one). David and Cheryl live near Toledo, Ohio, where David has served as pastor of Springfield United Brethren Church, Monclova, Ohio, since 1988.

sion on him by their selfless service. A small Indian church also made a lasting impression.

Now David is waiting for God to lead him to the next step in his service.

Nathan is our youngest.[4] His wife is Sandy Bennett. He also graduated from seminary in the spring and has become director of Christian education and youth ministry at Community Church in Bristol, Tennessee.

Sandy worked in an ophthalmologist's office and Nate painted houses (one built in 1691) to pay seminary expenses. One of Nate's best experiences was holding weekly Bible studies in a nursing home.

All our children are concerned for other people and involved in their lives, especially those who don't yet know Jesus Christ. The three who have homes demonstrate the gift of hospitality.

Mary Lou[5] and I are aware that all this represents the grace of God, but also that for ourselves and our children the road hasn't ended.

Yet we know that both by His severity and by His goodness God has shown consistent faithfulness. God is good. He is worthy of all trust and glory. Amen.

---

[4] Nathan and his wife, Sandy, now have four children: Cassie (ten), Sarah (eight), Frances (five), and David (five). Nathan and Sandy live in Bristol, Tennessee, where Nathan has served as pastor of Cornerstone Chapel since 1986.

[5] Mary Lou Bayly ("Mud" to her children), lives in Bartlett, Illinois, in the home in which she and her Joe shared together many winters and summers. Mary Lou loves to garden, travel, take part in neighborhood Bible studies, and snooze in a chair while dreaming she's writing letters to her loved ones.

This is the ordination charge Joe Bayly gave to his son, Tim, on October 23, 1983, in First Presbyterian Church of Pardeeville, Wisconsin.

Ordination Charge

My BELOVED SON Timothy,

I charge you as you enter upon your ministry.

Have faith in God, Who has called you. Seek to fulfill His expectations first of all, not those of His people, or your own. Build the church for His glory.

Use the talents and training and gifts He has given you to the fullest, but don't depend on them. When your experience increases, don't depend on that. Depend on God Who has called you, to fulfill your calling. Depend on the Holy Spirit to work through you.

Do the work of an evangelist as one who himself has experienced deliverance and redemption. Carry the keys to the kingdom of heaven in your hand at all times. Be ready to give your time and life for one lost sheep as earnestly and diligently as you would for a thousand.

Tend the flock of God. Seek the lost ones, the defeated ones, the soul-sick ones, the wandering ones, and lovingly restore them. Then send them back into the battle.

Preach the Word of God, not avoiding those parts that are unpopular, or that cut across the grain of accepted opinion. Be prophetic, but exercise judgment upon yourself and your own actions first of all.

Respect authority, submit to authority, as to those appointed by God.

Be a careful counselor. Listen with your heart, guard the confidences you receive. Avoid and discourage gossip.

Pray for your people. When you work, *you* work; when you pray, *God* works. Never doubt that God can change people and situations, can resolve conflicts and bring peace where there has been trouble.

Love your people, care for them, have compassion on them. Encourage them to serve the Lord with joy and freedom. Share the Lord's work with them, train your laypersons to work in the fields of the Lord with you.

And enjoy your people. You are their servant, but you are also their friend. Share their lives, their joys as well as their sorrows, even as our Lord Jesus shared the lives of His disciples.

Be a responsible citizen in your community. Let your influence for ethics and morality be felt, always remembering that the community cannot be held to the standards of Christ's church.

Model love and care for your wife and children. Don't sacrifice them and your responsibility for them on the altar of your work and leadership in the church. Determine not to preach to others and see your own children castaways.

Guard your thoughts. Praise and worship God as a man, not just as a pastor. Don't covet another's position or possessions.

Enjoy God. Look for His fingerprints on every part of life. Cast your burdens on the Lord; don't bear them yourself. The battle is not yours, but God's. Find joy in the service, the place, the people God has given you.

Tonight you are being asked, "Wilt thou?" Some day you will be asked, "Hast thou?"

As an undershepherd, serve the Great Shepherd so that you may answer in that day, "I have fought the good fight, I have finished my course, I have kept the faith."

Index

1984, 181

AIDS
  causes of spread, 229
  necessity of protection of public health, 229
Abednego, 116
Abolitionist Movement, the, 230
abortion, 181-84, 189, 214-17, 221, 225, 229
  antislavery movement and, 183
  baby's pain in, 220
  compared to the Holocaust, 230-231
  eugenics and, 181
  opposition to, 182-83, 230
  Pandora's box opened, 216
  population control and, 183
  profitability of, 214-15, 220
  Roe v. *Wade* and, 220-221
Abraham, 149, 189, 192, 258, 259
academic community, 161
  attack upon Christianity in, 161
  silence of Christian witness within, 162
academic freedom, 161
Acts, 93-94
  2:38, 194
  20:21, 194
  25:11, 201
Adam, 187, 192, 263
adoption, 183
adultery, 152, 204, 213, 219
  (*see also* sexual immorality)
Advertising Age, 180
affair, 189, 205
  (*see also* adultery)
African-Americans
  civil rights of, 156
  illegitimacy rate of, 156
  moral decay among, 156, 158
  need for prophetic voice among, 157-58
  (*see also* black; Negro)
agnostic religion, 230
Ahab, 188
alcoholism, 124, 178, 197, 209, 262
Amazon Indian tribes, 212
America, 166, 169-70, 171, 172

Christian, 168, 170, 213, 215, 223
  decline of, 170
  in moral decay, 152-53, 204, 221-22, 225-26
  (*see also* American; United States)
American, 166, 179-80, 203, 207, 213
  (*see also* America; United States)
American Bible Society, the, 182
Amos, 102
  5:15, 21, 23-24, 206
anarchy, 121, 176
Anathothburg, 153
angels, 252, 257, 259, 261
antiabortion, preferable to pro-life, 221
anti-intellectualism, 223
antinomianism, 168
apologetics, 175
Apostles' Creed, the, 141, 214
arbutus, trailing, 158-9
archaisms, 204-07
Arctic, 260
Atonement, the
  moral influence theory, 200
  substitutionary, 200
Aucas, 151
Auden, W. H., 173-74
Augustine, 171
Austria, 221
Avis, 131
awe, 205

Babel, 263
baptism, infant, 170-71
Barnhouse, Dr. Donald Grey, 104, 265
Bayly, 235-238, 266-269
  Cheryl (McHenny), 267
  Danny, 235-38, 242-43, 258
  David, 197, 236, 267
  Deborah, 237, 266-67
  Elizabeth, 267
  Hannah, 267
  Heather, 267
  John, 237, 258
  Joseph, the V, 235-38, 258
  Joseph, the VI, 267

Mary Lee (Taylor), 267
Mary Lou, 102, 112, 121-22, 151, 196, 236, 256, 258, 266, 267, 268
  Michal, 267
  Nathan, 267
  Nathan Curtis, 237, 268
  Sandy (Bennett), 268
  Taylor, 267
  Timothy, 216, 236, 267, 269
Berlin Wall, 223
Bethlehem, 144, 145
Bible, 98, 101, 111, 116, 150, 184, 219
  authority of, 95, 114, 163, 165, 174-76, 182, 187-88
  changes in stories in, 188-90
  conformed to evangelical thought patterns, 173
  favored parts of, 165
  gender, teaching on, 182-84, 187-88, 191
  inerrancy, 174-76
  inspiration of, 155, 165, 173, 174-76, 186, 187, 201
  interpretation of, 173, 211, 218
  marketing of, 155, 171-72
  memorization of, 126, 172
  paraphrases of, 154, 171-73
  private interpretation of, 209
  punishment, teaching on, 198-202
  reading of, 211
    to children, 167, 180, 211
  Synoptic Gospels, the, 162-5
  teaching of, 92, 104, 105, 108, 124, 126, 127, 129, 130, 151, 158, 167, 188
  translation of, 154-55, 171-74
  use in public worship of, 172
  versions of
    American Standard, 173
    Amplified Bible, the, 154, 173
    Beck, 172
    Berkeley Version, the, 154, 172
    Douay Version, the, 172
    God Is for Real Man, 172
    Jerusalem Bible, the, 172, 174
    King James Bible, the, 154, 172, 173
    Knox and Confraternity, 172
    Living Letters, 173
    New American Standard Bible, the, 172
    New English Bible, the, 154, 172, 173
    paraphrases, 154, 171, 172-73
    Philips, the, 154
    problems and questions in, 154-55
    Revised Standard Version, the, 154, 171, 172, 173, 190, 218
    Teen-Age Version, the, 155
    Today's English Version, the, 172
    Verkuyl-Berkeley, the, 154
    Williams, the, 154
Bible Study Fellowship, 224
Big Brother, 181
Bill of Rights, the, 31
birth control, 182, 229
black, 185
  (see also African-American; Negro)
Blaine, Graham, 179
Blanchard, Jonathan, 230
Bloomington, Indiana, 267
Boise, Idaho, 107
bookstores, Christian, 225
Boston Common, 214
Boulding, Kenneth, 184
Bowen, Catherine Drinker, 181
Bradburn, Samuel, 91
Brahams' First Symphony, 104
Bristol, Tennessee, 268
bus ministry, 118

Caesar, 185, 221
Calvary Baptist Church (New York), 194
camping, Christian, 222, 224
Campus Crusade for Christ, 224, 227
Camus, 139
Canada, 92, 121, 163, 168, 216, 221
Cape May, 263
capital growth
  in Christian organizations, 227
capital punishment, 198-202
  and racism, 201
  and the poor, 201
  and voyeurism, 198, 201-3
Carmichael, Amy, 120
Carson, Johnny, 180
Catholic, 166, 172, 220, 223
Catholicism, 172
Central Park, 214
Chamberlain, Eugene, 188
Chester, Pennsylvania, 249
Chicago, 99, 121, 131, 134, 266, 267, 268
  inner city kids, 212
Chicago and Northwestern Station, 132
Chicago Tribune, 99
child abuse, 215
Child Evangelism Fellowship (CEF), 224
childbirth, 181
  Lamaze, 216

Children's Hospital (Philadelphia), 235-36, 242
China, 34, 121, 153, 170, 203
China Inland Mission (CIM), 160, 202
Christian Businessmen's Committee, 224
Christian education, 117-18, 213
Christian Endeavor, 224
Christian Herald, 224
Christian Legal Society, 224
Christian Medical Society, 224
Christian Service Brigade, 224
Christian witness, 162
Christianity and Crisis, 162
Christians
  and church loyalty, 225
  and consistent living, 225
  and entertainment, 225
  and pacifism, 186
  and perfection, 160
  as agents of moral change, 29-32, 235
  as citizens, 29-32, 220, 228-30, 270
  as salt and light, 161, 162, 167
  complacency of, 238
  hindrances to growth, 149
  lowering level of ethics of, 165, 173, 175, 230
  narrow, 178, 238
  silence against attack, 161-62, 229, 230
Christmas, 131-47, 214
church growth, 148
Church of England, the, 27, 166
Church, the, 154, 213, 270
  and age-level activities, 226
  and building programs, 224, 228
  and family togetherness, 226
  and money, 227
  and persecution, 211, 214, 227
  and politics, 149, 226, 227,
  as patriarchal, 226
  as witness against evil
    silence of, 220-22, 229, 230
  building, 125, 223
  Daily Vacation Bible School in, 225
  decline of doctrine of, 164-65, 225
  Early, witness of, 94, 163, 222
  electronic, 22-26, 205, 213, 224, 227
  its capitulation to moral decay, 170, 228
  lay workers in, 227, 228
  materialism in, 213
  small groups in, 226
  social justice in, 201
City of David, 145
civil religion, 226
civil rights, 156-58

cleave, 205, 207
Club Aluminum, 119
College Church (Wheaton, Illinois), 148
colleges, Christian, 175, 180, 190, 213, 224, 227
Communion, 47-49,
Communism, 31-32, 34-44, 160
  demonic, 169
  evils of, 168-70
    atheistic, 169
    family, 169, 181
    gender roles, 169
    state control of children, 169
    persecution of Christians, 121, 202
  revisionists, 191-92
Community Church (Bristol, Tennessee), 268
compassion, 124, 270
conception, 215
conferences, Bible, 164
confirmation, 170-71
Constitution, the, 186
conversion, 170
Cook, David C., Publishing Co., 103, 121, 265
Coolidge administration, 152
Corinthian church, 199
Cornerstone Chapel (Bristol, Tennessee), 268
cosmetics, 184
counseling, 210, 213, 270
Craig, Clarence T., 199, 218
Creation, the, 187, 192, 257
Crete, 157
criminals, punishment of, 152, 198-202
Cuban refugees, 212
Culley, Ruth, 182

Dagon's temple, 188
Daily Vacation Bible School, 225
Dallas Seminary, 218, 226
dancing, 222
Daniel, 261
David, 147, 189, 216, 244, 249, 258
death, 109, 208, 210, 214, 239-40, 241-53, 256-64
  of a son, 236-38, 242-43, 252, 254-55
  right to die, 96
  laboratory of, 187
  related to sin, 199
  denial of, 246
"Death Be Not Proud", 251, 252-53
decisions for Christ, 168, 170, 176-78
Depression, the Great, 223
Detroit News, the, 180

Deuteronomy
  19:11, 13, 200
  23:21-23, 207
discernment, 209
disciples, 192, 210, 213, 258, 259, 270
discipleship, cost of, 238
discipline, 199
  lack of, 149
  loving, 150-51
divorce, 169, 178, 185, 202-3, 205, 213, 217-19, 225
doctorate, 213
doctrine, 125, 149, 174, 205, 211, 217
  deteriorating, 164
  fundamental, 165
  need for integrity of to be guarded, 230
  rebirth needed, 205
  shallow treatment of, 166-67
  standards of, 164
Donne, John, 253
Doxology, the, 141, 187
drugs, 156, 185
DuPage County (Illinois), 102
Duty, Guy, 217

Ecuador, 196
Eden, 261
education, compulsory for four-year-olds, 169-70
Edwards, Jonathan, 171
Egypt, 117, 157
Eli, 189
Elijah, 162, 258
Elliott, Elisabeth, 151, 174
Emmanuel, 144
end times, 166
England, 91, 92, 121, 153, 166, 222
entertainment, 179-81, 202, 225-26
environmentalism, 183-84
  endangered species, 212
Ephesians
  6:10-17, 186
  2:1, 249
Equal Rights Amendment, the, 186
Esau, 190
Eskimo, 260-61
eternal destiny, 178, 198
eternity, 150, 212
Eternity, 152, 263
ethics, 184, 204, 222, 270
  in business, 118-19
  lowering level of among Christians, 165, 166,

175
eugenics, 181
Europe, 161, 222
evangelicalism, 211
  authority in, 163
  doctrines absent within
    Law, the, 166
    sin, 166
  immediacy of salvation, overemphasis of, 167
  sick, 218
Evangelical Community Church (Bloomington, Indiana), 267
evangelicals, 172, 174, 217-18, 222
  agenda for new generation, 226
  and acts of religious formality, 170-71
  and compromise, 230
  and divorce, 205, 218
  and pietism, 203
  and risks, 227
  and Roman Catholics, 223
  attitudes toward Bible versions, 173-74
  authority, 163, 165, 174
  indifferent, 220-23, 226
  lowering level of ethics of, 165, 166, 175, 222, 230
  not known for love, 164
  passing the torch, 223, 230
  shallow treatment of sin and law, 166
  spiritual and doctrinal integrity, 230
evangelism, 50-89, 213, 240, 269
  bus ministry, 118
  concern for lost souls in, 178
  lifestyle, 86-89, 177
  repentance and, 168, 206
  Sunday School, 117
    need for fresh emphasis on, 118
  tears and, 168, 206
  urgency in, 178
Eve, 187, 192
Exodus, the, 246
Exodus
  20, 167
  21:12, 14, 200
  20:14, 205
  33:13, 246, 238

faith, 120, 128-31, 173-76, 178, 181, 194, 208-09, 218, 239, 246
  heroes of, 149
family, 210, 225
  altar, 117
  children

concern for, 219, 270
Bible reading with, 117-18, 180, 211
death of, 235-40, 266
fruit of love, 159
government indoctrination of, 168-70
providing safe moral climate for, 229
rebellious, 166, 171
training of, 150, 169-70, 188, 223
  for persecution, 210
unbelieving, 168
Christian, 159-60
divorce (see divorce)
ethics, 119-20
fatherhood, 180, 187
  attacked by television, 180
large, 160
love in, 159
marriage, 168-69, 178, 191, 194, 205, 210,
211, 217, 225
  ceremony, 207, 219
  divorce (see divorce)
  feminism, legitimate complaints, 181-84,
190-91
  interracial, 184, 185
  love in, 158-60, 202-3
  nitpicking in, 175-76
  vows, 202, 207, 219
  motherhood, 169, 1803, 181-84, 187, 191
  put-down of by feminists, 191
  patriarchal, 226
  remarriage (see remarriage)
  single parent, 185, 225
  togetherness in the church, 226
  wedding, 207
Far East, 126
Federal Constitutional Court of Germany, the,
221
feelings
  with truth, 121
  overemphasis on, 211
fellowship, 112
feminism, 182, 186-88, 191-92, 213
  editing the Bible, 190-92
  legitimate complaints of, 181-84, 190-91
  marriage, 191-92
  motherhood, put-down of, 181-84, 191
  unisex, 187, 191
  women in combat, 186
fences
  man's or God's, 183-86
fetus, 214-16, 221-22
First Corinthians

11, 192
15:26, 245
First Evangelical Free Church (Fullerton,
California), 267
First John
1:9, 199
First Presbyterian Church (Pardeeville,
Wisconsin), 267, 269
First Thessalonians
2:4-13, 92
5:17, 195
First Timothy
2:12-14, 187
6:10, 215
Fitzgerald, F. Scott, 253
Flood, the, 189, 201
forgiveness, 102, 193, 220
Fort Lauderdale, 163
France, 153, 221-22
freedom of religion, 29, 213
Freedoms Foundation, 153
friendships, 149
Fuller, Charles E., 224
Fullerton, California, 267
fundamentalism, 154, 163
Fundamentals, the, 163-65
fundraising, 228

Gaebelein, Frank, 174
Galatians
3:11, 208
Galileans, 194
Gallup, George, Jr., 206
Garrison, William Lloyd, 230
gender
  differences, 191, 218
  roles, 187, 191-93
  teaching of Bible on, 187-88, 191
  unisex, 187, 191
Genesis
1:1, 155
9:6, 200
3:19, 249
German Lutheran, 202
Germany, 153, 185, 221, 232
  Nazi, 220-21
Gettysburg, 94
Gilmore, Gary, 198
Glen Ellyn, Illinois, 133
Glennallen, Alaska, 265
Gloucester, 91

God
  and abortion, judgment for, 221
  and holiness, 148, 162
  and punishment, 199-201
  and sin, judgment for, 249
  and suffering, 239-40, 245-46
  and war, 186
  banished from Russian life, 169
  Communist attitude toward, 169
  compared to a mother, 192
  goodness of, 266, 268
  is love, 239, 247
  primary work of, 239-40
  severity of, 265-66, 268
  sovereignty of, 239, 246-47, 255, 266
  uses doubts to convict, 171
Good Samaritan, the, 122
Goodman, David, 159
grace, 193, 194, 212, 218
  cheap, 163, 166
Graham, Billy, 180
Gray, 165
Great Awakening, the, 166, 171
Great Depression, the, 223
Greer, Germaine, 191
growth
  hindrances to, 149, 203
  overemphasis on, 204, 221
guilt, 191, 195, 200, 205, 221
Gulliver, 220

Hagar, 189
hair, 184
Hammerton-Kelly, Dr. R. G., 216
Hammond, Canon T. C., 166-67
Handel, 262
Harlem, 257
Harvard University, 179
hate, 205
Haverford College, 184
Havner, Vance, 119
Hawaii, 261
Hayakawa, S. I., 179
health and wealth gospel, 149, 150
Health, Education and Welfare Department, 170
Hearst, Patty, 197
heart, hard, 217
heaven, 128, 149, 173, 178, 189, 206, 230, 236, 240, 249, 250, 252, 255, 256-64, 269
Hebrews, 150, 165

12, 149
12:2, 149
12:10, 151
5:12, 204
Hebrides Islands, the, 168, 194
Hefner, Hugh, 166, 187
hell, 178
heresy, 98, 165, 203, 211, 212
Herod, 192
Hitler, Adolf, 181, 185, 187, 216
Hitt, Russell, 265
Hodge, Charles, 199, 201, 246
holiness, 148-51, 162
Holocaust, the, 187, 216, 220-21, 230-31
  of abortion, 220, 225
Holy Spirit, the, 93, 105, 127, 151, 155, 168, 171, 176, 182, 187, 209, 210, 214, 215, 226, 227, 240, 259, 269
homicide, 200
Hosea, wife of, 192
human life, value of, 212
humble, 206, 210-11
Hundred Texts, The, 166
Hungary, 153
Huxley, Sir Julian, 161

Illinois, 200, 243
In Death and Life, 248
In Understanding Be Men, 166
Incarnation, the, 261
incest, 229
India, 120, 124-25
indifference, 220-23, 226, 230
infant baptism, 170
infanticide, 215
intellectuals, Christian, 162
interdenominational activity, 164-65, 184
InterVarsity Christian Fellowship, 159, 166, 224, 227
Ireland, Northern, 200
Irish Church Missions, 166
Isaac, 259
Isaiah, 261
  59:19, 121
  28:9-10, 125
  7:14, 172
  44:2, 183
  53:2, 183
  58:13-14, 207
  25:8, 264
Israel, 131, 133, 137, 139, 141, 239, 246
Italy, 221

Jacob, 190, 207, 259
James, 165, 258
  3:17, 212
  5:14-15, 236
Japan, 185
Jeremiah, 104-5, 153
Jerusalem, 134, 145, 201, 257
Jesus
  and care for the lonely, 113
  and holiness, 148, 150
  and judgment, 212, 230-31
  and love of the brethren, 164
  as only road to God, 178
  as teacher, 110-11, 122-24, 186, 189
  as unlikely hero, 213
  call of, 108
  deity of, 165
  exalted view of, 168
  humanity and unity of nature of, 165
  if here today, 213-15
  importance of the individual to, 110-11
  low view of, 166, 176
  return of, 126, 218
  rewriting the life of, 189
  sensitivity as teacher, 97
  suffering of, 247
  teaching of on divorce and remarriage, 217-18
  type of, 167
Jewish/Jews, 30-31, 133, 144, 145, 169, 185, 187, 207, 217, 221, 222, 230-31
Jezebel, 188
Job, 246-47
  31:15, 183
  18:14, 244
John, 109, 165, 167, 215, 258-61
  3:16, 95
  3:7, 167
  7:37, 190
  2:1-4, 214
  10:10, 249
  11:25, 249
  19:26, 250
John the Baptist, 188, 193
Johnson, President Lyndon B., 170
Jonah, 206
Jonathan, 188
Jones, E. Stanley, 196
Joseph, 143, 145, 147, 190
Joshua, 143
Judas Iscariot, 194
Judges, 167
judgment, 102, 178, 197-201, 207, 212, 219-

20, 221
Judson, Adoniram, 171
Jungle Aviation and Radio Service (JAARS), 196
justice, 184, 191, 199, 205, 222
  injustice, 152, 207, 222
  punishment inflicted to satisfy, 199-200

Kennedy, Robert F., 244
Kerner, Governor Otto, 197
King, Martin Luther, Jr., 244, 266
Knox, John, Presbytery, 269
Kraft, George, 202-3
Kraft, Pearl, 202-3

Lake View Academy, 266-67, 268
Lake View Presbyterian Church (Chicago, Illinois), 266
Lamaze childbirth, 216
Lamentations
  3:33, 247
Las Vegas, 257
Law, the, 157, 163, 165, 166, 183
  as schoolmaster, 167
  shallow treatment of, 166-67
  penalty for violation of, 199, 205
lay involvement, 227, 270
Lazarus, 247
leadership, 209-10, 213, 223, 224, 227, 270
  speaking out against evil, 218, 226
Lebanon, 197
legalism, 184
legislating morality, reasons for, 228-30
Leviticus
  19:2, 148
  24:17, 200
  6:4-5, 205
Lewis, C. S., 104, 247
liberalism, in shambles, 223
libertarians, 228
literacy, 211
Lloyd-Jones, Martyn, 193
Lord's Day, the, 207-08, 211, 226
  (see also Sabbath; Sunday)
Lord's Supper, the, 123
lost sheep, 122
love, Christian, 164, 219
Luke, 142, 188
  2, 100
  16:8, 161-62
  18:8, 181
  13:2-3, 194
  6:37, 212

2:39-50, 214
1:41-44, 215
1:79, 249
6:21, 23, 264
Luther, 248

McDonald's, 204
Macaulay, Joseph C., 168, 194
Machen, J. Gresham, 175
Mark
  10:21, 123
marriage (*see* family)
Martin, Dean, 180
Mary, 143-47, 214-15
materialism, 121, 170, 180, 212
Matthew, 108
  6:26, 92
  6:28, 92
  28:19, 93
  12:20, 97
  5:48, 149, 155
  5:13-14, 162, 167
  7:6, 163
  10:22, 190
  27:3, 194
  19:5, 205
  12:41, 206
  12:30, 212
  12:46-50, 214
  7:3-5, 219
  23:29-34, 231
  27:46, 247
Mayo Clinic's Methodist Hospital, 256
media (*see* television)
Meshach, 116
Messiah, 143, 144, 145
Mexico, 187
Middle East, 132
Miletus, 188
Minnesota, 110
Mission Aviation Fellowship (MAF), 196
missionaries, 124, 138, 149, 151, 192, 223,
  226, 236, 238
  prayer for, 100
missions, 181, 224, 229, 240
  financial support of, 33-42
  matriarchal, 226
  Moravian, 203
Mississippi, 121
Monclova, Ohio, 267
money, 215
Monica, 171

Moody Bible Institute, 160, 264
Moody, Dwight L., 98-99, 121
moral absolutes, 161-63
moral influence, theory of, 200
moral relativism, 122, 161
moralism, 165
morality
  Christian, 157, 162, 184, 206, 213, 222, 270
  decline of, 166, 167, 175
  legislating, 229
  New Morality, the, 181-82
  quickening of, by revival in the church, 166
Moravian missionary movement, the, 203
mortality, 208
Moses, 117-18, 149, 162, 192, 238-39, 246,
  258, 259, 263, 264
motherhood (*see* family)
Mount of Transfiguration, the, 258
movies, 179, 184, 202, 206, 228
Murray, John, 220

Naomi, 167
National Council of Churches, the, 224
nations under judgment, 230-31
Nature, 161
Navigators, the, 227
Nazareth, 143
Nazis, the, 220-21, 228
Negro, 156-58
  crime, 156-59
  discrimination, 156-58
  immorality, 156-58
  leaders, 157
  (*see also* black; African-American)
Neighborhood Bible Studies, 224
Netherlands, the, 208, 228
Nevada, 229
New Hampshire, 95
New Republic, the, 183
New Testament, 194, 201, 218
New York, 193, 232
New York/City, 119, 124, 134, 194, 199, 209,
  257, 260
New Yorker, the, 195
Newsweek, 200
Niagara Bible Conference, the, 164
Niagara Platform, the, 164
Nicodemus, 92
nihilism, 176
Nineveh, 209
Nixon, Richard, 193
Noah, 189, 203

Noah's ark, 153, 195
Nobel prize, 212, 241
nuclear weapons, 219
Numbers
  35:16, 200
Nurses' Christian Fellowship, 224

O'Hare Airport, 131, 142
Oklahoma City, 216
"Old-Fashioned Revival Hour," the, 224
Old Testament, 141, 150, 183, 189, 200, 201, 217, 221, 244, 246, 250, 259
  embarrassing to pacifists, 186
Ontario Bible College, 168
ordination, 269-71
  of women, 187
Orr, 165
orthodoxy
  dead, 203
  test of, 154, 165
Orwell, George, 181
"Out of My Mind", 152
overpopulation, 183-84
Overseas Missionary Fellowship (OMF), 202-3

pacifism, 186-87
parachurch organizations, 204, 224-25
Pardeeville, Wisconsin, 267, 269
Parent's Guide to the Emotional Needs of Children, A, 159
pastorate, the, 269-71
  and divorce, 202-3, 213
  counseling, 213, 270
    dangers of, 210
  pastors' silence against abortion, 221
  pastors' silence against effects of television, 179-81
  preaching, 268
    in streets, 214-15
    prophetic, consequences of, 152-53
    on repentance, 193, 195, 206, 222
  qualifications for, 215-17
patriarchal (*see* church; family)
patriotism, 185, 187
Paul, the Apostle, 92, 130, 157, 162, 163, 166, 186, 187, 188, 189, 190, 192, 199, 201, 212, 218-19, 244, 249, 258
  attack upon by feminists, 187-88
  taught repentance, 194
peace, 208, 239, 246, 256, 266, 270
penalty
  for violation of law, 198, 199, 205

Pennsylvania, 94, 158, 196, 249
Pennsylvania Bible Society, 182
Pentecost, Day of, 194
periodicals, Christian, 224
persecution, 213, 216, 229, 262
personal morality, 222
Peter, 109, 194, 258
Philadelphia, 156, 182, 236
Philippians
  4:11, 130
  4:7, 208
physicians, Christian, 220, 239
pietism, 205-6
Pilate, 194
Pioneer Ministries, 224
Playboy, 166
Pleasant Valley, Pennsylvania, 158
pollution, 183, 208, 229, 230
pollution, moral, 206, 229, 230
Polycarp, 171
poor, the, 102, 152, 185, 189, 208, 209, 213, 219
  and abortion, 215
  and capital punishment, 201
  widow, 122
pornography, 229-30
Potiphar's wife, 190
poverty, 157, 183-84, 200
Powell, Father John, 220
prayer, 104, 106, 108, 113, 124, 195-197, 206-7, 237, 252, 270
  list, 126, 195
  for missionaries, 100, 126, 129
  for children, 100, 235-36, 238
  for fellow Christians, 115-16, 126, 235-36
  for teaching, 128-29
  within home, 117-18, 211
preaching, 204, 214, 270
  and repentance, 193, 195, 206
  doctrinal, 225
  expository, 225
    emphasis on prophecy, 225
  on success, 225
  prophetic, consequences of, 152-53
  relational, 225
    emphasis on success here and now, 225
  street, 216-17
pre-evangelism, 176-78
Presbyterians Pro-Life, 267
pride, 210
Priscilla, 263
prison camps, 30

prisoners, 189, 208
Problem of Pain, The, 247
Prodigal Son, the, 122, 192
Prohibition, 230
Promised Land, the, 146, 189, 264
proof texts, 209
prophecy, Old Testament, 97, 141
prophets
  persecution of, 231
  call for Negro, 156-58
propitiation, 198
prostitution, 186, 228-29, 241
Protestantism, 172
Proverbs, 167
  23:7, 203
Psalms, 169
  34:8, 178
  139:13, 183
  16:6, 183
  33:8, 205
  51:5, 216
  118:23, 225
  23, 238
  55:4-5, 244
  103:7, 239, 246
  22:1, 248
  23:4, 249
public education, compulsory, 169
public relations, 225
public school, Bible reading in, 169
publishing, Christian, 224
Pulitzer prize, 212
punishment, purpose of, 197-202
  compared to chastisement, 199
  eternal, 198

Quito, Ecuador, 196

racism
  capital punishment and, 198-9
  interracial marriage and, 184-85
radio, religious, 224
Raikes, Robert, 91, 121
Rayburn, Jim, 226
Reasoning Faith, 166
rescue missions, 124
relativism, 162
remarriage, 185, 213, 217-20
repentance, 193-95, 206
  lost grace of, 193
  necessity of preaching it, 223
Resurrection the, 248-53, 257, 259

retribution, 198-200
Revelation, 157, 165, 190, 261
  2:16, 194
reverence, 205
revisionists, Christian, 190-91, 218
revival, 166, 168, 194
rich, the, 189, 201, 213
righteousness, 184, 199, 205, 221
Riso, John, 245-46
Rocky Mountains, the, 261, 263
Roe v. *Wade,* 220
Roman, 144-46, 162
Roman Empire, the fall of the, 181
Romans
  7:13, 163, 165
  7:7, 166
  1:16, 173
  10:17, 175
  2:4, 194
  3, 200
  13:4, 201
  8:35-39, 208
  1:17, 208
  6:11, 249
Rome, 229
Rosedale, Wisconsin, 267
Rosedale Presbyterian Church (Cambria, Wisconsin), 269
Rowan and Martin, 180
Russia, 152-53, 168-70
Ruth, 167
Ryrie, Charles, 217

Sabbath, the, 207-208, 211, 226
  (*see also* Sunday; Lord's Day)
Saint John's University, 110
salt and light, 161, 162, 167
salvation 166, 173, 176, 177, 189, 209, 249, 269
  obsession with immediacy of, 167
  security of early decision, 168
  assurance of, 171
  goal of, 178
  refused, 201
Samson, 188
Samuel, 189
San Francisco, 229
San Francisco State University, 179
Sarah, 192
Satan, 129, 150, 186, 190, 192, 201, 227, 247, 249
Saturday Evening Post, the, 224

Saul, 188
Scotland, 168, 194
seal hunt, Canadian, 220
Second Chronicles
  7:14, 206
Second Coming, the, 164, 251
Second Corinthians
  7:10, 193
Second Peter
  2:20, 206
Second Timothy
  3:16-17, 167, 201
  4:7, 271
Secret Life of the Unborn Child, The, 215
secular humanism, 229
self-centeredness, 149
self-esteem, 148
seminary, 213, 224
Senate, the, 197
SEND, 267
sentimentality, 203
Sermon on the Mount, the, 112, 123, 149
sexist language, 190-92
sexual immorality
  Abraham and Hagar, 189
  adultery, 152, 205, 213, 219
  affair, 205
  among Negroes, 156-58
  child sexual abuse, 229
  fornication, 161-63, 175, 185
  homosexuality, 218, 228-30
  incest, 229
  pornography, 228-29
  prostitution, 186, 228-29, 241
Shadrach, 116
Shinto-shrine worship, 185
Siberia, 153
Simeon, Charles, 149
simplistic answers, 209
sin, 149, 152, 178, 186, 200, 206, 207, 213, 220, 221
  mourning over, 193-95
  of indifference, 220-21
  of pride, 209
  related to sickness and death, 198
  shallow treatment of, 166-67
Singapore, 129, 202
Singapore Bible College, 203
single adults, 213
singles ministry, 221, 222
slavery
  white, 157

Negro, 230
Slessor, Mary, 149
Smith, Anita, 267
social justice, 221-22
Socrates, 244
Sodom and Gomorrah, 198
Solomon, Song of, 173
soul, origin of, 215
soul-winning, 177, 213, 240
South American Indians, 260
Southern Baptist Sunday School Board, 188
Spain, 153
spiritual dependency, 210
Springfield United Brethren Church (Monclova, Ohio), 267
Spurgeon, Charles Haddon, 96, 120-21
Stam, Betty Scott, 160
Stanford University, 216
state, the
  purpose of punishment by, 198, 200
Steinem, Gloria, 187, 191, 192
Stephen, 188, 258, 262
Sterrett, Jerry, 237
Steward, Jennie, 252
students, ministry to, 159-60, 161-63
substitutionary atonement, theory of, 200
success, 150, 206, 209, 213, 218, 225
  overemphasis on, 204
Sudomier, Kathy, 180-81
suffering, 245-46, 261
  as road to holiness, 150
  Christian response to, 239-40, 247
  God's purpose in, 175, 239, 247
  in marriage, 202-3
  permitted by God, 247
Summit Books, 215
Sunday, 206-9, 211, 228, 249, 257
  (see also Sabbath; Lord's Day)
Sunday School, 90-130, 169, 180, 188
  as standard raised by God in crisis, 121
  curriculum, 103, 188
  health of, 120-21
  lessons taught as salvation lessons, 167
  nature changed from evangelism to education, 117
Sunday School Times, the, 224
Supreme Court, the, 30-31, 214, 221-23
  equal treatment under the law, 201
Swarthmore College, 237
Swindoll, Chuck, 267

TWA, 131, 142

Taiwan, 205
Taylor, H. J., 119
Taylor, Hudson, 149
Taylor, Kenneth, 172
Taylor, Maria, 149
television, 179-81, 210, 224-25
  advertising, 180-81
  and violence, 201-2
  as pollutant, 206
  effects of, 179-81, 210, 223
  fatherhood, attack upon, 180
Texas, 259
theocracy, 221
theology, 111, 207, 214
  accommodated to present world, 198
  biblical, 203-4
  black, 220
  contemporary, 149
  homosexual, 218
  liberation, 149, 218
  relational, 149
  women's, 149, 218
Thielicke, Helmut, 248
Third Reich, 220, 230
Thomas, 165
Thomas Bread Company, 119
Tim, Tiny, and Vicki, 180
Time, 197, 225
Timothy, 189
Titus
  2:9-10, 157
tolerance, 178, 211, 218
Tolkien, J. R. R., 174
Toronto, 216, 257
Torrey, 165
treasures in heaven, 260
Trophimus, 188
Turkey, 153

Union Seminary, 199, 218
United Nations, the, 31
United States, the, 92, 102, 121, 162, 163, 166, 170, 181, 185, 186, 207, 206, 216, 221, 230
  (*see also* America; American)
unjust judge, 122
Updike, John, 174
Ur, 192

values, 180, 201, 225
Vander Puy, Abe, 196
vasectomy, 183

Verny, Thomas, 215
Virgin Birth, the, 155
Virginia, 119
vow, 207
vows (*see* family)
voyeurism, 198, 201-2

WLS, 136
war, 262
  and death, 244
  and pacifism, 186
  Civil War, the, 94, 121, 230
  God permitting, 186
  Vietnam, the, 187, 206
  women as combatants in, 186
  World War II, 182, 187, 209, 216, 220, 221-22, 226, 229
    (*see also* Hitler; Holocaust; Nazis)
Watergate, 193-94, 197
Wattenberg, Ben, 183
Webster's New Collegiate Dictionary, 1975 ed., 207-10
wedding (*see* family)
Wesley, John, 91, 171
Wesleyan Revival, the, 91
West Coast Lumber Company, 119
West Germany, 181, 221
West Philadelphia High School, 169
Wheaton, Illinois, 132-43, 149
Whitehead, Alfred North, 128
Wilberforce, William, 230
wine, 123, 135, 189, 213
Wisconsin, 267
witness
  Christian, 226
    instead of holiness, 149
    Jesus' example, 124
    salt and light, 161, 162, 167
    sexual immorality in, 230-31
    silence of, 15, 27-28, 232-33
Wolman, Dr. Irving, 242-43
womb, 146, 183, 215, 252, 260, 263
women
  Equal Rights Amendment, the, 186
  equality of, 181-84
  in combat, 186
  ordination of, 187
  role of, 226
  sexism and, 190-92
  Women's Lib, 186-88, 191, 212
    (*see also* family; feminism)
Woods, Stacey, 226

Wycliffe Bible Translators, 196

Young Life, 224
Youth for Christ, 224
youth work, 213, 217, 224-25

Acknowledgments

Selections in *A Voice in the Wilderness* are copyright by Joseph Bayly unless otherwise noted. Reasonable care has been taken to list original publication dates with the titles.

Christmas Voices: 1974

The Gospel Blimp: 1960

Heaven: 1977

How Silently, How Silently: 1968, 1973 (including other parables not listed separately)

I Love Sunday School: © 1987 by David C. Cook Publishing Company

I Saw Gooley Crash: 1985

The Last Thing We Talked About: Originally published as *The View from a Hearse*, 1969

Out of My Mind columns: These appeared in *Eternity* magazine from 1962-1986

Psalm on the Death of an Eighteen-Year-Old Son: From *Psalms of My Life*, 1987

When a Child Dies: 1966

If you liked *A Voice in the Wilderness,*
check out this exciting title from
Chariot Victor Publishing...

WINTERFLIGHT
by Joseph Bayly
ISBN: 1-56476-786-8

Set in the not-so-distant future, this chilling tale
challenges readers to consider how America's apathy and
inaction may soon lead to a society of legal terminations
and genetically perfect populations. A suspenseful look at
what tomorrow could bring, this novel inspires Christians to
respond to the issues of their day with conviction, courage
and truth.

Another inspirational title from Chariot Victor Publishing...

PSALMS OF MY LIFE
by Joseph Bayly
ISBN: 1-56476-785-X

These thought-provoking daily reflections on such everyday topics as newspapers, hotel rooms and wild flowers inspire personal prayer and greater observation of the things God is doing. Joseph Bayly helps readers discover how they can write their own psalms of their lives.

If you like John Grisham thrillers, check out this contemporary novel from Chariot Victor Publishing...

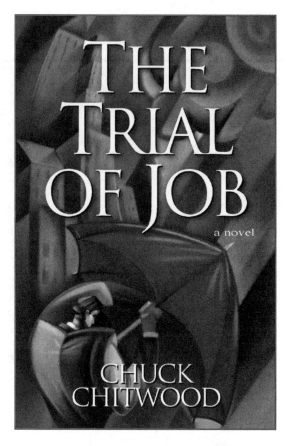

THE TRIAL OF JOB
by Chuck Chitwood

ISBN: 0-78143-308-8

Thirty-four-year-old attorney Charlie Harrigan had it all. A beautiful wife. A precious daughter. A nice home in an excellent neighborhood. And then it happened. Without warning, his family was suddenly taken from him and now he must choose between a fragile, immature faith and a road of vengeance he appears to have every right to pursue.